International Business Foundations

Robert Sweo, Ph.D.
Shelley Gordon, Ph.D.
University of Central Florida

Kendall Hunt
publishing company
4050 Westmark Drive • P O Box 1840 • Dubuque IA 52004-1840

Cover images provided by Jennie Sweo

Contents

What Is International Business?

To many, the question of what constitutes international business seems to have an obvious answer. The intent in this book is to help you start to understand how complex the world really is and how sophisticated you must become to be able to deal with it. Seemingly, simple questions like What constitutes international business? can have very complex answers. To begin to understand what is and what isn't international business, therefore, it helps to consider why international business is different from business conducted within just one nation.

HOW IS INTERNATIONAL BUSINESS DIFFERENT?

International business has a number of special issues and added complexities that a company doesn't face in a single country. Those differences include:

Currencies—Most countries have their own unique currencies. International businesses often deal in multiple currencies, making their financial situation more complex. There is financial risk associated with exchanging currencies, holding assets in other currencies, and trading on prices set in other currencies. All these risks, and endeavors to reduce the risks, add to the turbulence and difficulties the businesses face.

Government/Laws—Dealing with multiple governments and laws adds another set of opportunities and risks. Having multiple legal systems offers a company the opportunity to choose laws that best fit its business model, which can make it much more profitable. All those contrasting laws can also be a substantial challenge to a company, however. An international company must be able to deal with multiple political systems with contrasting goals and methods. It is not uncommon for a company to be told by one of its governments that it must do something and at the exact same time face another government telling it it can't do it. The inevitable conflicts must be resolved and this can be very costly.

Different Accounting Systems—Business activity is measured and controlled by companies through their accounting systems. However, each country has different laws that dictate accounting rules. International companies are thus required to maintain multiple sets of books and follow multiple sets of rules as they establish their accounting systems. Employees and customers from different countries may be confused by how company budgets, billing, or other accounting systems operate.

Different Languages—Operating in multiple languages provides international companies another set of opportunities and risks. Risks come from the chance that mistakes will be made as product instructions, packaging, marketing, and business procedures are translated among languages. Beyond just getting the words incorrect, entire approaches to thinking embedded in languages can cause a great deal of misinterpretation and harm a business. The company that accurately translates its business to other, lesser used, languages can sometimes find niche markets to exploit profitably.

Different Cultural Perspectives—Cultures go far beyond language in controlling how people think and respond to the environment around them. It can be difficult for a person from one culture to truly understand someone from another. The challenge is to create business practices and policies that consider a wide range of practices that work well in each culture without alienating customers, suppliers, employees, governments, or the communities in which they operate.

Different Economic Systems/Cycles—Although the world economy is globalizing and becoming more interlinked all the time, different countries still have different economic systems and cycles that can be used to diversify risk and gain opportunities. Most of the world's population does not live in a stable, capitalistic democracy. Other economic systems exist, each with strengths and weaknesses. International companies can choose to use those different strengths to make a stronger overall company. Varying economic cycles between countries also provide companies a chance to diversify away some of the economic risks faced in an economic cycle when operating in only one country.

Differing Geographies—Even the country's physical geography can have a substantial effect on its business practice. For example, consider Switzerland and Singapore—both are small countries with strong business orientations but because of their physical geographies they must take different approaches to business. Switzerland is a landlocked, mountainous country with cold weather most of the year. Singapore is mostly surrounded by water leading into a strategic strait of Asia. Switzerland has specialized in banking and other intellectual trades that utilize a highly educated work force. Singapore has used its year round warm waters to become the world's largest shipping port and international trader. It is important to consider natural resources for competitive advantage.

Higher Risk Until Diversified—All of the above items show international businesses face many more problems than a company operating within just one country. All those problems mean international companies face substantially greater risks. As you learned in finance class, however, risk is not always a bad thing. Companies are rewarded for taking risks. The trick is to make sure that the risks you face are diversified. That means the company that operates across many countries can be far safer than companies operating in just one or two. Management of risks is crucial to success.

WHAT IS AN "INTERNATIONAL" BUSINESS?

Given all the differences that go into making an international business, the next question we face is which kinds of companies face these differences. There are four categories of companies that most regularly deal with these kinds of differences and therefore need to be considered international business. They are described below.

Companies with Operations in More than One Nation

The company no one has trouble recognizing as an international business has operations running in more than one country. The scales of these companies range from the largest companies in the world, such as General Electric, IBM, Siemens, and Toyota, to small companies with operations in multiple countries. In the last few years we have even seen a large number of entrepreneurial companies initially start up in multiple countries. Whether gigantic or very small, all these companies face similar international issues.

Businesses Selling Products across National Boundaries

Another group of companies most people easily recognize as being international are those companies that sell their products across national boundaries. Companies that export their products to other countries face almost all the same issues as companies with operations in more than one country. They must deal with multiple currencies, cultures, governments, and other international business differences.

Businesses that Rely on International Suppliers

A group of companies that many don't think of when listing international businesses are companies that rely substantially on international suppliers. But if a company gets many of its important supplies from overseas, it must be considered an international business. A company dependant on international suppliers' costs is still based on foreign currency transactions; other countries' government's actions can affect its business; language and cultural misunderstandings can easily affect product supply and quality. If a company does not operate as an international company by choosing the best sources for supply, it risks competitors that will gain price advantages and better links to customers which they can use to eliminate any business trying to ignore its international dimensions. If you consider all companies that have substantial international suppliers to be international businesses, you can see the number of companies not considered international becomes very small.

Businesses that Are Affected by International Competitors

The last group of companies that must be considered international are those having large international competitors. Even if a small company were able to substantially limit its international suppliers it will still face international problems if its competitors are largely international. Consider, for example, a small, local hamburger restaurant. Even though the restaurant may buy all of its supplies locally, it still faces international risks. Because the restaurant's biggest competitor is likely to be McDonald's, it must successfully compete against McDonald's. McDonald's is one of the world's most international businesses. When a major currency weakens against the dollar, the price of beef to McDonald's drops. McDonald's can use that lower priced beef to lower the cost of its hamburgers. If the local hamburger restaurant does not follow suit it will lose substantial business. Therefore, for the local company to survive it must pay attention to international trends that affect its competitors. Thus, for all intents and purposes, international competition makes it an international business.

If businesses with operations in more than one nation, businesses selling products across national boundaries, businesses that rely on international suppliers, and businesses that are affected by international competitors are all international businesses then an obvious question is, What isn't an international business? There isn't an easy answer, but there are a few companies that should be considered.

WHAT ISN'T INTERNATIONAL BUSINESS?

Not Much!

The first answer when asked What isn't international business? has to be, Not Much! There are not many companies that don't use a substantial number of international suppliers. Even fewer don't have large multinational competitors. Most companies, therefore, are in international business. Every serious business person needs to understand how to succeed in international business. There are a few exceptions, however, and some are considered below.

Isolated Real Estate

It would be wrong to consider the real estate market one that doesn't have substantial international dimensions. If you look at a market like Miami, where so many customers come from outside the United States, prices are largely driven by international currency factors, cultural preferences, and even foreign taxes and other policies. But there are isolated markets where international considerations have little to no affect. In markets with no large international employers, no substantial tourist trade, and few other international effects, real estate can remain independent. In these isolated markets the real estate tends to have lower values.

Non-Transportable Products

There are some goods that are so large, heavy, or unstable that they simply cannot be transported from one country to another. These goods are not considered international. Do be careful when considering these, however, since many of these goods are often handled by international companies. Particularly with goods that are very unstable, few companies will have the expertise to handle the products and many of the companies that do so have taken their expertise with the products to an international level. So, even though the products may not be international, the companies that handle and service them still could be.

Highly Perishable Goods

Much like the situation with non-transportable goods, some goods have too short a lifespan to be moved internationally and sold. There are some fruits and flowers for instance that can only be sold locally because they ripen and spoil in just a couple of days, making it too difficult to market them internationally.

Local Services

Some service industries use limited international suppliers and have few or no international competitors. These companies could be considered not to have an international dimension. Companies putting themselves in this category however, must be very careful. More and more international service businesses are arriving every day. If one of them shows up in what you considered to be your local market, they will likely cause havoc with a local business before it even knows what has happened. For example, just a few years ago most people considered accounting to be a local or, at best, national business. Now large international companies completely dominate the accounting industry. A lot of companies that didn't see the transition coming were killed by the large multinationals as they arrived. Call centers offer another example.

WHY IS INTERNATIONAL BUSINESS IMPORTANT?

The fact that almost all business is international business makes it pretty clear why one needs to understand how to work through the intricacies of international operation. But it isn't the only reason one should study how international business differs. There are several other reasons international businesses are crucial.

World Growth

One reason international business is so important is that world growth is largely dependent on it. For a country as rich as the United States, growth may not seem that important, but few other countries have the luxury of thinking that way. For the more than one billion people who are living subsistence lives, barely able to feed themselves, economic growth is critical for survival. For the four billion people living above the deepest poverty but still far below standards available in some of the richest countries, growth may not be a matter of life and death but most people still feel a desire to be able to live like those they see in the western world. For all these peoples economic growth is their route to a better life. That route is dependent upon continued improvements in international business. The richest countries must lead the way to global growth.

Survival (We Must or They Will)

Another reason studying international business is so important is that international business provides many competitive advantages. As competitive as the business world is, if the other companies in your industry are using international business to lower their prices and improve their understanding of customers, those companies will be learning techniques that they can use to win. Companies that are not in the game will constantly be falling behind and eventually dying. All one needs to do is look at how dominant international companies have become in international business to see just how true this has become. You either do international business or someone else does it to you.

World Equalization

A significant advantage of international business that most people do not consider is that improving world business climates helps create a more equal world. Yes, it is true international business has created a large number of billionaires. And it is also true that there are still more than a billion people living in absolute poverty. But those in absolute poverty are there because they are disconnected from the world of international business. It is international business that has helped the four or five billion who are living better lives get there. Successful international business creates profit-making opportunities across a large spectrum of needs and skill sets. It is the sharing of those profits among workers, governments, and providers of capital that has created a large population of wealthier people. Does world growth attempt to lift all boats? Think of it as countries with ladders against the wall. All are trying to climb up. Politics, tax policies, and laws decide whether there will be concentrations along the middle of the ladders or whether some will reach the top and others will be left miserably at the lowest rung.

World Peace

An even more surprising outcome of increasing international business is increasing world peace. Given the highly competitive nature of international businesses, many people might think it increases conflicts in the world but the opposite is true. If you look at a map of the world and look to where wars have occurred or are highly likely, two issues usually stick out. One is that countries that wage war with each other are usually geographically close. The second is that countries that wage war with each other usually have very little trade with one another. Countries that trade with one another develop ties to make that trade possible. They form bonds of trust through regular interaction. Most importantly, they create a class of business people with a strong motivation to prevent hostility from breaking out. When business people see their country threatening to fight with countries that are significant customers they are generally not happy. They will strongly lobby to try to prevent escalation. Given the wealth available to the business class and the wealth needs of the political class, business people are usually highly influential. The buildup of trust over time, and the necessity of cooperation, can prevent wars.

HOW DO YOU VIEW THE WORLD?

Hopefully, the combination of a growing world economy, successes of businesses, improving wealth equalization, and increasing world peace are enough to motivate anyone with a desire for a career in business to make a careful study of international business. If you find yourself thus motivated, there's one more important consideration you should make before diving in. That consideration is that it can be difficult to study international business because it is hard for us as human beings to see things beyond our own perspectives. There are three perspectives or viewpoints that are particularly influential in the way people see the world and thus see international business. Each perspective clouds all thoughts and makes it difficult to see the world from the other two perspectives. Every person and every company tends to adopt one of these in their thought process. It is important that you identify right now which thought process you use. It will be necessary for you to clearly see, otherwise you'll never be able to understand the thoughts coming from the other two perspectives. The three perspectives are identified in the following paragraphs.

Multinational Perspective

The first of three perspectives that tend to dominate some thoughts is called the multinational perspective. The multinational perspective is most easily understood through company examples. Consider a company like McDonald's. McDonald's was born in the United States and perfected its business methods here. It took those business methods to the rest of the world and, with very little modification, made them work. Its approach to business was to find the very best answer to a problem and its culture and then sell that answer to all the rest of the world's cultures. Coca-Cola is another example. This approach is very common in many industries and the countries that dominate them. It is the dominant approach in many American companies and in many American's minds. The approach, however, is really more British. There's a phrase they use in England that describes the perspective perfectly, it is "Make the world England."

Multidomestic Perspective

Companies that take the multidomestic perspective have a different view on the world. Multidomestic companies believe that every country is different. Multidomestic companies, therefore, try to completely change their business practices, products, and services to meet the needs of each market. There are individuals who think the same way. They don't believe there is a right way as suggested in the multinational perspective. Telefonica, a Chilean-based phone company that has grown to become the second largest in the world, is a good example. Telefonica owns phone systems in many different countries. It adapts its business system so well to other countries that most people think it is a local phone company. People who think multidomestically believe the best way to act is to use whichever way people in that market want it. The phrase that best captures the multidomestic perspective is "When in Rome do as the Romans do."

If your personal perspective is the multinational perspective or the multidomestic perspective you're probably now thinking the other perspective is so obviously wrong. That is why these perspectives are so powerful. If you believe in one perspective, it is very hard to see the world from the other. But both perspectives have great strengths and weaknesses. Companies using the multinational perspective are able to use one business process all around the world. This can be incredibly efficient and profitable. However, it may make it difficult for your products to succeed in some markets. Therefore, the multinational perspective can limit the breadth of markets to which your product can apply. The multidomestic perspective allows companies to apply their products to a much broader set of cultures. It does so at a far higher cost, however. Each time a company modifies its business practices or products it adds substantial expense to those products. Multidomestic products are thus often overpriced and customers are frequently not willing to pay the required premium.

Global Perspective

The global perspective tries to gain from the strength of both the multinational and multidomestic perspectives. In the global perspective a person or company tries to find the best answer to any issue from anywhere in the world. They then try to use that answer everywhere they operate. The global perspective sounds like an improvement but it doesn't just gain the advantages of the multinational and multidomestic perspectives, it also gains their problems. The search for the best answer all around the world can be expensive. It can thus significantly increase the company's costs. At the same time the company tries to apply one answer to the entire world. That can mean the product will not meet local tastes and is therefore rejected in many markets. A global approach, therefore, only works in a small number of industries and is far less common an approach in most people's thinking. The classic example of a global product and company comes with the Sony Walkman. The Walkman was the world's first small, portable, music player. Because it was first of its kind, no cultures had a preference for different kinds of products. That allowed Sony to take good ideas from all around the world and put them into one product sold to the entire world.

Whichever approach you use personally, it is very important that you constantly remind yourself of the other two perspectives as you study international business. It may not be clear yet, but as you study international business you will discover that you have a very hard time accepting some of the ideas presented. It is probably because they come from one of the other two perspectives. If you understand the perspectives and can try to see the world from the perspectives other than the one most natural to you, you will probably find it much easier to learn ideas you initially find challenging.

 NOTES

The following spaces for notes are provided to help you prepare for tests. Tests are primarily comprised of three kinds of questions: 1) questions that test your knowledge of definitions of key terms, 2) questions that test your ability to recognize information categories, and 3) questions that test your ability to apply the concepts to examples. In our experience, students who fill out and study the tables below are much more successful on tests.

The concepts below are directly derived from PowerPoint slides used in class lectures. It is easiest to fill them in while watching class videos. Some categories and definitions are slightly different than presented in the body of this book. The differences are intentionally provided to help you have more perspectives on diverse issues.

One final note on the notes section: With a large class, it would probably be easy to find someone else who has already filled in these notes. In our experience, copying and studying someone else's notes is usually poorer preparation for tests then creating the notes yourself, especially for the questions that test your ability to apply examples.

Concept	Definition	Example
Why Is International Business Different?		
Currencies		
Government/Laws		
Different Languages		
Different Cultural Perspectives		
Different Economic Systems/ Cycles		
Differing Geographies		
Higher Risk Until Diversified		
What Is an "International" Business?		
Companies with Operations in More than One Nation		
Businesses Selling Products across National Boundaries		
Businesses That Rely on International Suppliers		
Businesses that Are Affected by International Competitors		
What Isn't International Business?		
Not Much!		
Isolated Real Estate		
Non-Transportable Products		
Highly Perishable Goods		
Local Services		
Why Is International Business Important?		
World Growth		
Survival (We Must or They Will)		
World Equalization		
World Peace		

Concept	Definition	Example
What Are International Businesses' Bigger Problems?		
Economic Growth		
Who Wins/Who Loses		
Income Inequality		
Are $ Figures All That Count?		
How Do You View the World?		
Multinational Perspective		
Multidomestic Perspective		
Global Perspective		

Defining Culture

To be successful at international business, there are special concerns that a business person must consider. The most important one is culture. With the exception of geography and natural resources, culture underpins all the other differences between countries. If you can get a good understanding of how cultures differ and how those differences affect business, you will have an excellent foundation for predicting business conditions and behavior in a country.

Cultural issues will be covered extensively in the next two chapters. Chapter two defines what a culture is and, in the process, explains how important culture is to understanding international business. Chapter three defines important cultural traits that help differentiate countries from one another. Culture then runs throughout the rest of this book, showing up as it influences government, market, individual, and group behavior. If you develop a particularly keen sense for culture, you can predict much of what goes on, not only in international business but also in business in general and, for that matter, anything else concerning human behavior.

WHAT BUSINESS CULTURE ISN'T

Before defining what is meant by culture, it is important to define what is not meant. Culture is one of those words used in different contexts in English. It is important to separate two other definitions commonly implied from what is meant here.

Cultra vs. Culture

The most commonly used definition of culture speaks only to what is sometimes more narrowly described as high culture. High culture, cultra, refers to things like opera, ballet, sculpture, and painting. Most cities have a cultural district that usually houses the town's theater and museums. We didn't invent this word "cultra." It has been used by others faced with the same situation of trying to separate the high arts definition of culture from the broader understanding that is meant in this book.

List of Habits

Another commonly used definition of culture is really a list of cultural habits. For example, if you type "Japanese culture" into Google you would most likely get back a long list of Web sites that describe interesting but minor habits of the culture. The list will tell you that Japanese traditionally bow instead of shaking hands and that business cards are very important to them. Understanding these minor habits is useful to being able to do business in the country but they are not the more important trait of culture where we will focus. Therefore, we want to separate out these lists of habits from culture as well. One must be careful. There are many people out there calling themselves cultural experts who know the basics of the language and a collection of these habits and who then deem themselves cultural experts. That information will do you little good in the total understanding of culture.

CULTURAL COMPONENTS

Cultural components define how a culture comes to be. These three cultural components explain how a culture comes to influence our lives and why the process is unavoidable.

Culture Is Learned

The first component of culture that one must know to understand culture is that all culture is learned. That means it is not part of your genetic makeup. If you were born with it, it isn't a part of culture. The best way to emphasize this point, and its importance, is to remind you that, genetically speaking, you're absolutely no different than a caveman. There have been no significant genetic modifications to humanity for thousands of years. Any human child separated at birth from the rest of humanity but who was still provided a way to survive would revert back to thoughts and behaviors that are, in fact, less sophisticated than cave men had, for even cave men had rudimentary cultures. That means everything you know and everything you do beyond those behaviors of cave men come from your culture. You know how to do things because someone before you figured them out and they were taught to you. This is hugely important and cannot be understated. Biologically, we are animals who have learned from others in our own culture and from what we see or experience of other cultures. Learned is the key operative word in culture.

Culture Is Interrelated

The second important component of culture is that all cultural aspects are interrelated That means that no cultural traits truly exist in isolation. The important implication of this is that you can't just change one piece of a culture without other changes occurring. Any attempt to change one part of the culture is going to have significant effects on other parts of it and may result in unintended consequences.

For example, many times modern civilizations have bumped into less evolved earlier cultures. As this happened in more recent times, sometimes the modern civilizations tried to "help out" the ancient culture without damaging it. This most frequently happened by the modern civilization providing some basic medicines or cleaner water to reduce infant mortality and other needless death or to bring the right religion to them. The attempts to improve basic health without substantially changing the culture were all failures. It was quickly discovered that even the simplest of medicines drastically changed infant mortality and created huge population booms in the more primitive cultures that sometimes resulted in starvation instead. These population booms then required substantial changes in methods of food production and housing. Where the modern civilizations then "helped" with better farming techniques and systems of governance they quickly erased the primitive culture. The primitive cultures soon depleted natural resources and had to find other ways to live again including waging war and havoc on surrounding cultures. This still resulted in quickly destroying their previous traditional way of life.

Culture Is Shared

The last component necessary to understanding culture is that all culture is shared. That means that if a particular thought pattern or behavior is truly unique to the individual then it is personality, not culture. Culture defines the shared behavior patterns of peoples. Anything that is truly unique to the individual doesn't count, but, as you'll see as we go through cultural dimensions, a huge amount of what you considered to be individual behavior, isn't. There is far more commonality in what you do than most of you could ever believe.

CULTURAL DIMENSIONS

Dimensions of culture make a culture powerful. These psychological, social, and historic components are what make culture impossible to avoid or control. This is true at the individual level, the collective level, and the aggregate level through historical changes.

Psychological

The psychological dimension of culture tells us that most of what we consider to be our personal makeup is really just a derivation of culture. It is quite impossible for modern men to have even a single thought not controlled by their culture. The easiest way to prove this is to ask you to think of your favorite activity.In doing so, you've had a thought. But now consider how you had that thought. First of all, that thought came to you in English (or possibly another language) but was confined to the words of that language. We think with our vocabulary. The larger your working vocabulary, the more you are capable of sophisticated thought. Thus, if your language doesn't have a word for an activity, most people can't think of it because almost all conscious thought in modern man is done through words. That is not part of your genetic makeup. Language is one of the more important tools of culture. There are others that similarly control who we are even at the individual level. Consider your clothing or your tools for eating your food as individual choices but they still are culturally determined.

Social

Culture also fully defines our social context. What one means by family changes significantly as one moves from culture to culture. How work relationships are defined and practiced similarly are controlled by culture. What is acceptable behavior in even your most intimate relationships is defined by culture. All social interactions, including the rules of social engagement, public behavior, governance, and family life come from culture. Because international business participants are expected to behave appropriately in different cultural settings, they must learn to live by multiple sets of rules and mores for social interactions in small groups or in the larger cultural settings. Nuances of behavior can matter greatly. Interactions can change significantly from culture to culture and present a particular challenge to international business.

Historic

One of the more confusing dimensions of culture is the historic dimension. The historic dimension tells us that culture was never planned. It tells us that culture accumulates and changes through events and time with no real guiding principles. The rules of the culture are what they are because of idiosyncratic events that led to cultural changes. That means that cultures contain self-contradictory elements, elements that are destructive to the culture, and elements that simply make no sense whatsoever to people viewing them from outside even though the culture makes perfect sense to people who grew up in it. Consider Santa coming down the chimney with a roaring fire in the grate, for example, and stuffing toys into stockings and then, with only a finger beside his nose, escaping into the night. This makes perfect sense and must be promoted to the next generation in the U.S. culture.

CULTURAL TRAIT STABILIZERS

Given how diverse the world is and how history accumulates one would expect culture to be a constantly changing entity and it is...but it changes slowly! There still is a tremendous amount of continuity within it. That continuity is protected through a number of stabilizers built into most cultures. The trait stabilizers work to draw a culture into a consistent pattern of behavior. Cultures tend to change slowly because they are constantly drawn to the mean or normal behavior on the bell curve. This equalizer, or reversion to what the majority do or believe, i.e., the mean, keeps the culture more constant. Trait stabilizers vary from culture to culture but those listed below are strong influencers in almost every culture.

Verbal Communication Patterns

Verbal communication patterns are a powerful trait stabilizer that uses language to try to influence cultural thinking. For example, earlier, the psychological dimension of culture was defined. The words in the definition of the psychological dimension of culture were patterned in such a way as to get you to see your individual psychology differently than you had seen it before. If it succeeded, that definition has allowed you to see the world differently and behave differently because of it. Almost all teaching, writing, and speech are similar tools used in an attempt to pattern your thoughts in a desired direction. Where it succeeds, verbal communication stabilizes a culture by getting more and more people to see the same events in a similar fashion. This is often called brainwashing or prejudice inducing. Consider the political ads in the recent Presidential campaign. All are intended to influence and reinforce your thinking within the culture. Culture is passed down from generation to generation in tradition and the comfort of doing what we've always done. Change in the culture is more commonly evolutionary, not revolutionary. Consider your religion or political party. Where did you learn to accept those? Have you even considered rethinking your positions? Barring some significant outside event, likely not, because they have been part of your culture since you were young.

Nonverbal Communication Patterns

Even more powerful than verbal communication patterns are nonverbal communication patterns that attempt to stabilize cultural traits without the use of words. As powerful as verbal communications are at influencing people, nonverbal communications are even more powerful. Psychologists will tell you to look to the behavior, not the words, in assessing what is really going on and what is meant. Do the words and the behavior match up? Mission accomplished. Nonverbal communications can be simple behaviors such as a wink or a nod, or eye contact or lack of it, or more complex behaviors. Facial expressions, for example, tend to convey information far more quickly and accurately than a long speech. Consider the statement the Chinese student made in 1989 by standing in front of rolling tanks as the Chinese government tried to quell a student rebellion. Nonverbal rituals within the culture are powerful reinforcers; we stand as the American flag passes.

Religion

Religion is another powerful trait stabilizer in most cultures. Religion embodies cultural answers to the important questions of life. What is the meaning of life? Why am I here? How did I get here? How should I behave? These are all questions religion attempts to answer. Where a religion is able to create a consistent set of beliefs with a population, the religion can have a substantial stabilizing effect on its culture. If a religion can get many people to believe in a specific purpose in life, for example, then the adherents of that religion are likely to behave in particular ways. The specifics of requested behavior change from religion to religion and even from local implementation of the same religion, but where consistency of belief is created, some level of trait stabilization tends to occur. The church enforces its own norms of individual and collective behavior among its members. When most of a society is part of the same larger religion, such as Christianity for example, then that religion's influence on the country as a whole is even greater. Because the United States does not have a national religion, arguments and disagreements are still a part of the cultural fabric of this nation. Another country might have a national religion that determines much of its culture.

Social Enforcements

Social enforcement mechanisms are behavioral patterns formed after social norms coalesce that punish people who do not comply with expected behavior. The social enforcement mechanisms work extensively throughout a culture. Each culture has its own ways for clearly demonstrating to people that they are outside acceptable cultural boundaries. For minor transgressions usually a disapproving facial expression or quiet word suffices. Consider the confinement in the stockades in early New England for someone disgraced by their behavior. The taunting of the passers-by was sufficient. For major transgressions much stricter responses like jail confinement are likely. For international business people operating outside their own culture, three levels of cultural enforcements are recognized. International business participants must pay careful attention to these social enforcement mechanisms to ensure they avoid offending host nation employees, customers, and governments.

Cultural Imperatives—Cultural imperatives are behavior patterns that everyone within a culture is expected to display. Being an outsider is no excuse for missing a cultural imperative. Each culture has its own unique set of cultural imperatives that international business people must know and within which they must behave properly. Most cultural imperatives are minor issues; failure to follow them will only lead to lost business. But most countries have a few cultural imperatives that are important to their culture regardless of whether the issue is unimportant or even unknown to other cultures. Failure to meet these can lead to being ostracized or even imprisoned.

Cultural Adiaphore—Cultural adiaphore are behavior sets popular in a culture that people from outside the culture are allowed to participate in but are not required to. A good example of a cultural adiaphore in the United States is being a sports fan. Most Americans participate as a sports fan at some level. Foreigners who come to the United States are usually offered the chance to participate as well and that may help create business relationships. If the foreigner chooses not to participate there are no negative consequences. Cultural adiaphore are strictly optional for foreigners. Care must be taken though as your perception of what is optional may, in fact, not be.

Cultural Exclusives—Cultural exclusives are the most difficult social enforcements for international business people to handle. The cultural exclusive is something in which everyone within the culture is expected to participate but in which people from outside the culture are not allowed to participate. This is a particularly great problem for international business people because it can be hard to know how to behave in a new culture. Most international business people therefore learn to act slowly. They let their hosts do things first and they simply copy behavior. It is usually a safe way to get by. Cultural exclusives, however, cause a great problem for this approach. When a host national performs a cultural exclusive and the international business person copies their behavior, the international business person has created a transgression. The best example of cultural exclusives in the United States is criticism of our government. Virtually every American criticizes our government. In fact, there are a number of trait stabilizers in the United States that encourage us to do so. But criticizing the U.S. government is a cultural exclusive. Foreigners who criticize the U.S. government are looked at harshly and might even be deemed enemy combatants.

CULTURAL TRANSMISSION

Even though the trait stabilizers are powerful, cultures still evolve or change. Many things can move a culture but, by far, the most prevalent change agent is cultural transmission. Cultural transmission occurs when different cultures interact. As people in one culture see behaviors or outcomes from another culture that they like, they tend to copy them. Even though the copying culture almost never makes an exact duplicate of the behavior from the copied culture, the copying culture still changes. In the large scale interactions of cultures many people see many different things. Each of those people comes from a slightly different cultural base. As they copy from each other there is a constant swirl of cultural adaptation. Wars, trading, university exchanges, and even formation of new countries such as the United States form the melting pots of influence, and eventually, of cultural transmission. Cultures can affect each other through mechanisms, the most prevalent of which are described below.

Direct Interaction

Direct interaction of cultures is a very powerful cultural transmission device. As people interact with others they learn from them. They see things that work and they try to copy them or to export the belief to other cultures. They see people more or less happier than they are and try to learn from what they do or have. Or they try to influence another culture to behave in the "right" way. Because of the overwhelming power of direct interaction, expansive cultures tend to try to promote direct interaction. Such systems as student exchanges, diplomatic exchanges, and missionaries are all designed to promote direct interaction and cultural transmission. International business itself is a system primarily targeted at promoting change through direct interaction. The reason business people are sent from one country to another is to try to guide behavior in the host country toward behavior patterns more profitable to the company. In many instances recipient countries are happy to have the benefits gained through direct interaction. There are several exceptions, however. For example, missionaries have not always been welcome in many countries. American business practices are, at times, similarly rejected when the host country doesn't consider that it is benefiting also.

Communication and Technological Devices

Communication devices such as the Internet, television, radio, and movies all play a significant role in cultural transmission. People often see desired behaviors and outcomes in these cultural transmission tools and try to copy them. Sometimes this happens with comical effect. For example, many countries of the world have seen the portrayals of American wealth in American movies and television. Some believe those portrayals are true to American life and try to copy behaviors in the movies on the assumption that those behaviors led to wealth. Seeing other people copy the outrageous clothing and actions portrayed lets one know just how powerful, and at times damaging, cultural transmission can be. International business plays an important role in developing cross-cultural communication devices. Poorly guided attempts to sell communications devices into an unprepared culture can have disastrous effects that will have negative consequences to the adopting culture and will usually lead to retribution against the company introducing the device.

Political Devices

Political systems are another mechanism through which cultural norms are transmitted. Sometimes they are adopted because they seem to improve the desiring culture. Sometimes political devices are forced on other cultures. Because all cultural elements are interrelated, political changes lead to other changes, some desirable some not. The attempts to persuade Middle Eastern countries to adopt a capitalistic, democratic model and the many positive and negative repercussions are a good example of how political devices try to promote cultural transmission.

Cultra

The high arts defined as cultra are another cultural transmission device. The exchange of ideas through fine arts, dance, theater, and other cultra experiences can change cultures. Particularly music is a cultra device that can have a strong transmission affect. A significant number of the people who speak English as a second language began to learn English listening to American music.

Business Processes

The area in which international business has the most direct impact in cultural transmission is through the exchange of business processes. Business processes are themselves complex cultural mechanisms. Embedded within any business process are hundreds of cultural traits from the country in which the process was developed. For example, consider the introduction of the assembly line process. The assembly line requires people to work together closely in monotonous, repetitive tasks. When the assembly line was first introduced very few cultures could adopt it. Cultures that did not already use mass education techniques like classroom teaching and accept hierarchical leadership structures had to change substantially before successful adoption of assembly line techniques. Even though the assembly line was a drastic improvement in efficiency, many cultures resisted its adoption because of the significant cultural changes it required. More modern business techniques such as TQM and data warehousing are meeting similar resistance.

ALL RIGHT ALREADY, SO WHAT IS A CULTURE?

After the extremely lengthy introduction provided, we're now ready for a definition of culture. As you may expect from all you have seen to this point the definition itself is pretty vague. Because the word culture can only be defined within a culture a somewhat ambiguous definition is inevitable.

> **Culture Definition—A fuzzy set of mostly shared traits within a defined population.**

The definition of culture has three important components. First is the idea of a **fuzzy set**. A fuzzy set is a set with a somewhat ambiguous outer edge. Think of the circles that are used to portray a set in a Venn diagram. Every drawing of a Venn diagram you have ever seen has the edges of the circles drawn with a very clear line. That is because it is assumed there is a very clear definition of what belongs in the set and what does not. Cultural traits use a fuzzy set because exactly where the edge of what is within the culture and what is outside it is not so clear. Therefore the edge of the circle is a bit smudged. There are outliers of individuals and groups outside of the fuzz, but overall, the center holds the majority and thus defines the overall culture.

The second important part of the culture definition is **shared traits**. Traits are patterns of behavior or thinking which are shared within a culture. Measurement of traits is the primary yardstick upon which cultural comparisons are carried out. Therefore, understanding where a culture is on any group of traits is how we develop an understanding of the culture itself and how that culture compares to others. Chapter three presents many of the more important business traits and helps you develop an understanding of how different trait measurements affect international business.

The third piece of the culture definition is within a **defined population**. It is important to understand that cultural traits must be measured within a defined group. Because cultural traits are such fuzzy sets you would never be able to decide whether an individual belonged inside or outside a culture unless you started with a population defined by geography, political system, or some other reality that defines them. Your family has a culture, your neighbourhood has a culture, your city has a culture, your state has a culture, your region of the country has a culture, etc. These are defined populations and, depending on your largest defined population, the others become subcultures.

SUBCULTURES

Now that you have a definition for culture it is important to understand that every culture is made up of many subcultures. Any large culture can be broken down to many more elements which have distinct cultural elements of their own. Therefore, understanding a culture as large as a country usually requires understanding the interaction of a large number of subcultures. It is also important to know that many subcultures cross national boundaries. So even though we may focus on countries as cultural elements in international business we will often find countries like Switzerland which is really a combination of French, German, Italian, and a very small actual Swiss component. It would be impossible to understand Swiss culture without understanding how all the subcultures interact.

As one learns to understand and predict a culture, it is also important to know that among the many subcultures within a large culture one or more subcultures is almost always a counterculture. A counterculture is a culture that lives in direct opposition to an important trait of the majority culture. Countercultures are important to the health of majority cultures. Countercultures challenge dominant views and are the primary mechanism through which cultural innovation occurs. That said, many countercultures are destructive and, at times, even self destructive. That does not diminish their importance to the health of the overall culture. This is because communication and disagreement promotes innovation.

NOTES

Concept	Definition	Example
What Business Culture Isn't		
Cultra vs. Culture		
List of Habits		
Cultural Components		
Culture Is Learned		
Cultural aspects are interrelated—you can't change just 1 part		
Culture Is shared		
Cultural Dimensions		
Psychological		
Social		
Historic		
Cultural Trait Stabilizers		
Verbal Communication Patterns		
Nonverbal Communication Patterns		
Religion		

Social Enforcements
    Cultural Imperatives
    Cultural Adiaphore
    Cultural Exclusives		

Cultural Transmission		

Cultures affect one another through:
    Direct Interaction
    Communication and
      Technological Devices
    Political Devices
    Cultra
    Business Processes		

Concept	Definition	Example
All Right Already, So What Is a Culture? A fuzzy set of mostly shared traits within a defined population		
Subcultures		
Most nations include many subcultures		
Many cultures and subcultures cross national boundaries		
One or more subcultures is almost always a counter-culture		
Cultural Traits		
There are many hundreds— they vary by culture		
Several important dimensions have been defined to help study business interactions		

Cultural Traits

Chapter 2 outlined what culture is and how important it is to someone trying to function within international business. The definition called culture "a fuzzy set of mostly shared traits within a defined population." Given that definition, it is important to understand the traits that make up national cultures.

There have been hundreds and possibly thousands of cultural traits defined across the social sciences, but only a small number of those are of great importance to international business. Below you'll find descriptions of the most important traits that help define international business.

HOFSTEDE'S FOUR DIMENSIONS

Geert Hofstede is a renowned international business expert who, years ago, defined four cultural traits that have become the most commonly analyzed traits in international business. These four traits underlie the most important differences between countries. Understanding them and their implications will bring you a long way toward understanding how business will function within a country. Descriptions of the four dimensions and their most important implications follow.

Uncertainty Avoidance—The Rejection of Risk

The first dimension defined by Hofstede is uncertainty avoidance. That avoidance is a measure within a culture of how willing people are to take risks. Uncertainty avoidance is the negative measure of the more commonly considered term in the United States, risk acceptance. Knowing how willing people within a culture are to take risks is important to understanding their approach to business. Cultures that freely accept higher levels of risk will have more dynamic stock markets, investment communities, and research and development facilities. Countries that score high on uncertainty avoidance will be far more reliant on traditional methods and long accepted practices. Differences in uncertainty avoidance can be clearly seen in how cultures handle investments and social interaction.

Investments—A culture with a low uncertainty avoidance score, such as the United States, tends to have dynamic investment markets. People in a low uncertainty avoidance country are generally willing to put their money at risk if it can generate a higher return. Stock markets, derivatives, hedge funds, and futures markets are all associated with low uncertainty avoidance countries. In high uncertainty avoidance countries finance and investments will be far more conservative. Banks and other safer, more traditional investment approaches such as savings accounts tend to dominate. Japan is an example of high uncertainty avoidance; they move cautiously.

Social Interaction—Social interactions are another area where the uncertainty avoidance score clearly affects business practice. In a low uncertainty avoidance country, new social relationships and business relationships are easily created. People are generally willing to trust and work with people they have just met. The American business person who flies halfway across the world, has a couple of days discussions with a potential overseas partner, then signs a $20,000,000 contract at the end of the meeting is showing low uncertainty avoidance. In a high uncertainty avoidance culture, months, years, and sometimes even decades are required to develop the trust needed to initiate a new business relationship.

Power Distance—The Psychological and Social Distance between Superiors and Subordinates

Power distance is a measure of how people with different levels of power are seen. In a high power distance culture a person in a position of power is seen as significantly different from someone in a lower power position. For example, a secretary in the high power distance country would expect to do what he is told exclusively. He would not commonly act on his own initiative, raise problems to his superior, or expect to be consulted on any issue of importance. In a low power distance culture people see themselves as equals regardless of power positions. In a low power distance culture the lowest level employee would feel comfortable raising issues and problems with people in the most powerful positions. Power distance has significant implications across most of the international business landscape. Within subcultures inside a country such as the United States, power distances vary and the ability to speak up without negative consequences can change with circumstances. In some cultures it is immutable and might result in jail or death if one were to speak up. A few of the most important considerations are described below.

Employer/Employee Relations—As one might expect, power distance has a significant effect on employer and employee relations. In a low power distance country open communication helps identify and solve problems quickly. It also provides an easily identifiable path for developing new managers. If everyone in the organization sees himself as equal, it is easier to train employees to move up within the organization. Companies in countries with high power distance use more hierarchical systems of management. Instructions come from high level managers and lower level employees are expected to do what they're told. The system is usually more efficient but much less adaptive. Does the organizational structure work from the top down, or bottom up? Is it flat or bloated with many layers of management? Is it an organic, free-flowing team or a bureaucracy? In Hungary, a high power differential country, I witnessed an interpreter stand with his hands in his pockets while one clerk tried to do all necessary to help 26 people buy and ship wine. This frustrated the U.S. customers and he truly did not understand why. He was told his job was to give a tour in English; end of story.

People to Government Relations—Similarly, high power distance cultures tend to create high perceived barriers between governments and their people. In low power distance countries, concepts like government by the people and for the people will commonly prevail. In high power distance countries the people are more often seen as the workers there to support the government's power. International businesses frequently struggle in adapting to the various forms of governments that grow within cultures substantially different from their own on power distance. It can be hard for a company formed in a free-flowing democracy, common in low power distance countries, to understand how to work in the more totalitarian regimes often found in high power distance countries, and visa versa. Once business is underway, the ground rules of geopolitical power differentials can change, causing more uncertainty.

Parent to Child Relations—Even parent-child relationships are affected by the level of power distance in a culture. In fact, the parent child relationship is probably the foundation through which power distance is learned within a culture. In a low power distance culture like the United States, for instance, it would be common to try to sell toys by advertising to children. It is assumed that if you can convince the child to want the toy, the child will be able to convince their parents to buy it. In a high power distance culture that approach would never work. Even if you were able to convince the child to want the toy, the child would have no hope of swaying parents. The implications suggest an American company would need to learn a whole new approach to dealing with families in a high power distance culture.

Collectivism vs. Individualism

Collectivism versus individualism is a measure of what a culture considers its base unit of importance among its people. In a collective society, the group or culture itself becomes the important unit of analysis. Individuals are often seen as expendable in service of the greater good for the entire population. Collectivistic cultures focus on serving the needs of the entire population. If a few individuals are hurt in the service of the greater good that is considered a price that must be paid. By contrast, in an individualistic culture the individual is the most important unit of consideration. In individualistic cultures it is assumed doing what is right for individuals within the culture is the best approach for taking care of the culture itself. Individualism suggests people should work on their own behalf and markets of accumulated individual behavior will take care of the collective needs. How much the culture looks to its collective well being vs. how much it looks to the well being of its individuals has serious implications for many important business functions. A few are described below.

Teamwork—It may seem counter intuitive, but individualistic cultures are best at teamwork. A leader will emerge who will propel the group into action. This culture is more attuned to getting the task accomplished. In the collective culture more attention is paid to the nuances of the group and to not hurting feelings or stepping outside of your defined boundaries. Leadership is lacking. Collectivistic cultures have difficulty with teamwork because they tend to have defined jobs and roles that are separate and distinct.

Rewards Systems—Team reward systems need to work very differently in collectivistic and individualistic cultures. For example, in United States' very individualistic culture it is common to assign work to a group and expect that group to work together in getting the job done. It would then be common, however, to assign rewards of different values to different people based on their input to the team. That would never be accepted in a collective society. In fact, trying to reward performance differentially in a group in a collectivistic society would so upset the group that work would quickly stop. Interestingly, those people who were rewarded more than the others would be the ones who would be most upset by differential rewards.

Innovation Management—The style of innovation management in a country is also significantly affected by how collective a culture is. Societies that are individualistic tend to be good at developing breakthrough technology. Breakthrough technologies usually grow from an individual who first tries something a little different from common practice. And the individual can continue reiterating change until what has been developed is drastically different from what came before. Essentially, the individual breaks out of the box or even operates with the mindset, "what box?" Those drastic differences become what are known as breakthroughs. Collectivistic societies tend to be better at incremental change. Because everyone is always working so closely together with confined expectations, it is hard for any one person or group to change something drastically. Collectivistic societies therefore become much better with the incremental changes commonly described in the TQM process.

Masculinity vs. Femininity

The last of Hofstede's original four dimensions is a measure of how masculine vs. feminine a culture is. The masculine culture is a culture that is said to display an assertive desire for rational control and power. A feminine culture is said to be more modest and focused on the group's well being, happiness, and, ultimately, the nurturing of the company and culture as a whole. It is important to remember that we're not discussing the sexual make-up of the population. That tends toward 50% male and 50% female in any society unless gender cleansing has occurred. The question is whether a culture emphasizes more of the roles we traditionally identify as masculine vs. feminine. The international business functions most affected by entrenchment of masculine or feminine culture are the organizational structure and rewards used within the country.

Organizational Structure—The masculinity vs. femininity measure is an important determinant of what types of organizational structures will work within a country. Highly masculine countries tend to prefer more rational and consistent structures. Masculine countries tend to prefer the order and consistency available in a multi-layered, hierarchical structure. Feminine countries tend to prefer much more organic and flowing structures. Emphasis is placed on making relationships work out and keeping everyone happy. The approach typically improves morale and effectiveness but is an efficiency challenge.

Rewards—Rewards are also significantly affected by how masculine or feminine a culture is. A highly masculine culture tends to prefer objective measures of performance and incremental rewards based on those objectives outcomes. The straight 10% sales commission is the type of reward system that would do very well in a highly masculine culture. In a feminine country rewards are often very different. Rewards are often geared towards improving employee morale and are usually less monetary. In a highly feminine country you would more likely see more flexible work schedules, time off, or possibly improvements to health care as a reward rather than direct monetary compensation. Rewards are more equally shared. In France the top 25% make about 4 times what the bottom 25% make. Here, the top 1% makes 20% of the income. French companies also routinely grant 6 weeks of vacation. France has a feminine viewpoint where rewards are more equally shared.

OTHER IMPORTANT TRAITS

Beyond the four Hofstede dimensions, other cultural traits have been measured across a large number of countries and have been found useful for predicting people's behavior in international business. The most important of those additional traits are described below.

Material Wealth

Material wealth is a measure of how important controlling physical assets and other services is to a culture. Cultures that score high consider being rich good in itself. Cultures with high material wealth scores would usually be willing to trade away other values such as free time to gain wealth. Countries that score low on material wealth hold other values to be more important than money. Rewards in a country like the United States that has high material wealth scores are almost always cash or equivalent. In countries with low material wealth scores you'll be far more successful rewarding people with things like more vacation time. Material wealth is a particularly important issue to understand for American business people who are often surprised that people in other countries don't understand the "inherent good" of increased profits and that those same people aren't willing to work harder to gain them.

Achievement

Achievement is a measure of how important it is for people to move to higher level positions throughout their life; to move up on a career ladder. In a high achievement country people believe they should be constantly progressing towards their higher goals. In low achievement countries people are generally satisfied to stay where they are, perhaps with a family heritage in a trade or skill. The ultimate example of a low achievement culture is the caste system embedded in the Hindu religion. In a caste system people are seen as being born into their appropriate place in life, their destiny.

The combination of America's high material wealth and achievement scores can make it difficult for American managers to understand workers from low material wealth and achievement countries. It is a constant challenge for American managers overseas and the attitude is often confused with lack of motivation.

Time

Some countries have a very strict sense of time. Being even a minute late in a country with a high time score can destroy a business relationship. In a country with a low time score, being 15 to 20 minutes late is often the norm and sometimes showing up within a week of when promised is fine. Countries with high time scores tend to be more efficient because they can more intricately schedule activity with fewer conflicts. That does not always increase their effectiveness, however. Intricately scheduled timing systems often leave no room for creativity or adjustments to situational changes or the development of trust.

Change

Attitudes toward change is a cultural trait which tells us how desirable change is to a people. Some countries with very high change scores consider change to be the norm and people within the cultures are often irritated when change slows. For example, in the United States one of the more important measures of success is how much better your life is than that of your parents. That measure is a clear indication that Americans expect continuous change and expect to do better because of it. In many other countries change is considered a negative thing. In countries with low change scores people generally have diminished expectations and feel that their parents did well, their grandparents did well, the great grandparents did well, etc. If their parents and grandparents were fine then there's no reason living the same lives themselves wouldn't be just fine also. In cultures with low change scores, the very process of international business is not desired.

Subjective vs. Objective Decision Making

In an objective decision-making process, decisions are based as much as possible on factual information. Someone trying to make a $1,000,000,000 decision in an objective culture will ask for a marketing report, finance reports, feasibility studies, and other analyses in an attempt to bring the decision down to a rational number. The hope is that all of the analysis will lead to an informed decision. A subjective decision process is based far more on subconscious considerations. Someone from a subjective culture, if asked whether or not to make the $1,000,000,000 investment, would lean back, think about how the investment makes them feel and come up with the decision based upon gut instincts. Americans are often horrified when they see important decisions being made subjectively. But it is important to note that many studies show that there are kinds of decisions that are better made subjectively. Subjective decisions also have the advantage that they can be made quickly. Military battle decisions often must be made this way due to time constraints.

Family

Another important trait for international business people to understand is how important family is to a culture. In cultures with low family scores, like the United States, families are considered to consist of two spouses and their children but the family is not ranked highly in decision making. In countries with high family scores, families are extended and include spouses and children along with grandparents, aunts and uncles, and other relatives all living in one household. In that case, the family is the most important concern in decision making. Many international companies have been challenged because they grew up on the American model in which workers are trained to seek higher level positions by transferring or moving for training within the company. In countries with high family scores the process can't work because workers are unwilling to move away from their extended family.

Authority

Attitudes toward authority is a measure of how much respect people in a country give to people in positions of official authority. In countries with high authority scores, official authority is highly respected. A first year police officer, for example, in a high authority country could expect to give a command to anyone in the country and have them obey it. In a low authority country, little to no respect is given to official authority. The president or head of the military in a low authority country could give a command and would probably expect very few if any of their people to follow it.

Trust

Trust is a measure of how willing people in a country are to accept claims made by others. In high trust countries people generally expect others are telling the truth and will readily work with others they know little about. In low trust countries people are much more suspect. People are generally not willing to trust someone they have not known for a very long time. Trust is an important foundation of international business. To move millions of dollars worth of products from country to country with no governmental oversight outside that provided by the two countries within their own domains requires a great deal of trust. Countries with high trust scores tend to find it much easier to create the relationships necessary for expanding international business. Trust misplaced can result in negative consequences, however. Consider the recent declines in our stock market where investments were based on trusting the system. When it broke down, trillions were lost. Countries with low trust scores tend to keep business within family groups and smaller well known networks. It can be difficult for new companies to break into those tight networks. When they do, much can be at risk. Witness when Russia repatriated its oil business. Many international oil companies lost billions in investment money because they trusted the Russian government.

Future Orientation

Future orientation is attending to the time frame where a culture is comfortable. For example, the United States is future oriented. People of the United States tend to constantly ask "what's next?" They are focused on looking to the future and trying to make the future a better place. There are countries in the world that are much more past oriented; that look to the past to help them make decisions. Past oriented countries focus on precedents and how things were done before. Business decision processes in future and past oriented countries are different. If an important investment decision is needed, a future oriented decision maker will try to project the likely outcomes of a decision into the future and choose the one that creates the most positive outcome. The decision maker from a past oriented culture with the exact same question would instead look to the past for situations that were most like what they currently face and try to repeat the behavior that worked best. There are a small number of present oriented countries. Present oriented countries focus almost entirely on the here and now. Present orientation has some strong religious foundations but is a challenge for the business community and has tended to weaken adherent countries' economies. Thus, it remains a weak force in the modern world.

Fatalism

Fatalism is a measure of how much people within a culture believe they control their own destinies. In a highly fatalistic culture people believe that the future is largely already written. People in highly fatalistic cultures generally see their lives as playing out their assigned roles. Many believe nothing they do in life will change anything. Low fatalism cultures believe that people control their own destiny. People in low fatalism cultures believe that each action they take will have ramifications for the future. Business implications of fatalism are far less clear than many would imagine. Many people from high fatalistic cultures prove dynamic and creative. They also tend to suffer from far less stress. People from very low fatalism cultures will often work harder to affect change but often do so with a very high cost in stress. Moving mountains takes more effort than one might imagine.

Monochronic vs. Polychronic Information Processing

Someone from a monochronic information processing culture tends to process information one piece at a time. People from monochronic cultures prefer to handle a task to its completion and then begin another task. This is often thought of as linear processing. Work such as science and mathematics is usually better done in monochronic cultures where precise concentration is required. People from polychronic cultures are the ultimate multitaskers. They are able to accept, filter, and process multiple threads of information all at one time. People from monochronic cultures are usually more useful in tasks that require timely completion and attention to detail. People from polychronic cultures tend to work better in environments with high interrupt opportunities and consequences, such as air traffic controller might encounter.

Combined, the above traits will provide a reasonably clear picture of international business techniques employed by a country. It takes a great deal of experience to recognize where each culture lies on each trait and understand the business effects of interactions of each trait within each culture. This can prove useful in deciding which cultures or countries might lead to good business opportunities for a particular company or product. Pay careful attention and you will find that, over time, you can develop quite a skill at anticipating how markets, governments, and peoples will respond to business activities by understanding the countries' traits.

SOURCE

Hofstede, Geert (1984). *Culture's Consequences: International Differences in Work-related Values.* London: Sage.

NOTES

Concept	Definition	Example
Culture Definition (reminder) A fuzzy set of mostly shared traits within a defined population		
What Are the Traits (reminder)		
There are many hundreds— they vary by culture		
Several important dimensions have been defined to help study business interactions		
Hofstede's Four Dimensions		
Uncertainty Avoidance—The Rejection of Risk Investments Social Interaction		
Power Distance—The Psychological and Social Distance between Superiors and Subordinates Employer/Employee Relations People to Government Relations Parent to Child Relations		
Collectivism vs. Individualism Teamwork Rewards Systems Innovation Management		
Masculinity vs. Femininity Organizational Structure Rewards		

Concept	Definition	Example
Other Important Traits		

Attitudes Towards:
  Material Wealth
  Achievement
  Time
  Change
  Subjective vs. Objective
    Decision Making
  Family
  Authority
  Trust
  Future Orientation
  Fatalism		

Monochronic vs. Polychronic Information Processing		

Government and Political Systems

POLITICAL SYSTEMS

To understand the government of a country, one must first understand the political systems through which a government is built. International business often finds itself dealing more with the political systems governments are embedded in than with the government itself. It is therefore critical that an international business executive clearly understand political systems and how they operate.

Let's start with the definition: **A political system is a complete set of institutions, the relationships between those institutions, and the norms that govern their function.** There are three important components to the definition of a political system.

First, a political system is a complete set of institutions. That means that as you try to study a political system like the government it is not enough to study the executive branch or the executive and legislative branch or any other subset of the institutions that make up the political system. Without understanding all of the major components, such as the cabinet ministries, lobbying industry, and other major influencers, you'll never be able to understand the full extent of how a political system interacts and functions.

Next, understanding the institutions within a political system is not enough to understand the political system. You must also understand the relationships between all the institutions to understand how individuals make decisions within each institution. Any one institution may have many of its rules written down so everyone can see and understand them. But the institutions do not operate in isolation. The other institutions in the political system can have substantial impact on what happens inside one particular institution. The rules for the interactions of institutions are rarely ever written making predicting the relationships between institutions far more challenging. It is the unwritten influence system and its nuances that are powerful.

Finally, the definition of a political system also includes the norms that govern the function of institutions. It is important to note that the definition includes the word norms not rules. Rules are often written, clear, and ignored. It is the norms of repeated behavior within the institution that one needs to understand if you are to understand the political system.

With this definition in place it is now important to consider what constitute political systems. Governments and their related institutions clearly qualify but if you think about it so do companies. In fact, so do universities, fraternity systems, high school classes, and a huge number of other loosely defined human organizations. Governments are a particularly focused type of political system but it is important to remember they function just like most other political systems and are not in any way separate from them. That encompassing totality is an idea that is critical to understanding how international business interfaces with governments.

Now that you know what a political system is, it is important to consider why they exist. Political systems have been around for as long as human beings have been gathering into groups and have felt the need for structure and organization. Many would even argue that baboons, chimpanzees, apes, and other advanced species have rudimentary political systems as well. With such a long history, it is clear that political systems play an important role in human life. There are three primary functions political systems serve. They are described below.

FUNCTIONS OF POLITICAL SYSTEMS

Focus on Distributing Power

The primary function political systems serve is to distribute power. To understand that statement one must consider what is meant by the word "power." Power in this context means the ability to get other people to do what you want. American culture often teaches us power is a bad thing. Our high individualism rebels against having others tell us what to do. But power is an absolutely necessary function for groups of people to live with one another.

Without power we could not decide whether we should drive on the right or the left side of the road, or which days to take off from school, or how to proceed with any of the thousands of other transactions we accomplish in a day that require some level of integration and coordination between people. Political systems decide who gets to tell others "in America we drive on the right side of the road," or "we don't have classes on Sundays or holidays." Political systems give us an organized way to decide who gets to decide what. They prevent every decision a person makes from being a unique instance. They keep us from having to make every decision every day and fight (and fight physically in the absence of political systems) for our solutions if others disagree.

Establish Boundaries between Groups

The second most important function provided by political systems is the establishment of boundaries between groups. Governments tell us this is the border of Mexico and this is the border of Canada. Companies tell us you work in marketing or finance but not both. Companies then define what a marketing person does and why and how that is different from what the finance person does. Political systems thus define the borders that people use to define themselves.

Include Specified Members

Finally, political systems define who is a member of the group and who isn't. The power to control who belongs within a political system is immense. Consider the difference between being born in San Diego or a mile away in Mexico. The rights and privileges one gains are drastically different because of how political systems have defined who belongs and who doesn't. You'll see the same power in who belongs and who doesn't to which sorority or fraternity, who works for which company, and who is or isn't a member of a particular church.

GOVERNMENT

With a solid understanding of what a political system is, we're now ready to turn our attention to governments. Governments perform all the functions of political systems. They distribute power, established boundaries between groups, and define their membership. Governments are a particular form of political system with specific roles to play, however. Those roles are described below.

GOVERNMENTS' ROLES—UNIVERSALLY AGREED

There are many different approaches to governments in the world. There is a set of universally agreed roles for government, however. A political system that fails to take on the universally agreed roles will not be considered government. The universally agreed roles for government follow.

Create and Maintain a Monopoly on Violence

The role that defines a political system as being a government is that it must create and maintain a monopoly on violence (Weber 1919. That statement comes as a shock to many people so it is worth further consideration.

First, to accept the statement one must accept that all power ultimately derives from violence. Someone may not be able to force you to do what they want using violence, but if they are willing to kill you and you cannot prevent it, they can prevent you from stopping them doing whatever they want. All other power therefore derives from the willingness and ability of a person or group of people to defend themselves from violent attempts to enforce their will. Think about centuries of human conflict that determine power and its influences.

The Middle Ages provides an excellent model for how modern government developed. Prior to that, in the dark ages, Roman authority disintegrated and for many areas of the world governance was in disarray. People were free to live to the extent of their abilities to defend their own lives. Given the inherent instability and danger in that situation, people started looking for ways they could be protected when they were weak. They started recruiting the best fighters among themselves and paid them to protect the people in their villages. In Europe these defenders became the early knights. As groups of people ran into each other, their knights inevitably took to fighting one another to gain control over larger groups. Some knights were very successful and other knights made contracts with them to protect the weak knights and their people. These very successful knights became Kings. The Kings held contracts with all their local knights which basically said that the King would protect the knights and their territories so long as the knights agreed that if the king went to war the knights would join him. That is the foundation from which modern European governments grew.

Many would argue that governments have taken on so many other roles that a monopoly on violence is no longer the core requisite to being a government. But consider a political system that loses its monopoly on violence such as happens in coups, civil wars, and revolutions. If the system does not win it is no longer the government. It is also worth noting that there are still several governments in this world that do little more for their people than hold a monopoly on violence. There are a large number of governments who freely murder and steal from their own people. These governments are still recognized as governments because they hold a monopoly on violence. Think about the many African nations and the powerful but inhumane governments who are in charge until the next rogue group holds a violent coup and becomes the new government.

Regulate Areas that Might Otherwise Degenerate into Violence

After a monopoly on violence, there are very few things everyone on the planet would agree are legitimate roles of a government. One other universally agreed role if you expect government to maintain its monopoly on violence is that you must permit it to regulate areas that would quickly degenerate into violence if they were not regulated. What each culture defines as areas that would degenerate into violence differs but there are many similarities. For instance, most cultures have some concept of personal property. Regulation against theft of personal property, however defined, is therefore well accepted as an appropriate role for government. Most cultures are protective enough of their concept of private property that violations of it usually lead to violence.

Tax

The only other universally agreed upon role for government is tax. Although most people do not like being taxed, and taxing itself has led to a great deal of violence, pretty much everyone understands that they must pay those who hold the monopoly on violence in some way. That payment is called tax. Once the government takes on the role of taxing, however, most governments have extended their reach far beyond their role of controlling violence to include sponsoring their definition of the greater good of the society.

GOVERNMENTS' ROLES— NOT UNIVERSALLY AGREED

Once a government has taken on the taxing role it most quickly moves into other areas of its country's economy and asserts control. There is no universal agreement on what other roles a government should take. There is enough consistency among many of the world's large countries to identify some broad categories of activities governments have undertaken. They are described below.

Support Areas of Natural Underinvestment

Many governments have chosen to support areas of natural underinvestment. There are things that are good for a group but which are less clearly good for any individual in the group. These activities tend to lead to natural underinvestment. Activities such as schools for the young bring benefits to a society, such as higher national income, a more dynamic economy, greater equality among people, and a general reduction in violence. It takes a very long and large up-front investment for any individual to see personal gain from education, however. Therefore, when left under individual control, most families underinvest in their children's education. Many governments have stepped in, taxed people, and then used that money for schools, forcing more investment in education. Many governments repeat that pattern for any area they consider an area of natural underinvestment. Support for arts programs, languages, public parks, and numerous other activities are justified as being support for areas of natural underinvestment.

Support for Projects that Require Full Citizen Participation

Another role governments have stepped into is support for projects that require full citizen participation. There are some projects, such as building roads and bridges, where everyone in a community gains when the project is built. But if everyone were allowed to decide on their own many people would choose not to invest in the project even though they would gain from it. The government, therefore, steps in with its monopoly on violence and taxing capability to force everyone to participate. Again, the range of products put under this heading is huge. Although many of the projects really do support everyone in the community, some projects, such as statues and sports stadiums, are done purely to stroke the egos of the politicians suggesting them.

Maintain Cultural Values

Many government projects can be described as existing to maintain some cultural value held by the government or some section of its people. Many countries, for example, have official language ministries that define the legal and acceptable use of their language in the country. Museums, cultra programs, and other culture-enforcing mechanisms fall within this category.

Control Economy

Some countries have gone so far as to say their monopoly on violence and the culture they say they're defending gives them the right and obligation to run their entire economy. Given the lack of innovation that tends to occur under such a command economy, few countries go so far as to try to run the entire economy from government offices but many countries still have government playing by far the majority role. This is a centrally planned country where innovation is discouraged.

Etc. Etc. Etc.

The Etc. Etc. Etc. category must be included here because once a political system has established its monopoly on violence it becomes very difficult to prevent that political system from doing anything it pleases. The only sure-fire alternative to accepting a role the government chooses for itself is to overthrow the government. Democracies have tried to make that task easier but it is still far from easy. In countries without democracy, violence is often needed to prevent the government from doing whatever it wishes. That means governments have taken on an incredible range of roles. Some have been beneficial; many have been extremely destructive.

MAJOR FORMS OF GOVERNMENT

With that understanding of what governments do, let's now take a look at the structural forms governments use to do it. These structural forms are prototypes. Most countries use modified or mixed forms of each. But it is worthwhile for international business people to develop a solid understanding of each form of government because international business is often faced with different issues and opportunities depending on the form of government with which they're dealing. The major forms of governments are listed below, broken into two major categories—democratic and autocratic forms of government.

Democratic

The democratic forms of government attempt to give people more say in how they are governed. The first three forms are all representative democracies. In representative democracies people are not asked to govern themselves, but instead they're given the chance to have some input into who will govern them. The first three forms of democratic government progress from giving people the greatest say in who governs them to the least say.

> **Presidential Republic**—In a presidential republic, as in all representative democracies, people are not asked to govern themselves. That right is still reserved for an elite few. People, however, are given input into who governs them. In a presidential republic people have the greatest say in who rules them. In most presidential republics people choose a number of legislative representatives who are responsible for creating law, handling government budgets, and reviewing

government activities. Prosecuting the laws and managing the implementation of government activities is usually left to an administrative branch. Because administering and implementing government activities centralizes a great deal of power, the chief administrator is very powerful. In a presidential republic the people vote to choose that chief administrator themselves. That elected president is usually very powerful within their country. He or she has control over the implementation of government and can claim a mandate from the people when negotiating with the legislature.

Parliamentary Republic—Like a presidential republic, parliamentary republics divide control of government between a legislature and chief executive of administration. The big difference is in a parliamentary republic is that the people of a country do not choose the chief administrator. The legislature reserves for itself the right to choose the chief administrator, usually called a prime minister. The prime minister is usually in a weaker position than a president because they cannot claim a direct mandate and the legislature can replace them at any time. In practice, the prime minister usually ends up weaker still due to party politics. In presidential republics party systems usually develop that include only two major parties. Given the importance of the presidential position, only two parties typically survive the evolutionary process of trying to elect a president. In parliaments, more parties usually survive because a prime minister can build a coalition of many small parties to get elected within the legislature. Having their position dependent on several small parties weakens a prime minister, however, because if a smaller party chooses to leave a ruling coalition the prime minister will often lose his or her position. Thus, more small parties gain voice in a parliamentary republic, weakening the prime minister.

Totalitarian Democracy—A totalitarian democracy is often democracy in name only. In most totalitarian democracies a president or other chief administrator was once fairly elected, but they then used their centralized power to distort the democratic process to favor themselves and their parties. When this happens, democracy typically survives in name only and totalitarian democracies often end up as dictatorships in practice.

Direct Democracy—In a direct democracy, people vote on all important government actions directly. There's not a system of elected officials with centralizing power. Currently there are no countries using direct democracy for all of their operations. However, it is still important for international business people to understand this sysrem. There are several smaller towns and cities operating under direct democracy and your business could end up operating in one of them. Direct democracy is also growing as a concept as more and more people become used to having a say in a far broader set of issues due to the internet. Consensus building on issues is easier than ever before for large groups.

Autocratic

In autocratic forms of government, people are not given any official say in who overns them or how they are governed. In practice, even an autocratic form of government listens at least somewhat to the desires of the people if for no other reason than to reduce the risk of a revolution. The forms of autocratic government follow.

Dictatorship—In a dictatorship, a single person and the associates have grabbed control of the monopoly on violence. They can then use that control for whatever purposes they see fit. Some dictators are actually very good leaders, focused on helping the people that they govern. Others are violent, self-absorbed people stealing as much for themselves as they can get. A benign dictatorship is actually an efficient form of government. Only one person must be consulted to get a decision made. Many international businesses find great advantage in dealing with dictators who have their own people's interests at heart. The major problem with a dictatorship is that there is no mechanism in place to pass control to the next person when a dictator dies. That frequently means civil war. Thus, that effective dictatorship only works in the short run.

Monarchy—Monarchies are an attempt to fix the dictatorship problem of passing on control by setting up a system of hereditary succession. Monarchies generally developed when a dictator was powerful enough to place his own son in control when he died. If a family were successful enough they could pull that off for a few generations so people became accustomed to it and it became generally accepted within the culture. There are many longstanding monarchies still running countries today. Monarchies can have the advantages of a dictatorship if the monarch is capable. Unfortunately, monarchies have an "idiot son" problem. If the next person in line happens to be incompetent, they still end up a leader. Monarchies are then faced with potentially decades of incompetent leadership or revolution. Many of today's monarchies are monarchies in name only. There are legislative branches of government and prime ministers that really run government operations. The United Kingdom is an example. There are still several strong monarchies, however, where the ruling family still runs the country. Saudi Arabia is probably the best known example.

Theocracy—A theocracy is a country in which a religious order has taken control of government. Theocratic governments usually follow religious texts as their guiding principle. Theocratic governments, therefore, tend to be conservative and intolerant because most of the religious texts being followed are thousands of years old and are highly rule-bound.

Failed States—Failed states are countries in which no one group has been able to gain and maintain a monopoly on violence. That leaves competing groups struggling for control and the country in civil war. As many problems as other forms of governments may face, none tend to be nearly as bad as having competing groups struggling to gain the monopoly on violence. The vast majority of people in the world who die from starvation, genocide, or curable diseases usually live in failed states.

POLITICAL RISKS

Although international businesses can have a substantial impact on government, they typically do not control it. Therefore, they must learn to deal with the risks that arise from a political environment. There are a number of risks that companies face. Major ones are listed below.

Expropriations

In an expropriation, a country takes over an individual company. The takeover can occur because the company was failing or because it has made the country politically unhappy. It is not uncommon when a country expropriates a company for the company to be paid very little, or nothing. Therefore, the company takes a complete loss on all assets that were in the country. Such large losses are obviously unpopular with shareholders so companies will typically do whatever they can to prevent them. Sometimes the expropriation occurs because of something the company did and the company can head off the problem by modifying their behavior. Other times an expropriation has little to do with the company and more to do with that country where the company is based. In these situations, the company must recognize issues before they arise and must move resources if necessary.

Nationalization

In a nationalization, a country takes over an entire industry rather than just one company. This happens most frequently with natural resource industries like oil but this industry-wide takeover has occurred in financial and other industries. Since the entire industry is being taken over there is probably little a company can do to protect itself other than make sure it sees problems coming and move the resources before it happens.

Socialization

In a socialization, a country takes over its entire economy. Socialization is uncommon now but the risk still exists. Individual companies have no real opportunity to prevent socialization so their only strategy is to see them coming and move ahead of them.

Social Upheavals

Social upheavals are events such as riots, revolutions, or other outbreaks of violence where the government temporarily loses their control over violence. Sometimes limited property damage occurs in these upheavals. Sometimes many people die. It can be very difficult for a company to be stuck in such an upheaval. Property and employees' lives are at risk. It is imperative that the company predict the events as best possible and provide appropriate protections.

Political Attacks on Foreign Companies/Industry

Political attacks on foreign companies frequently occur when a government is looking for a scapegoat. When the economy is not going in the direction politicians would like, they will usually look for someone else to blame. Foreign companies are easy targets because they are obviously somehow involved in the economy and they have limited political rights within the country. Companies need to do all possible to make sure they're not easy targets for such attacks. Maintaining positive public images in each country in which they operate helps. Companies must still understand that these attacks rarely have anything to do with the company itself. Frequently they're attacks on the country in which the company is based. The company's best hope for such situations is to make sure they're popular enough with the people and the politicians within the country so that another company is chosen for the attack instead.

War

Although very large and powerful companies may be able to influence the decision to go to war, most companies, like most people, are merely victims of that choice. War can be disastrous for company operations within affected countries. Employees stuck behind warring lines are at great physical risk. Most companies' operations are destroyed, at least while the fighting is nearby. Companies, therefore, have a strong motivation to avoid being caught in warring countries.

THREE PHASES OF WORLD POLITICS

Given the drastic impact of war on a company, most companies would prefer to avoid being in warring countries. Fortunately, there are theories that help a company predict where wars are likely to break out. The most prevalent of these theories is set in the three phases of world politics (Little, Smith 2006). This theory tells us that the world tends to rotate between three phases. Each phase is controlled by a different international power structure. This theory is well documented and supported all the way back to the 1400s and the birth of the modern nation state. Understanding which world phase you're in helps you better predict which types of wars your company is likely to be threatened with. The three phases are defined below.

Bipolar

The bipolar phase of world politics is characterized by two approximately equal military powers who largely dominate the rest of the world. This phase occurred most recently roughly between 1950 and 1990 when the United States and the USSR dominated world politics, but it has existed at other times. Spain and England, France and England, and other countries have controlled bipolar phases. The bipolar phase is the most stable of the world phases. It is stable because the world is largely divided between two major powers and there is little motivation for those two powers to fight. The only kind of wars typically seen in the bipolar phase are small wars in fringe countries as the two major powers test each other's resolve and capabilities. After the bipolar phase has run its course, one of the two powers typically self destructs. The weaker economy of the two bipolar powers usually collapses under the strains of trying to maintain a military equal to the stronger economy.

Monopoly Power

A monopoly power phase begins as one of the two countries in a bipolar phase self destructs. In a monopoly power phase one country is left to dominate the world. This is the phase we now live in with the United States dominating world military and economic activity. England, Spain, and other countries have enjoyed similar situations in the past. In the monopoly power phase, the kind of wars that are most common are civil wars. The dominant power has a motivation and the capacity to prevent wars among its friends and trading partners. It has little motivation to stop small civil wars in countries with which it has little trade, however. The power vacuum left often leads to break out of unresolved hostilities bottled up during the bipolar phase. It is therefore dangerous to be involved in countries peripheral to the monopoly power. The continent of Africa plays that role in the current phase. Eventually, a monopoly power disintegrates from within. As the monopoly power disintegrates, several weaker countries usually step up, creating the multi-power phase.

Multipower

In the multipower phase, several countries climb to fill the power void left as a monopoly power disintegrates. The multipower phase is, by far, the most dangerous phase. In the multipower phase there are five, six, sometimes even seven powerful countries in the world. Those countries form alliances to try to gain control of world politics. The smaller countries in the alliance have a strong motivation to switch alliances. By doing so, they play a role far more important than their power dictates. As alliances shift, however, world wars break out as one alliance attacks the other to prove its dominance. World War I and World War II were the outcomes of the last time the world faced a multipower phase. Eventually, two countries grow in power to dominate alliances after warfare. Those two countries become the bipolar powers that start the cycle of world phases again.

POLITICAL RISK STRATEGIES

Companies have had to develop methods to control their political risks given the substantial jeopardy a company faces in dealing with numerous national governments. There are five important things that companies can do to try to protect themselves. They are listed below.

Have Own Panel of Experts

The most expensive option for a company looking to control its political risks is to hire its own panel of experts to predict where international political risks will occur. The company will typically set up a panel for each region of the world within which they operate. The panel's job is to constantly monitor political events in countries to discover threats to the company long before they occur. Most companies will have four or five people who regularly interact with one another, trying to see how political events will affect the company, their customers, suppliers, and employees. Such a focus group can usually offer valuable insights and help the company avoid problems in the country. They are expensive, however, so they are only used by very large companies with significant overseas operations.

Hire Outside Assessments

A significantly less expensive option for monitoring political activities in a country is to hire outside assessments. There are many consulting companies that exist exclusively to study political risks of countries or regions of the world. Many companies hire specific or more general reports from these consultancies to learn the risks they face. Although these reports are less expensive than having your own panel, they're usually also less specific to your company so they're not as useful.

Use U.S. and European Government Reports

The discount option for discovering political risks is to review government reports. The U.S. and European governments put out numerous reports about political risks in other countries. The reports are often useful for discovering general country risk but offer little in industry-specific intelligence. Managers are therefore left to predict company-specific risks themselves.

Have a Plan for Each Possible Change

As a company determines specific country risks, it needs to develop plans for what it will do if risks progress to negative events. Given each major risk, the company needs a plan for how it will handle a country rejecting its employees, or attacking its assets and reputation in the country. Detailed evacuation plans are needed because if a company needs to get employees out quickly, people are unlikely to be thinking clearly. Plans for protecting proprietary information are also critical if a company is going to need to abandon physical assets.

Have an Overall Plan for Unforeseen Change

Along with all the plans for predictable risks the company faces, it also needs a plan for all the risks it hasn't predicted. It is impossible to predict every possible occurrence. Therefore, the company needs some generalized plans for what to do in case it needs to evacuate employees, remove assets from a country, or abandon a country altogether.

SOURCES

Weber, Max. 1919. *Politics as a Vocation*. Speech given at Munich University. Out of Print.

Little, Richard, and Michael Smith. 2006. *Perspectives on World Politics*, Routledge, London.

 **NOTES**

A political system is a complete set of institutions, the relationships between those institutions, and the norms that govern their function.

Concept	Definition	Example
Political Systems		
Primarily focus on distributing power		
Establish boundaries between groups		
Include specified members		
Governments' Roles— Universally Agreed		
Create and Maintain a Monopoly on Violence		
Regulate Areas that Might Otherwise Degenerate into Violence		
Tax		
Governments' Roles—Not Universally Agreed		
Support Areas of Natural Underinvestment		
Support for Projects that Require Full Citizen Participation		
Maintain Cultural Values		
Control Economy		
Etc. Etc. Etc.		
Major Forms of Government		

Democratic
   Presidential Republic
   Parliamentary Republic
   Totalitarian Democracy
   Direct Democracy		

Concept	Definition	Example

Autocratic
   Dictatorship
   Monarchy
   Theocracy
   Failed States		

Political Risks		
Expropriations		
Nationalization		
Socialization		
Social Upheavals		
Political Attacks on Foreign Companies/Industry		
War		
Three Phases of World Politics		
Bipolar		
Monopoly Power		
Multipower		
Political Risk Strategies		
Have Own Panel of Experts		
Hire Outside Assessments		
Use U.S. and European Government Reports		
Have a Plan for Each Possible Change		
Have an Overall Plan for Unforeseen Change		

International Law

Chapter four provided a description of how governments function as sets of political systems. Governments must codify their practices and rules into law to increase the efficiency and consistency with which they govern behavior. This chapter will look at the types of legal systems implemented by various countries as well as the international alliances that affect international business. Remember that laws are expression of political will. The level to which a country attempts to create legal consistency within its rules and their application across an entire population varies greatly. Written laws may not be enforced and unwritten laws may still mean prosecution. That said, knowing the laws and underlying legal systems is still critical for understanding the rules of local governance.

TYPES OF LEGAL SYSTEMS

Countries operate under different legal systems that provide a unique mindset for those practicing law within a country. No country follows any of the legal systems perfectly. There is enough consistency within each country, however, that understanding the legal systems provides a useful basis for understanding how a government thinks about controlling its people. Here are the five major types of legal systems.

Common Law

Common law approaches rule writing with the understanding that a government can never predict all the ways things can go wrong. It also recognizes that rules prevent innovation. It tries to guide behavior with general guidelines that people are expected to interpret and then act upon in a manner consistent with the guidelines.

Law by Precedent—Governments that use common law write laws that are fairly general. They then let the country operate and as long as everything goes well, they don't intercede. Eventually something doesn't go well, however, and someone is hurt physically, financially, or emotionally. Common law allows that person to suggest who they think hurt them and sue them. The person who was hurt and the person(s) who they think hurt them are brought before a judge to tell their stories. That judge's decision is then entered in the law books as precedent. Any time anyone else sues, saying the same thing happened to them, the next judge is supposed to look at the precedent and judge the same way. Thus, common law is built by a series of lawsuits that build precedents.

Influence of England—The countries where common law is most prevalent are the countries most influenced by England historically. England built an extensive empire and brought common law with them to most of their colonies. After the United States broke from England, it kept common law as its primary system of laws and helped spread the legal system to countries where it has the most substantial commercial influence.

Interpretation by Judges—Legislatures provide basic guidelines but judges are expected to analyze specific situations and determine how to best apply those general rules. Allowing judges so much leeway for local interpretation keeps common law alive. It is constantly adapted through judge's interpretation of the specific situation compared with similar precedents. Conflicts in interpretation by different judges often occur.

Disadvantages of Time and Costs—A major problem with common law systems is that they require a huge number of lawyers to work through intricacies and delays and are thus time consuming and expensive. Because laws are written broadly, interpretation is vague. The only way to find out if something is legal is to wait for someone to sue someone else and see what happens. And then, of course, there are appeals—appeals of appeals—appeals of the appeals of appeals. The legal system becomes an expensive luxury in common law countries and frequently becomes neglected in poorer common law countries.

Advantage Is Innovation—The major advantage of common law, however, is that it is easier to innovate when you don't have to wait for the government to make something legal. If you discover a new possibility and believe it to be safe, you can generally just try it. As long as no one is hurt you can profit from it immediately. Therefore, common law countries tend to be more innovative and have more dynamic economies.

Uncertainty—Overall, common law keeps people guessing because you can never know for sure whether what you are doing is legal or not. For the most part, people can sue any time over anything. The risk associated with the open-ended nature of common law is an irritant. The improved opportunities for innovation can make it worth the cost however, at least for companies in dynamic industries.

Civil Law

Civil law takes the stand that people should know exactly what is and is not illegal. It is practiced by countries that believe in directing behavior through precision and clarity.

Law by Code—Civil law is primarily code law. Code law sets specific limits for what is and is not illegal. In Norway, driving under the influence of alcohol lands one in jail. No exceptions. Code law tries to make as specific a guideline as possible for all legal situations.

Influence of France—Although code law is a German invention, it was primarily France that spread it to the rest of the world. Most countries that are heavily influenced by France or any of the ex-French colonies tend to operate under civil law.

Application by Judges—The judge's job in a civil law country is different from that of a common law judge. The civil law judge is expected to determine which side of the line you were on with respect to a particular law. For example, the judge in a civil law country would try to determine whether you were going 55 miles per hour as you say or 60 miles per hour as a policeman says. That is the only interpretation allowed, however. If you are determined to have been going over 55, you broke the law, and you're punished. The punishment is more clearly defined by law for the judge who has limited, if any, leeway.

Not Lawyer and Cost Intensive—It is easy to know what the law is by simply looking it up. If the legislature made it legal, it is. If it did not, it is not. No court interprets it. Courts are not clogged by appeals. Class status or ability to pay for top legal advice is irrelevant—theoretically.

Impediment to Innovation—The major problem with civil law is that it can become impossible for a legislature to stay ahead of its economy. If it requires a law for something to be legal then any innovation requires legal change first. That puts pressure on a legislature to understand the implications of any change and lengthy passage of time to write new laws. Legislatures are rarely up to the task, so innovation suffers by time delays and uncertainty of legislative intent and action.

Deliberate Linear Process—Clearing everything in advance through the need to have laws in place stifles innovation and slows the economy. If you look around French-influenced countries of the world you'll note most of them are fairly slow-growing economies because of this very problem. In fact, in the United States, 49 of the 50 states use common law. One, the state of Louisiana, uses primarily civil law. Even though it has a major international port, the state of Louisiana's economy has suffered and fallen behind much of the rest of the United States because of it.

Religious Law

Religious law is practiced in far fewer countries than common or civil law. It is common enough, however, that the international business person needs to understand it. Some major countries like Iran officially recognize religious law as its highest legal system. Many more countries that don't officially recognize religious law have embedded components of religious law in their secular legal system.

Law Based on Religious Standards—Religious law uses codes and guidelines found in religious practice and texts as the country's legal system. Because most religious codes and practices are open to several interpretations, religious leaders are usually the heads of their legal system. The commingling of law and religion tends to create conservative and slow to change legal practices. Because most religious codes were set down more than 1000 years ago they do not always apply easily to modern situations. Legal/religious scholars in religious law countries are therefore left to struggle with how to appropriately apply religious dictates to situations never imagined when the codes were created. For example, the controversy over stem cell research is an embedded religious issue within the common laws of the United States in the definition of personhood.

Common in Middle East—Religious law is most common in the Middle East and other parts of the world with a strong Muslim tradition. Religious law influences many countries in Asia, Europe, and the Americas, however. Even many U.S. cities and states practice some religious law. So-called blue laws that restrict things like selling alcohol on Sundays are an example.

Religious System Is Ultimate Judge—In a pure religious law system religious powers are the ultimate judges. For example, in Iran, there are civil laws and civil courts. Religious courts, however, can always overrule anything that comes from the civil system. Judges in a religious law system try to interpret religious texts and traditions to determine what is allowed or forbidden. Because of the complexity of religious tradition there is huge variance in how actions are judged.

Uncertainty in Interpretation of Actions—The dual religious and civil system in religious law countries can be a significant problem because international businesses will not know under which system they will be judged. The breadth of interpretation available in most religious texts allows many decisions in religious law countries to become highly political and open to bribery. Some people, and companies, are willing to buy the religious interpretations they need for legal advantage. Another method of coping is to form alliances among producers in several countries, like OPEC, so that rules apply more broadly and there is a larger base of protection from the uncertainty.

Indigenous Law

Indigenous law is rarely found at the national level. It is still common around the world at the village, tribe, or town level. Indigenous law relies entirely on the cultural understanding of its people for law. This creates uncertainty that is not conducive to business dealings.

Law by "Elders"—Unwritten indigenous law assumes everyone affected by the law is a member of the culture and knows what is right and wrong. Village Elders are assigned as judges whenever disputes arise. If ever two people, families, or companies disagree on what is allowed, the dispute is arbitrated by someone who is seen to be highly experienced in the culture. Sometimes that experience is made official through a title, like mayor or official village Elder, but sometimes it is a person to whom others have customarily learned to turn. The village Elder's role is to listen to both parties before using his best judgment to decide the dispute. End of story.

Lack of Consistency—Because disputes are resolved by a village Elder's experience, there's lack of consistency between Elders or frequently even with one Elder's decisions. There is no written law that Elders need to follow so they're free to make whatever decisions they think best. Their decisions can wisely consider all relevant issues, but sometimes their decisions are misinterpretations that do great damage to all parties concerned. This inconsistency provides an unknown environment making it difficult for businesses to thrive.

Interpretation and Influence—Without written rules, Elders are free to interpret standards and rules however they see fit. Favoritism can be rampant. That tends to make indigenous law systems open to bribery and other attempts to affect decision. International companies facing indigenous law constantly struggle between how much they should use their economic power to influence the local system to bring it closer to world standards vs. how much they should allow existing tradition to reign supreme.

Innovation Is Stifled—Because tradition is the legal standard, the system is inherently against innovation. Lack of innovation seriously slows economic development within the region where the system is used. For some cultures, that slow economic growth is expected and people are happy to move within their traditional lives. For peoples who wish the benefits of economic growth, however, the lack of innovation within indigenous law can be stifling.

Bureaucratic Law

No country declares itself to have bureaucratic law as its primary legal system, but every long-established country has a large component of it. As you move from country to country you must recognize how much bureaucratic law has taken over the country's other legal systems. In many countries, bureaucratic law has completely taken over to the point where bureaucrats run the country and politicians have little power to control them. In other countries the political class still dominates the legal power structure but bureaucrats still control many of the lower level functions of the country.

Decisions Made by Bureaucratic Departments—The feature that most distinguishes bureaucratic law is that law is made and enforced by departments with a narrow focus of responsibility within the government. This means the laws being written and enforced are optimized to fit that particular department's needs but not the entire countries. Think of the word bureau which means chest of drawers. Top drawer is the highest and best, but every drawer is defined with its own distinct territory and laws. Rarely is any consideration given to big picture issues within bureaucratic law.

Contradictory Answers—Because each department writes and enforces its own rules, there's no need for the departments to coordinate rulings. That frequently creates situations where one department says an action is legal while another says it is not legal. Worse, it is common for one department to tell you that you must do something while another department tells you it is illegal to do it. In a strong bureaucratic system there is no one to resolve such contradictions. Bureaucrats simply leave it to each individual affected to figure out their own way through the problem. People and companies are caught and hurt in bureaucratic legal traps with no higher authority open for appeal and no legal method to resolve the contradiction.

Bribery Is Rampant—The small bureau nature of decision making means that inherent in bureaucracy is the opportunity and expectation of bribery. Bribery is harder to catch and there is not much incentive to root it out. Individuals and companies caught in a bureaucratic trap find their only way out of it is to bribe one or more of the conflicting bureaucracies. Some countries will purposely design conflicting rules to force bribes as a primary method of funding governance and self-indulgent wealth. The bribery system inevitably does substantial damage. Relying on a system of bribery means people with money face different legal systems than those without money. A series of bribes adds frustration, cost, and time to trying to do business.

Stifles Innovation—The more bureaucracy the more difficult it gets for innovation to survive. If there are a small number of bureaucratic offices to navigate, a company will usually be able to work with the offices and push new innovations through. When a company must deal with a large number of bureaucratic departments, it can become impossible for the company to work changes through all the bureaucratic systems. Most companies give up and keep doing what they have already been doing. Stifled innovation eventually crushes the bureaucratic systems' economy.

TYPES OF INTERNATIONAL LAWS

As a company works its way through the legal systems it must remember that few countries have just one legal system. For example, in the United States a company must follow city law, county law, state law, and federal law. Each legal layer has its own laws that frequently contradict laws at higher or lower levels. Once a company gets through one country's laws, however, it is not done with legal analysis. There are four more levels of laws of concern for an international company. It is critical for a company to know about and understand any agreements or treaties that affect their industry.

Bilateral—Two-nation Agreement

Bilateral laws are laws agreed upon in treaties between two countries. It is common for countries to have a number of specific agreements tied to individual industries. For example, the United States and Japan have agreements that dictate how they will trade automobiles, foodstuffs, and many other goods. These treaties become a layer of law that supersedes all the federal, state, and local laws of both countries.

Regional Laws—NAFTA, EU, etc.

The complexity of every country needing to have bilateral agreements with every other country led many countries to develop regional laws. Regional laws are intended to supersede all bilateral and national laws. The North American Free Trade Agreement (NAFTA) and the European Union (EU) are the two best known of these regional legal systems but there are many others.

Multinational Laws—WTO, etc.

Multinational laws attempt to cover trade across almost the entire world; they try to create rules that apply to everyone. The World Trade Organization (WTO) is, by far, the largest attempt at global trade law. World Trade Organization laws are said to supersede all other legal systems. The WTO and similar systems do create some consistency in basic trade but there are enough loopholes and enough areas where WTO rules do not apply that regional and bilateral laws still largely dictate country trade rules. Most importantly, the WTO has few mechanisms for enforcing laws, so trade violations by powerful countries are rarely addressed.

United Nations

The United Nations has its own set of laws that are meant to cover most nations of the world. The intent in establishing it after World War II was for it to be a global policy-making body with absolute veto power by five nations. That vision has not fully materialized. An international business, however, should recognize which laws of the UN apply to it.

LAWS YOU MUST KNOW

Companies entering a new country will usually start their legal analysis with the type of legal system they face and the bilateral, regional, and multinational laws that will affect their industry. Once the overall legal ramifications are understood, they must learn the specific national and local laws that will affect their business. Major categories are listed below.

Ownership

Most countries restrict foreign ownership in some way. There are three primary questions the company will ask.

How much is an individual or a company allowed to own? Every country has some sort of antitrust laws. Rules on how much of a national company a foreign company is allowed to hold are designed to prevent a company from having too much power in the market. What too much power means changes from country to country. In civil law countries, foreign companies are frequently restricted to owning no more than 49% of a company In common law countries like the United States, the restriction can be vague but still enforced. Other countries allow no foreign ownership. Some allow business ownership but not land ownership.

How much can we own in our industry? Most countries also have ownership laws that are specific to industry. Every country has a few industries that it most carefully protects. Ownership laws in the protected industries are usually more strict than in industries where the country may be trying to attract investment.

What form can ownership take? As a company investigates ownership laws, it must also pay careful attention to what forms ownership can take. The United States, for example, has created legal entities like corporations, partnerships, and sole proprietorships with specific laws relating to them. Some countries allow any investment ownership by foreign countries but not management control. Other countries permit almost any form of ownership. It is critical that an international company understand what is permitted and its ramifications as far as controlling the company's proprietary technology and image before deciding to enter a country.

Taxes

The second legal issue when deciding to enter a country is taxes. Taxes can have a huge effect on pricing and profitability in a country so it is paramount the company understand this before making an entry decision. Tax questions the company must research include:

Does the nation favor or punish FDI? The tax code can readily identify whether or not foreign direct investment (FDI) is favored. If a country does not want FDI, foreign companies will often find tax rates that are prohibitively expensive. When tax rates are low for foreign companies it usually means the country is trying to attract investments. Countries with such low tax rates will often provide other assistance to win new investments. Countries so willing to help are often better investment choices.

What method of taxing is used? There are techniques companies can use to minimize taxes by using multiple countries' taxing systems against one another. A company will want to understand how any one country fits its overall tax puzzle. Does a country use income taxes, or value added taxes, or combinations? Does the country tax individuals, or companies, or both? What form do tariffs and other trade barriers take in the country? All are important considerations for profitability. The United States is often criticized for having high nominal corporate gains taxes relative to other countries but the reality is that few companies pay them due to other tax manipulations that are legal. The issue is complex, as you might expect.

What industries are encouraged? Finally a company will look to the tax code to discover the favored industries in the country. Favored industries will usually have lower tax rates. If a company is in one of the favored industries and there's not yet too much competition in the country, it is likely to be a good investment base. The United States offers tax-free zones for foreign investment as incentives to bring them here. If the industry is actively discouraged by the country, through the tax code, then it is likely a country the company is better off avoiding.

Personnel and Labor Laws

Personnel and labor laws tell a company what kind of employee costs, skills, and risks they will face. Companies will usually look to four specific areas for the personnel and labor law they need to understand.

Unionization Laws—The unionization laws of the country tell a company how much freedom it will have in dealing with its employees. If union laws are weak it is likely the company will be free to follow best practices for its industry. If union laws strongly protect wages, hours, and working conditions, then labor practices are likely to be negotiated, making changes in labor practices difficult. Therefore, most companies only enter strong union countries when there is a unique skill set they need or when they consider profitability is assured.

Mandatory Benefits and Wages—Mandatory benefits and wages will give companies a framework for understanding labor costs in a country. There are countries where the costs of mandatory benefits significantly exceed the costs of wages. Things like mandatory 4 week paid vacations and maximum 35 hour work weeks can drastically add to the costs of doing business. Many first world countries offer health care at the national level, thus allowing business to avoid the cost of health care. The company must understand both wage and benefit costs before making any entry decision.

Equal Opportunity Laws—Only a few countries have equal opportunity laws as strong as the United States. Sometimes weaker equal opportunity laws are a benefit the company seeks. But other times weak equal opportunity laws are a challenge because they make it difficult for a company to create consistent practice across its operation. The problem is particularly great in countries that require favoring one group over another. For example, some countries require that people from a powerful ethnic or cultural group or caste be favored in employment decisions. Such requirements can prevent a company from choosing the best qualified candidates.

Worker Safety—A company needs to take a careful look at worker safety rules within any country it is considering entering. Some countries do next to nothing to protect workers. It can often be difficult for international companies that provide worker safety to compete on price with local companies that do not consider safety. It is often better for multinational companies to avoid such countries.

Child Labor—Another concern for companies entering poorer countries are child labor laws. A company must know about the restrictions on this practice. They will also be forced to carefully consider their ethical position in countries with weak child labor laws. For example, is a company better off employing 14-year-olds in countries that have no high schools for the children to attend or are they better off leaving the children to fend for themselves? Either choice will have critics.

Antitrust Laws

As a common law country, the United States actually has few antitrust restrictions. Other countries have more specific rules. Most companies will do a quick antitrust analysis when doing their analysis of ownership laws. They usually want to circle back and do a more careful analysis of two antitrust questions in countries they are thinking of entering.

With whom are you allowed to associate? Many companies have rules that prevent competitors within an industry from having any contact with each other. Industry associations, standards groups, and often even trade shows that are common practice in the United States are illegal in many other countries. Those countries restrict companies from having any contact with each other. American companies need to be particularly careful with these laws because even though industry contacts may be occurring in the United States, they could still be antitrust violations in other countries.

What percent of the market can you hold? Although your ownership analysis should have told you how much of the company you can own, it is also important to consider how large a share of a market you can hold in a country. Particularly in small countries, it can be a challenge for a large multinational company to prevent their market share from exceeding limits. Sometimes multinationals will even have to help rivals or start up new competitors just to prevent themselves from making antitrust violations. Microsoft has faced antitrust violations in the EU and has had to change its products to accommodate the laws.

Property Protection

The level of property protection is of concern to American companies. Because American companies live or die by the quality of the new ideas included in their products, they cannot succeed in countries that do not provide adequate protection of proprietary knowledge. It is, therefore, critical that American companies understand the quality of patent and trademark protection offered. Although most countries have similar written laws for patents and trademarks, many countries do not enforce those laws. American companies need to beware.

Bribery Laws

Another place western companies must be particularly careful in their legal research is bribery laws. Most countries have laws against bribery. Many of them are never enforced.

Is bribery customary? As a company does research on bribery in a country it needs to analyze both how legal it is and how customary it is. If it is illegal but customary, international companies are at a great disadvantage against local competitors. Local competitors are likely to accept bribery as standard practice. Multinational companies have other concerns but may not be able to win business without bribery. The company needs to decide what it can, and is willing to, do in such a country.

Foreign Corrupt Practices Act—A particular concern for American companies is the Foreign Corrupt Practices Act. The Act makes it illegal for American companies to bribe overseas. It is a particular challenge because the U.S. government dictates how companies must behave in foreign countries regardless of those foreign countries' own laws or customs. That sometimes puts American companies in a situation where American law tells them they must not bribe in the country when the countries' own practices say they must. Fortunately, other western countries have copied the Foreign Corrupt Practices Act so American companies aren't the only ones in the bind.

Marketing Restrictions

Another area in which it is important to do a complete legal analysis is marketing restrictions. Most countries have restrictions on at least some products and how they can be sold within their country. Your company needs to know if any of its products are affected.

Product Type Restrictions—These tell us what products can be sold within a country and how they can be sold. For example, in the United States, it is illegal to sell heroin or a large number of other restricted drugs. It is legal to sell cigarettes and alcohol but there are age limits and marketing restrictions on each. Every country has its own set of despised products it will not allow. Some of these make little sense to other cultures but are important to the home culture of the country. These restrictions are often idiosyncratic enough to a culture that they cannot be predicted so the only way to know them is to look them up.

Restrictions on Types of Promotion—Countries also have strict regulations on the types of promotions that can be used. For example, in Great Britain it was illegal to interrupt a television show with a commercial. That made it difficult to market using TV advertising. Direct sales, promotions that include comparisons to competitors, and other promotional techniques are restricted or outlawed in some countries. If your company primarily relies on one of those techniques for selling its products, it may not be able to adapt well to a country that has made that technique illegal.

Price Controls—With price controls a country makes it illegal to sell a product above a set price. For most countries, price controls are only used on goods that are considered critical to their population. Basic foods such as rice, and energy such as gasoline, are the most commonly controlled goods but some countries use price controls on a far greater variety of goods. Utilities in the United States have regulated prices. Price controlled goods are often heavily subsidized by the government and foreign companies are often excluded from the market so it may be impossible to do business in a country with price controls on a company's product.

Distribution Channel Limitations—Countries also restrict how goods can be brought to consumers. Some countries will mandate that local wholesalers be used; others will have severe restrictions on retail outlets. A company needs to know what limitations it faces and whether or not it can adapt its business system to the limitation.

Environmental Control Laws

Environmental control laws vary greatly from country to country. Some countries are very strict, to the point where one Swiss village has made it illegal to drive a car in the town. Other countries have little or no environmental restrictions. Limited environmental restrictions in some countries can be useful for accomplishing business not possible in highly restricted countries. If an important industry requires processes that will not meet their own countries environmental standards, sometimes, by necessity, they will move the process to a less regulated country. This risk-reward trade off must be considered carefully. There are always unintended consequences.

Technology Transfer Laws

Technology transfer laws restrict militarily useful technology from getting to disfavored countries. The number and types of technology restrictions have shrunk significantly over the last few years but there are still many old laws that exist. With the rapid advancement of technology it is easy to get stuck in a situation where everyday technology is illegal to export to a particular country. For example, today many cell phones exceed the computing power limits set to prevent supercomputers from going to enemies 20 years ago. Any company with technology-oriented product needs to know all the rules that might restrict its shipments between countries. The commodity uranium and the technologies that accompany it are highly restricted for international transfer.

Import/Export Restrictions

Finally, every country has some set of restrictions on what products can be imported and exported. Any company doing international business needs to know all the restrictions for the products and subcomponents it ships to every country where it does business.

NOTES

Concept	Definition	Example
Types of Legal Systems		

Common Law
  Law by Precedent
  Common in English
    Influenced Countries
  Judge Create Laws through
    Interpretation
  Very Expensive—Lots of
    Lawyers
  Allows Innovation
  Keeps People Guessing		

Civil Law
  Codification of law
  Common in French
Influenced Countries
  Judges Apply Existing Codes
  Easy to Know What the
    Law Is
  Innovation Requires Changes
    to Law First
  Tends to Slow the Economy		

Religious Law
  Law Based on Religious
    Standards
  Common in Middle East
  Religious System Is Ultimate
    Judge
  Hard to Know How Actions
    Will Be Interpreted		

Indigenous Law
  Law by "Elders"
  Lacks Consistency
  Very Open to Interpretation
    and Influence
  Against Innovation		

Bureaucratic Law
  Decisions Made by
    Bureaucratic Departments
  Can Give Contradictory
Answers
  Encourages Bribery
  Completely Stifles Innovation		

Concept	Definition	Example
Types of International Laws		
Bilateral—Two-nation Agreement		
Regional Laws—NAFTA, EU, etc		
Multinational Laws—WTO, etc.		
Laws You MUST Know		

Ownership
    How much are you allowed to own?
    In what industries?
    What form can that ownership take?		

Taxes
    Does the nation favor or punish FDI?
    What method of taxing is used?
    Value added? Income?
Individual or Company? Form of Tariffs?
    What industries are encouraged?		

Personnel and Labor Laws
    Unionization Laws
    Mandatory Benefits and Wages
    Equal Opportunity Laws
    Worker Safety		

Antitrust Laws
    With whom are you allowed to associate
    What percent of the market can you hold?		

Property Protection Quality of patent and trademark protection		

Bribery Laws
    Is bribery customary?
    Foreign Corrupt Practices Act		

Concept	Definition	Example

Marketing Restriction
   Product Type Restrictions
   Restrictions on Types of
     Promotion
   Price Controls
   Distribution Channel
     Limitations		

Environmental Control Laws		
Technology Transfer Laws		
Import/Export Restrictions		

Economic Environments

Countries differ by their economic environments. Understanding how economies differ is another important step to understanding how business within a country is accomplished.

WHAT IS AN ECONOMIC ENVIRONMENT?

What is being considered when we talk about an economic environment? **The economic environment primarily concerns the underlying existing wealth of a region and how that affects the capacity of that region to produce new wealth.** Here is where the values of a country come into play. Although wealth is often equated with good in American culture, it is less so in most other cultures. When we look at how successful a culture or government is at producing wealth in its economic environment, we're not looking at how good a country is. We're looking at a snapshot of how rich it is and then how its values stimulate it to produce more wealth. The culture reflects individual values of wealth. Wealth is not all there is to a life; people with low to moderate wealth still can live productive, happy lives. Remember, as we look at rich and poor nations, we're not looking at good and bad, but instead, at economic values. Within the totality of studying a country, know that wealth is vital to producing more wealth. It takes money to make money, simply put, or it takes resources to grow more resources.

COMPREHENSIVE MEASURES

The wealth of a country can be measured in various ways for comparison with other countries or for internal analysis. The comprehensive measures of economic environment look at the big picture of how well a country is doing. They provide useful information about overall performance.

GDP—Gross Domestic Product—The Value of All Goods and Services Produced In a Country

Gross domestic product is the most comprehensive measure of the economic output of a country. Gross domestic product counts the outputs of all business activities that occur within the borders of one country. For example, when measuring gross domestic product and looking at the income generated by IBM and Toyota, all the income generated by IBM's and Toyota's operations within the United States are included in the U.S. GDP. All income earned by IBM and Toyota outside the United States is not included in the U.S. GDP. That makes GDP a fairly reliable measure of how much wealth is produced within a country. It shows how much money is being generated by U.S. workers and is thus available to pay in wages or use in other economic activity.

GNI—Gross National Income—The Value of All Goods and Services Produced by Companies Domiciled Inside a Country Regardless of Where Those Goods or Services Are Produced Around the World

Gross national income is a comprehensive measure similar to GDP. Unfortunately, press accounts often confuse GNI and GDP even though, for many countries, the figures are drastically different. Because GNI measures all the income produced by nationally-based companies, it is a measure of total economic power, not economic activity. For example, when measuring GNI and looking at income produced by IBM and Toyota, all of IBM's income would be included in the GNI regardless of where that income was earned. None of Toyota's income is included in the GNI even though some of its factories operate in the United States. Thus, GNI is a good measure for how rich, and therefore powerful, the companies based within a country are. The higher a country's GNI, the more that country's culture will be affecting the rest of the world through its business practices. Countries with high GNI also typically receive substantial profits from other countries and are, therefore, able to increase their wealth.

Although the press often uses GNI and GDP interchangeably, and at times confuses the two, they are significantly different measures. GDP is primarily a measure of how much wealth a country is producing. GNI is a measure of how economically powerful a country is. These numbers can be broken down into subsets of important information.

GDP Per Capita

Although GDP is an overall measure of how much wealth a country generates, it tells us little about how wealthy the individuals in the country are. A small country with a modest GDP could have a population with more individual wealth than people from a large population with a substantially larger GDP. The measure used to help determine how wealthy the people within a country are is GDP per capita. **GDP per capita is calculated by dividing the GDP by the country's total population.**

Countries with high GDP per capita are usually considered rich even if they are small and have a low total GDP. Countries with a low GDP per capita are considered poor. The range between rich and poor countries is astronomical. Many of the poorest countries have an annual GDP per capita of less than $1000. Some of the richest countries have an annual GDP per capita of over $40,000. If you can imagine what it would be like to try to live on less than $1000 a year and then try to imagine an entire country doing so, you can see that business needs to operate differently in poor countries than in rich ones. Business opportunities in a poor country look different than what you'll find in wealthy countries.

GDP Rate of Change

GDP rate of change is a measure of how quickly the country's wealth is increasing or decreasing. In many ways, GDP is a snapshot measure of the past. It

shows you how a country did last year. GDP rate of change is a measure applied to the future. It shows how quickly GDP is growing and, when compared to other countries, shows whether a country is doing better or worse than other similar countries.

A country that has prolonged periods of very low rates of change is in trouble. Its stagnation means that it is unlikely to be able to compete with other countries for long. Historically, the country with prolonged growth below 2% a year or so is probably growing too slowly to keep up with the rest of the world. High rates of change can also be a problem, however. They usually lead to high inflation and all the problems that come with it. Wealthy countries growing more than 4% a year or so are likely to spark inflation. Poorer countries can sometimes grow for periods at 7% or more and still be okay. Because poorer countries are making up lost ground, it is easier to grow faster and still be less likely to cause inflation.

It is important to remember the effects of scale when considering rate of change. For example, a country with a $40,000 GDP per capita may grow only 3% while a country with a $4000 GDP per capita grows 10%. It looks like the poorer nation is doing better. But people in the country with the $40,000 GDP per capita got an extra $1200 from their 3% growth. The people in the $4000 GDP per capita country only got an extra $400 for their 10% growth. It can be hard for a country to catch up once it has fallen significantly behind. It is hard to imagine how a country with a GDP per capita in the $500 to $1000 range can ever catch up unless it literally discovers that it is sitting on a richly veined gold/diamond mine.

HUMAN DEVELOPMENT MEASURES

GDP, GNI, and other comprehensive measures show which countries are rich and poor. It is often hard to understand why one country is richer than another, however. Human development measures are an attempt to explain how some of the wealth difference developed. These measures look at traits economists believe are important to the capacity to create wealth. They look for things one economy might be doing differently than others that might explain that economy's better or worse performance. Here are some ways to do that.

Freedom Scales

Freedom scales are one of the most commonly used human development measures. A freedom scale looks at how much influence people have over their governmental system, how free they are to pursue business without government interference, and how free they are to live their lives as they see fit. Countries that provide their people greater freedom generally do better economically. Countries that have traditionally constrained freedoms but start loosening constraints generally improve economically. As always, there are exceptions, but freer countries usually become wealthier countries. Therefore, freedom scales and changes in countries freedom scores are often used by international businesses to predict how well a country will do in the future.

Education Scales

Countries with a better educated populace also tend to have more successful economies. Higher levels of education generally increase the level of innovation. Because economic growth comes primarily through innovation, growth in an economy is highly dependent on the economy's education level.

There are many different education scales available. Most display significant bias toward the type of education favored in the culture where the scale originated. For example, education scales developed in the United States typically emphasize excellence. The U.S. economy is highly dependent on a small number of well-educated people who generate breakthrough technology and innovation. U.S. education scales therefore emphasize an economy's ability to produce the best educated. Notice the emphasis is on superstar schools like MIT and Harvard. Many European economies, however, are far more dependent on incremental innovation and production excellence. That requires an educational emphasis of the breadth of the European populace but does not require the superstars focused on in the United States. The European education scales, therefore, tend to emphasize the overall population's basic education.

Envy Scale

This is a useful cultural/economic concept concerning individual human motivation. Simply put, it measures how much people care about the wealth level of neighbors and others within their culture. Is equality valued or is it important to try to do better economically than others? In countries where one covets the neighbor's belongings, growth tends to happen through competition. Where people want to share equally, communes thrive, innovation is unimportant, and harmony and cooperation rule. Motivation to get ahead drives competition and innovation.

These scales are useful in predicting how well a country will do. They're not perfect, however. Mongolia, for example, is one of the most free countries in the world but one of the poorest. Combined, the human development scales do provide useful insights into why some countries do better economically than others. Human development measures slowly change in a culture and thus are good for predicting where an economy will be in a decade or two.

Religious Scale

Knowing the prevailing religion of an area or country helps a business decide the cultural values and to some extent, what will be bought or sold. How much of life and movement is dictated by the religion? Is the religion largely ceremonial rather than a way of life? To what extent are people free to think and explore "outside the box" or do cultural pressures forbid creativity? Knowing about the prevailing religion, and other major influences, will go a long way to understanding the country or areas within it.

PREDICTIVE MEASURES

While the comprehensive measures try to give us the broad picture of what the world has been like in the recent past, predictive measures look at smaller segments of an economy to try to estimate in which direction an economy is moving. Predictive measures are usually used for short term analysis of where an economy is headed next month or next year.

Inflation Rate

The inflation rate is a measure of how quickly prices are increasing or decreasing in a country. It is probably the most important predictive measure for international business. As you'll see in Chapter eleven, the inflation rate is a prime determinant of currency exchange rates.

Because currency exchange rates determine the relative value of goods between countries, currency exchange rates largely dictate what international trade will occur. Inflation in a country, therefore, drives how successful the country will be in international trade. A high inflation rate, generally considered to be anything over about 5%, will continuously devalue a currency. As the country's currency drops it will get harder and harder for people and companies within the country to afford goods from other countries. As goods from other countries become more expensive, people within a country are forced to purchase lower quality, higher priced domestic goods which reduce their satisfaction and the overall wealth of the nation.

Very high inflation rates are extremely destructive to an economy. Many countries have seen inflation rates over 100%. When inflation rates get that high credit markets cease to exist and the country's currency is seen as useless. Business activity falls to extremely low levels and the economy in general fails. Whenever international businesses see inflation rates climbing over 10% or so, the businesses will typically start looking for ways to protect themselves, which frequently leads to choosing to leave the country.

Somewhat surprisingly, extremely low inflation rates can be as damaging, or even more damaging, than high inflation rates. The problem with extremely low inflation rates is they create a risk that inflation may turn negative. Negative inflation, known as deflation, is damaging to an economy. The problem with negative inflation is that interest rates in credit markets are driven primarily by inflation rates. When inflation rates turn negative interest rates cannot follow. No one would accept a negative interest rate. People would be better off hiding money under their mattresses than to pay interest for someone to hold their money.

Negative inflation rates also strongly encourage people to save. Since their money will be worth more on purchases tomorrow than today most people decide they might as well wait until tomorrow. People's greater savings reduces inflation further and makes negative inflation even more negative. Negative inflation, therefore, becomes a downward spiral very difficult for an economy to escape. International businesses generally do not like to operate in negative inflation environments. They do usually like to borrow money from countries with negative inflation, however, because interest rates in negative inflation countries are often near zero. In the United States, in late 2008, with housing prices and interest rates falling, deflation is a real threat. With home prices decreasing, people wait to purchase until prices bottom, thus exacerbating the problem. People are hording cash. It is deemed, in the financial markets, a crisis that must be stabilized.

Unemployment

A country's unemployment rate tells what percentage of the country's population is seeking work but has not yet found it. The unemployment rate of a country tells international businesses useful things. First, a country's unemployment rate is an important factor in predicting future wage increases in a country. A country with low unemployment, generally 5% or below, is likely to see significant upward wage pressure in the near future. A country with high unemployment, generally 8% or greater, is unlikely to see significant changes as employment costs decrease. A country with very high unemployment, 15% or more, is often politically unstable because 15% unemployment leaves too many people out of work and frustrated. Some are likely to turn to crime or, in times of high national stress, rioting. International companies prefer to see countries in the more stable 5% to 8% unemployment range. This discussion is simplistic in that one must also take into account underemployment, or those who would like a part-time or full time job, but have given up trying and are not counted in the statistics. If the underemployment is very high, instability of the country could be the case, even if it does not show in the numbers. Not all nations measure unemployment in the same way.

The country's unemployment rate is also a good predictor of its inflation rate. Since the majority of wealth is generated through labor, a low unemployment rate suggests pressure for increasing wages and thus increasing inflation. A high unemployment rate, however, suggests there will be little internal pressures for inflation as long as the government is stable.

Debt

There are two levels of debt international businesses look at in a country. The first level of debt is a governmental debt. A government that is consistently running up large debts can eventually find it difficult, if not impossible, to pay those debts. It can grow its way out, or inflate its way out, of a high debt burden. In 2008, the U.S. government decided to print money to inflate our way out of the current crisis, hoping that growth will eventually help stop the bleeding. The current debate about whether or not huge government spending, creating massive debt, will ultimately stimulate growth or inflation, is ongoing. In the same way, countries unable to pay their debts will typically resort to printing money to pay their debts if the debts are in their own currency. Printing large amounts of its own currency sets off high inflation in a country. Growth is desirable; inflation is not. A government with a large debt in another currency isn't able to print its way out of debt, so it is more likely to default on the debt. When a country defaults on its debt, it is usually frozen out of debt markets for a long time. Being unable to access world credit markets substantially damages the country's economy. Therefore, a large governmental debt is seen as a very bad sign by international businesses and a signal that a business would be better off avoiding the country.

The second level of debt of concern to international businesses is the level of debt of consumers within the country. A high level of consumer debt suggests consumers will have a hard time borrowing more in the future and may suggest a weak future economy for the country. Extremely low consumer debt in a country is a more difficult signal to read. It could mean consumers have a lot of money to spend, a good sign, or it could mean there is a very strong cultural or legal impediment to debt, signalling that growth will be weak in the future.

Income Distribution

Most companies will also take a close look at how evenly income is distributed within a country. Luxury goods producers often find their best markets are the rich people in poorer countries. For the small number of companies that focus on goods for the poor, uneven income distribution is again the target. To the majority of companies that focus on products for a middle class consumer, uneven income distribution is typically seen as a negative indicator.

As a predictive measure, income distribution can be particularly useful to international businesses. Countries with unequal income distribution tend to be more traditional. Countries with more even income distribution tend to be more innovative and dynamic. International businesses typically find it easier to grow within the more dynamic, balanced income distribution countries. Think of the height of the bell curve and its concentration in the middle when you think of middle class; think of a bimodal curve, or haves and have-nots when you think of rich and poor. As a business are you looking for a large middle class or instead, a large rich or large poor class?

Poverty

Beyond the income distribution of a country many companies are interested in the poverty level within a country. High levels of true poverty, defined by the UN as people living on less than $2.00 a day, increases disease risk, malnutrition, and political risk. There are companies that specialize in dealing with such risks and have found ways to do so profitably. Most of the rest of international companies choose to avoid areas with such high risks associated with poverty, and because of that avoidance, the level of poverty and political instability likely increases.

Balance of Payments

The balance of payments is a comparative measure of how much a country sells to other countries in exports vs. how much the country buys from other countries in imports. It is assumed that, over the long run, a country will have to balance payments so that it has exported as much as it has imported. If over the long run the country needs to balance its payments and in the short run it is importing far more then it is exporting, there is a strong likelihood the country will need to reduce imports in the future. Therefore, a highly negative balance of payments is seen as a weakness for a country and is a strong predictor that the country's economy will suffer in the future.

That said, reality has not always worked out that way for every country. Some countries, most notably the United States, have run very large negative balance of payments for years with limited consequences. That may be because there are problems with how the balance of payments are measured or it may be that the United

States is a special case. Balance of payments does seem to work as a strong predictor for most other economies. You can wonder if this current world-wide economic crisis is causing the house of cards to collapse. The current effort in the United States to reduce dependence on foreign oil is, in part, an attempt to address this huge negative balance of payments.

Happiness?

Finally, it is worth considering what all this economic data actually means to people's lives. Although not accepted by all cultures, some cultures consider a pursuit of happiness as a primary purpose of the human condition. Particularly in the United States, happiness has come to be seen as the primary focus of life. It is, therefore, worth considering what all of this economic data means to creating happiness. Not too surprisingly, wealthier countries tend to be happier countries because the basic needs of humans are met or exceeded. The relationship is not perfectly linear however. There are quite poor countries like Mongolia that are still quite happy and several richer countries quite unhappy. Freedom and education scales explain part of the differences, as do religious influences, but in the end it comes down to the cultures and the values of the people.

 **NOTES**

Concept	Definition	Example
What Is an Economic Environment?		
The existing wealth of a region		
The capacity of a region to produce new wealth		
Macro Measures		
Comprehensive Measures		
GDP—Gross Domestic Product—The Value of All Goods and Services Produced in a Country		
GNI—Gross National Income—The Value of All Goods and Services Produced by "National" companies Regardless of Where Produced		
GDP Per Capita		
GDP Rate of Change		
Human Development Measures		
Freedom Scales		
Education Scales		
Predictive Measures		
Inflation Rate		
Unemployment		
Debt		
Income Distribution		
Poverty		
Balance of Payments		
Happiness?		

International Business Ethics

International business is rightly focused on what can be done and how to do it. To succeed in business, however, you must first consider what **should** be done. The question of what should be done becomes more complex. One chapter in a book could never do justice to what one needs to know to be good at making decisions under international business ethics. This chapter covers the basics to help you understand some of the important considerations.

WHAT IS ETHICS?

Ethics, as a field, attempts to define what one should do rather than what one can do. The attempt is to set moral standards for regulating right and wrong behavior. Defining right and wrong behavior is far more complex than one might think, however.

What makes something right? What makes it wrong? Although virtually everyone has some personal sense of right and wrong, most people are hard pressed when asked why they believe something is right or wrong. Codifying those choices to make standards for large groups of employees is even harder. Even more complex is doing so in an international environment. Most people's sense of what is right and wrong is directly derived from their own culture. Where cultures disagree, many people are lost when trying to figure out what to do. They often 1) follow their own culture, thereby upsetting people from different cultures, or 2) copy the other cultures dictates without any ability to justify the decision to home country audiences, or 3) create corporate wide policies that they hope will work around the world.

Fortunately, there are several moral theories that have been defined and are used around the world. These moral theories are long-derived foundations of ethical thought which have become embedded in most of the world's cultures. No one of them works in every situation but by understanding all of them you'll have a far better foundation for making an ethical decision. These moral theories attempt to create consistent philosophies of what is right and wrong. The major ones used around the world are described below.

VIRTUE THEORIES

Virtue theories suggest that the rightness or wrongness of a decision is dependent on the character of the person making the decision. Virtue theory thus suggests that the character of the person making the decision determines whether a decision is ethical or not. Under virtue theory, by definition, a decision made by a virtuous person is ethical. A decision made by someone who is not virtuous is unethical.

Good Habits of Character

Under virtue theory, ethical decisions are made by virtuous people. It is therefore incumbent on a person who wishes to be ethical to develop good habits of character. People who constantly strive for those good habits will understand the world well enough that decisions they make will be ethical. Evaluation of an ethical decision is decided by how virtuous the person who made the decision is. If a person making the decision is highly virtuous then, by definition, his decisions are ethical. If the person making the decision has bad habits of character the decisions he makes are unethical. It is important to note that the ethics of the decision is not determined by the decision itself but only by the quality of the person making the decision.

Western Cultures

Most people raised in America's culture think it's odd that the virtue of a decision be based on the decision maker. Yet even in America virtue theory underlies many of our ideas on ethics. For example, in our representative democracy, we elect representatives not by tallying the results of their past actions but by tallying collective belief about how "good" the person is. Voting on individuals is a form of virtue theory. Virtue theory also comes up in other areas such as using character witnesses in a trial or references in a job search. All are attempts to determine the character of the person being measured in the belief that a person with higher character will make more ethical decisions.

Plato's Virtues

One of the earliest known adherents of virtue theory was Plato (2008). Plato defined four virtues that he believed determined the character of a person. Those four virtues are:

> **Wisdom**—You must seek to understand the world to make good decisions about it.

> **Courage**—You must be willing to stand up to the consequence of a right decision, particularly a right decision that might be unpopular.

> **Temperance**—You must be willing to act visibly in good ways even when those acts are difficult.

> **Justice**—You must attempt to make sure each person gets that to which they are entitled.

Other Important Virtues

Later philosophers felt more virtues should be included. Five other virtues have been commonly valued in many parts of the world. They are:

> **Fortitude**—You must be strong enough to bear any difficulties right decisions might entail.

> **Generosity**—You must recognize and act with charity toward those who need help.

Self-respect—You must have the self confidence to make decisions with which others disagree.

Good temper—You must remain civil and not act out of anger.

Sincerity—You must be honest about your own feeling and thoughts.

Vices

In contrast to virtues that define good character, many later philosophers added vices which subtract from a person's good character. Most of the vices are negations of the virtues. The four most common follow.

Cowardice—Lacking the courage to face the pain or dissension that results from a right decision.

Insensitivity—Lacking the ability or motivation to understand how others will be affected by a decision.

Injustice—Willingness to see or promote unfair advantage of others or unfair punishment of others that results from a decision.

Vanity—Excessive belief in ones own ability to make or follow through on decisions.

DUTY THEORIES

Unlike virtue theories which determine the ethics of a decision based on the decision maker, duty theories base it on the inherent rightness or wrongness of an act. The challenge with duty theories is that they are dependent on having external sources to establish the inherent rightness or wrongness of the acts. For the most part, in reality they are based on religious practices. To the question "how do you know if it is right or wrong?" from duty theory comes the response that "our god(s) tell us so." In the few places where duty theory is used without reference to a god, some higher power must still be invoked to establish specific duties. Phrases like "natural law" which implies the universe itself establishes duties are often used where religious contexts are not accepted.

External Obligations

The base premise of duty theories is that there are external obligations every individual must meet. Much of the world's laws are written with duty theory as a base premise. Most of law itself is derived from duty concepts. Each time a new law is written, it establishes a new obligation that must be followed. Most ancient and many modern societies thus invoked special rights to their gods or the rulers have declared themselves gods in order to establish ethical dominion. Acts which meet duty obligations are ethical acts. Acts that fail to meet them are unethical.

In duty theory there is also room for acts which are neither ethical nor unethical because while they do not specifically address a duty, they do not work against others' ability to meet their duties. One of the major modern applications of duty theories come through rights theories.

Class Obligation

Rights theories originated in France but flourished and were spread throughout much of the rest of the world by the United States. Rights theories are a modern permutation of the ancient idea of "noblesse oblige" or a "noble obligation." Noble obligation implied that people who were born into positions of nobility had special obligations to protect people with less power and wealth. Rights theories turned noble obligation around and suggested people who are weaker and poorer have a "right" to demand that people who are richer and more powerful protect them.

The original concept of rights applied only to a physical protection from murder, beatings, and theft but those rights have been expanded exponentially. It has become popular in many countries for poorer or weaker groups to demand all sorts of things as rights. One of the major weaknesses of rights theory is that it requires a group to declare itself weak to deserve protection. Many groups that thus declare themselves weak ultimately regret the decision when all the ramifications of defending that weakened status are understood. Another major problem with rights theories is that because they are rapidly becoming disconnected from the religious or natural law obligations they were founded on, groups are declaring any strong desire that they have been unable to attain as a right. That said, rights theories are becoming a much larger part of the international business scene so companies must understand it.

Universal Obligations

Beyond rights there are other duties that various cultures and countries have accepted. Because these duties come from religious practice there is tremendous variation from culture to culture as to what is considered a duty. A number of duties have been recognized in so many different cultures they have become fairly widely recognized as natural duties of the human condition. Several of those duties are described next.

Fidelity—The duty to keep promises.

Reparation—The duty to compensate others when we harm them.

Gratitude—The duty to thank those who help us.

Justice—The duty to recognize merit.

Beneficence—The duty to improve the conditions of others.

Self-improvement—The duty to improve our virtue and intelligence.

Nonmaleficence—The duty not to injure others.

CONSEQUENTIAL THEORIES

While virtue theories look at the decider to determine if a decision is ethical or not and duty theories look to the specific act to determine how ethical it is, consequential theories look at the outcome of an act to determine whether or not it is ethical. In consequential theory an action is morally right if the consequences of that action are more favorable than unfavorable. Consequential approaches are popular among those trained in business because they seem similar to decisions based on profitability. No ethical theorist, however, would ever say a decision is more ethical because it is more profitable. Consequential theories have other measures for what should be maximized in outcomes. By far the most popular of the consequential theories is utilitarianism.

Utilitarianism

Utilitarianism as defined by its foremost proponent, John Stuart Mill (1863), says the action that creates the most happiness is the moral action. Utilitarianism thus requires an ethical decision maker to determine which action will have the greatest positive affect on the most people to determine what is ethical.

Utilitarianism as an approach to ethical decision making has the significant advantage that it allows one to make tradeoffs between competing demands. Duty theory cannot handle such tradeoffs. For example, if someone were to promise their retiring boss that they would help a favorite employee to move up through the corporation but then that employee performed horribly for the next two years, duty theory would leave the manager stuck. In duty theory there is no way to trade off ones duty of fidelity to their retired boss and their duty of justice to employees. Utilitarianism has no such problem. The manager can trade away the loss of happiness to the retired boss with the gain of happiness of current employees when they see a poor employee not promoted. Utilitarianism has another advantage in that to most people it makes sense. To make more people happy seems logically to be good.

Utilitarianism has problems, however. First, ethical decision making is difficult in that it requires a person be able to predict how their actions will affect the happiness of others. Secondly, you can never know whether a decision was ethical before you take action. No one can predict consequences perfectly. If things turn out very differently than anticipated, a person who tried very hard to be ethical may end up with an unethical outcome according to utilitarianism. There are two larger problems with utilitarianism however. They are:

Special Obligations—The first overwhelming problem with utilitarianism is special obligation. Special obligation says there are some people in this world to whom you have a higher obligation. For example, if you're driving down the street and you suddenly see three children playing in the road and you must swerve to avoid killing but they are grouped in such a way that no matter what you do you will kill either one of them if you swerve to the left or two of them if you swerve to the right. What should you do? According to utilitarianism you should swerve to the left because killing one child will probably subtract less happiness from the world than killing two children. But what if the child on the left is your only daughter? Most people, even if given plenty of time to think about it, would swerve to the right. That is recognition of special obligation, that is, you feel a higher obligation toward your own family and friends. Unfortunately, utilitarianism can't deal with the situation.

End Justifies the Means—The bigger problem with utilitarianism is it allows the possibility that some actions that would never be accepted as ethical under other measures may be okay under utilitarianism. For example, if you and your family of seven are living next door to a single retired person with no family and no friends or connections to the community who leaves their television blasting at full volume 24 hours a day seven days a week so your family can never sleep, it probably wouldn't be hard to create a utilitarian analysis that showed the world would be happier if you went next door and shot your neighbor. More happiness would be gained than lost.

Such "end justifies the means" analyses have been used to justify some of the worst atrocities in human history. Ethnic cleansing is justified by those involved under utilitarianism ethics. In fact, utilitarianism has a very hard time justifying the protection of any small minority. Therefore, utilitarianism has largely shifted towards rule utilitarianism in practice.

Rule Utilitarianism

Rule utilitarianism accepts the flaws of making ethical decisions based on individual cases and addresses those flaws by taking a rules approach. Under rule utilitarianism, an analysis of the effects on happiness is still needed for each type of situation but instead of solving each individual situation independently rules are created that apply to all similar situations. For example, consider free speech. Under utilitarianism it would be easy to show that each instance of unpopular speech would decrease happiness and therefore be considered unethical and banned. Rule utilitarianism looks at all free speech however and sees that although each instance of free speech may reduce happiness, the overall affect of allowing free speech increases happiness. The openness allows new and differing ideas to be aired and improved approaches to life to be learned. Rule utilitarianism would therefore create the rule that free speech is ethical and should be allowed.

Rule utilitarianism fixes many of the end justifying the means problems. It makes some inroads into special obligations problems but cannot fix all of them. Frequently, what is seen in many cultures is various approaches of rule utilitarianism being used.

SOCIAL CONTRACT THEORY

Given all the troubles with the three other ethical theories, social contract theory accepts that there may not be a purely philosophical way to dictate ethical behavior. Social contract theory thus states that, regardless of the underlying theory or motivations, there are certain minimum standards people must live by in order for society to thrive. Social contract theory then defines those minimum standards and essentially requires everyone follow them.

Social contract theory offers minimum standards for much of human experience. This being an international business text, only the standards most relevant to business are presented. According to Donaldson (1989) social contract theory requires that three standards must be met by every business in every country they do business. Those three standards are:

A productive organization should enhance the long-term welfare of employees and consumers in any society in which the organization operates.—This standard recognizes that the companies must focus on the long-term welfare of employees and the consumers of its products. The standard suggests short-term actions that have negative long-term affects are not ethical. It also requires businesses to resolve potentially competing needs of internal constituents (employees) and external constituents (consumers).

A productive organization should minimize the drawbacks associated with moving beyond nature to a controlled state of productive organizations.—This standard recognizes that nature is inherently chaotic and that businesses profit by making order out of nature's chaos. For example, a natural field is chaotic with all sorts a wild plants and animals intermixed in a fairly random array of interacting elements. When men come and turn that ecosystem into a farm they add substantial order which significantly profits people by allowing the field to produce more human food. Adding order, however, destroys the natural ecosystem. This standard requires that people understand the damage they do when they transform the environment to order, minimize that damage and where able, counter that damage in other places. The concept of carbon cap swaps in the utility industry is an example of this eco-neutral idea.

A productive organization should refrain from violating minimum standards of justice and of human rights in any society in which it operates.—This standard gets around duty theories problems with why, or even if, something is a duty given a particular cultural or religious standard by saying why it doesn't matter. The standard says minimum rules of justice and human rights need to be followed everywhere even if a particular culture or religion does not honor that particular standard of justice or human right. This approach clearly violates some standards within a culture. It does so because it is the only way to accept most of the standards a culture would apply to itself but not have to accept every cultural standard. Accepting every cultural standard in a cannibalistic tribe for example could be rejected while still trying to protect most of the tribes' culture.

APPLIED ETHICS

As you would probably predict from seeing the major ethical theories, it can be difficult to know how to act in any given situation. The mix of cultures one faces in international business makes the challenge greater. How does one react, for instance, when their home culture would clearly use rights theories to resolve an issue while the culture they are in would use a utilitarian approach which comes up with an exactly opposite solution. Because ethical theories are hard to apply to specific situations, several fields of applied ethics have grown to create policies of behavior which reflect careful thinking about ethical theory. For managers and international business people, many of the situations they will face have already been carefully considered and addressed in applied ethics. Although one can rarely look up an ethical solution in an applied ethics book that exactly matches their specific need, applied ethics does provide useful guides. There are sub fields within applied ethics that are useful to the international business executive. Some of the most useful are described below.

Business Ethics

Business ethics as an applied ethics field has addressed the most important questions international business people face. With a little research you can look up business questions which have been answered by people who have the time and background to consider the full ethical ramifications. An international business executive will want to have a couple of good applied ethics books. As you face cross-cultural issues the books can be invaluable. Understand, however, that the books will often recommend solutions that are ethical but not necessarily politically expedient. It will be up to you what you do in any given situation. You won't always be able to depend on people at the home office understanding the opposing pressures you face in cross-cultural situations. As the decider you face unique pressures.

Environmental Ethics

Environmental ethics is primarily concerned with protecting the natural environment. It is a growing concern for international businesses. Many countries in the world are more focused than the United States on environmental issues. As Americans first move overseas, particularly to Europe, they quickly have to expand their knowledge of environmental ethics issues. One must be careful when first entering environmental ethics, however, because there are extreme elements who present environmental arguments that do not fit well with the rest of ethical theory. Most pointedly, there are a few environmental ethicists who would argue, for example, that the life of a dolphin is equal to that of a human being. Given that premise the writer would declare that saving the life of two dolphins at the cost of one person is an acceptable trade-off. Although such ideas are seen frequently enough in environmental ethics groups, they are widely disparaged elsewhere. Nonetheless, environmental consideration and knowledge is important.

Computer Ethics

Computer ethics as a field frequently crosses over into issues of business ethics. Privacy, data protection, data storage, and other computer ethics issues have become business ethics issues. Since computer ethics is a comparatively new field there is far more disagreement about it as one moves from country to country. Companies will often be challenged because the Internet almost requires global computer ethics policies but each country wants different policies for themselves. It is up to international business people to find policies that work in each country and globally.

Corporate Social Responsibility

Corporate social responsibility as a field tries to determine what obligations a company has toward its communities beyond trying to maximize profitability and available wealth. Corporate social responsibility has two distinct camps. There are those that say a corporation should take on community projects and use its wealth for charitable purpose. There are others who strongly disagree and suggest corporate managers should not support projects that do not directly or indirectly increase profitability and shareholder wealth. They believe money should be returned to stockholders who can choose whether to use their money for charity or not.

INTERNATIONAL APPLIED BUSINESS ETHICS

International business meets several distinct challenges as it addresses ethics. Some of those challenges are described here.

Culturally Bound Theory Preference

Although most cultures use mixtures and variations of the ethical theories previously explained, each culture uses the theories in different ways. What is considered ethical in one culture can be considered unethical in another. It can be difficult to know what to do in such situations. If you follow home culture or global standards, you might trample the host country culture. If you follow a host country culture that has standards substantially different from home or global standards you will be attacked by the international community. It is incumbent on the international business person to be able both to defend choices and to work the political angles so that those who disagree with the decision are not able to undermine the company.

Conflicting Government and Cultural Requirements

Another problem arises when government and cultural requirements differ around an ethical issue. A government might adopt a law from international standards that directly conflicts with its own culture. Then the international business is stuck choosing between following the law or supporting the culture. For example, some poor countries have copied richer country rules that require workers be paid time and a half for overtime work. Most local companies ignore the law because it is cheaper to hire more employees to avoid overtime. They risk employees leaving to get overtime pay even if it is only at their regular rate. International companies that step into the situation are stuck. If they pay time and a half for overtime while local competitors do not, the costs are too high and they cannot compete with local companies. If the international company hires more workers to eliminate overtime, their workers leave for local companies that allow overtime at regular hourly rates. If they keep few enough workers to need overtime but don't pay time and a half, they're breaking the law and will likely be castigated in the international press. In short, it is difficult for them to succeed.

World Perspectives

Another challenge for applying business ethics to international business comes back to the world perspective of a company and its employees. Each world perspective suggests a different ethical approach.

> **Multinational**—Multinational companies are more likely to adopt duty theory approaches. That multinational company is projecting its culture to the rest of the world in the belief that its culture is in some ways inspired. Duties are the most culturally bound of the ethical theories and are tied to a culture's understanding of higher needs.

> **Multidomestic**—Multidomestic companies are much more likely to use consequential theories as a basis for their ethical analysis. A multidomestic company tries to adhere to the norms of the cultures it encounters.

> **Global**—The global business mindset is best supported by social contract theory and has thus been adopted by most global corporations. Modern social contract theory is, in effect, a global idea. The best minimum standards have been collected from around the world and applied to the entire world.

MAJOR ISSUES

As you have seen, ethical issues can be particularly difficult for international business. Understanding ethical approaches can help, as can understanding how applied ethics have been used in the past. In the end it always comes to international managers having to make intelligent, well-informed decisions. There are a number of issues that come up in international business for which you'll want to be prepared. They follow.

Environment

When and how to protect the natural environment is a major concern. It isn't only a matter of protecting wildlife because human life is at stake as well. Finding ways to serve both the needs of the environment and the needs of the poor communities is the best option. As an international manager, you'll constantly be asked to discover the best balance between long-term environmental needs and short-term human needs.

Employee Relations

There is no international consensus on how employees should be treated. As an international manager you'll constantly be challenged to balance home country needs, host country needs, and worldwide market needs to develop policies that work. Most people who don't understand business wonder why you just can't pay employees in poor countries more. They fail to understand that paying employees with limited skills more makes the products they are producing more expensive and makes it logical for the company to move the jobs to a more productive and more expensive country. That is good for the rich country but very bad for the poor one. The international manager will feel significant pressure from wealthy country unions for this very reason. Beyond pay, an international manager needs to figure out benefits packages and other employees' support that fit the culture and environment in which employees live. Ethical challenges abound.

Health & Safety

OSHA does not operate outside the United States. Many countries have few to no worker protections. In America a manager might spend $100,000 to protect a worker's life. In a poor country that $100,000 might pay for 50 more employees and keep their families from starving. The tradeoffs are never easy.

Interface to Religion and Other Cultural Practices

Because there is a reasonable consensus of what is acceptable behavior in the United States, companies are rarely faced with serious conflicts between religious or other cultural practices and standard business practices. In other cultures such conflicts are inevitable. Companies can often adapt to other countries' religious or cultural preferences with little cost. At times, however, the conflicts are substantial and the international manager will be forced to make a choice whether to accept the culture as it is or to try to change it. Either choice will have significant ethical implications.

Affects of Business on Local Culture

The very existence of international business will likely change the cultures where the businesses interface. That change in itself creates ethical dilemmas. Even when the company tries to accept a host culture as it is, the only reason international business succeeds is because it offers something not readily available in that country. Whatever else international business brings, it brings change that is both desirable and not desirable but always with unintended consequences.

Government Relations

International business will have interactions with host governments, particularly in smaller countries. The international manager will need to decide how much they should interfere or how much to be a force for good. Choices have ethical implications.

Corruption

One of the most challenging interfaces businesses have with governments come when dealing with government corruption. Wherever government officials put their own desires ahead of their responsibilities to their people, government itself is weakened and the country is made poorer. Businesses in countries with substantial corruption often cannot survive without a level of acceptance of the existing system. International business people need to take a careful look at the ethical implications of what they do and remember they will be held responsible for the long-term affects both inside and outside the country.

> **Bribery**—The demand for bribes Is particularly difficult. Although bribes are harmful to countries and their people, refusal to pay them can restrict or remove any possibility of doing business in a country. Simply refusing to do business in a corrupt country can be damaging to the country as well. International business people should understand ethical issues and be prepared to make hard choices regarding bribery.

> **Foreign Corrupt Practices Act**—The choices Americans make are particularly difficult because they face what are, at times, conflicting laws. The United States has implemented the Foreign Corrupt Practices Act which forbids American companies from paying bribes overseas. This creates challenges when the foreign countries' laws require bribes. Fortunately for American businesses most European and a few other governments have also outlawed bribery so American companies are not alone. Just because bribery in foreign countries is illegal does not mean it does not happen. Companies still need to carefully consider their alternatives and consequences.

SOURCES

Donaldson, Thomas. 1989. *The Ethics of International Business.* Oxford University Press, Oxford, U.K.

Plato and Robin Waterfield. 2008. *The Republic.* Oxford World Classics, Oxford, U.K.

John Stuart Mill. 1863. *Utilitarianism.* London: Parker, Son and Bourn.

 **NOTES**

Concept	Definition	Example
What Is Ethics		
Moral standards that regulate right and wrong conduct		
Most standards vary greatly between populations		
Ethical Theories		
Virtue Theories—Develop Good Habits of Character		
Duty Theories—Meet Obligations		
Consequential Theories—Seek Favorable Outcomes		
Social Contract Theory— Minimum Social Standards Must Be Adhered To		
Virtue Theories		
Develop Good Habits of Character		
Very Common in Western Cultures		
Plato's Virtues—Wisdom, courage, temperance, and justice. Other important virtues are fortitude, generosity, self-respect, good temper, and sincerity.		
Vices—Cowardice, insensitivity, injustice, and vanity		

Concept	Definition	Example
Duty Theories		
One Must Meet Obligations		
Rights Theories—Strong Must Protect the Weak 　We should not harm anyone's life, health, liberty, or possessions 　Obligations of the universe 　Fidelity—The duty to keep promises 　Reparation—The duty to compensate others when we harm them 　Gratitude—The duty to thank those who help us 　Justice—The duty to recognize merit 　Beneficence—The duty to improve the conditions of others 　Self-improvement—The duty to improve our virtue and intelligence 　Nonmaleficence—The duty to not injure others		
Consequential Theories		
An action is morally right if the consequences of that action are more favorable than unfavorable		
Utilitarianism—the action that creates the most happiness is the moral action		
Rule utilitarianism—measures rules of behavior rather than each act		

Concept	Definition	Example
Social Contract Theory		
The following minimum standards must be adhered to: That a productive organization should enhance the long-term welfare of employees and consumers in any society in which the organization operates. That a productive organization should minimize the drawbacks associated with moving beyond the state of nature to a state containing productive organizations. That a productive organization should refrain from violating minimum standards of justice and of human rights in any society in which it operates.		
Applied Ethics		
Tries to create policies of behavior from Ethical Theory		
Business Ethics		
Environmental Ethics		
Computer Ethics		
Corporate Social Responsibility		
International Applied Business Ethics		
Theory preference is culturally bound		
Companies often face conflicting government and cultural requirements		

World perspectives important
    Multinational
    Multidomestic
    Global		

Concept	Definition	Example
Major Issues		
Environment		
Employee Relations		
Health & Safety		
Pay		
Interface to Religion and Other Cultural Practices		
Affects of Business on Local Culture		
Government Relations		
Bribery		

Corruption
   Bribery
      Foreign Corrupt Practices Act		

Now What?		
This will be one of your biggest problems in International Business—START STUDYING		
Golden Rule—Do unto others as you would have them do unto you		
Platinum Rule—Do unto others as they would have you do unto them		

International Trade Theory

International trade is as old as nations. People have always benefited from being able to trade with others that can make a product better or more cheaply. Understanding international trade means understanding how and why countries might constrict trade even when they are harming themselves. This chapter will look at the development of international commerce and the resultant types of international trade currently employed.

MERCANTILISM

To understand why the international trading system works the way it does, you have to understand some of its history. The history of international trade is best understood by first understanding mercantilism. Mercantilism is the buying or selling of commodities for the gain of both parties. In reality, it is a system through which a few tried to take advantage of many.

Pillage Other Lands

It is important to remember that the history of the world is far more about city states than countries. Until countries arose, trade was done between city states. City states were almost always run by a king or some other form of land owner or dictator. That dictator's goal was generally self-enrichment rather than to enrich a larger country or public. With that as the goal, the natural extension was to pillage and plunder the lands of others for self gain.

Import Barriers and Export Subsidies

One way a dictator enriches himself is by constricting trade to maintain a monopoly on it. Kings of old created their monopolies using the two tools of import barriers and export subsidies. By creating high import barriers the king could ensure that goods from other countries could not be sold in his lands, thus forcing his people to purchase goods from him at prices he set. He could subsidize the exports he wanted to sell in other city states in order to under price competition and build monopolies.

King's Wealth, Not Consumer Satisfaction

Because of the king's policies designed to enrich himself, his people could not get cheaper or better quality goods from other countries. That meant they were paying more for lower quality. The King's subsidies used money that might otherwise have been available to improve the lives of the people of the country. Thus the mercantilist system made the King richer but the King's people far poorer. Life as a peasant was usually one of poverty. The satisfaction of the subjects didn't matter.

Neomercantilism

As the era of Kings waned and democracies started taking hold around the world it became more difficult for a King to defend his mercantilist policies. Mercantilism did not completely die, however. Even in democracies there are politicians who can gain by favoring one minority over the needs of the majority of the people. Many democracies have thus adopted neomercantilist policies. Neomercantilism is a more recent strategy of countries that use protectionist trade policies in an attempt to run favorable balances of trade and/or accomplish particular social or political objectives. Like mercantilist policies, neomercantilist policies take from the many and give to the few. Neomercantilism simply tries to hide that fact or justify the policies in other ways.

ABSOLUTE ADVANTAGE

Mercantilism was fairly universal policy around the world for several thousand years. It was not substantially challenged until the 1700s. The theorist who most successfully attacked it was Adam Smith.

Adam Smith (1776)

The year 1776 was not only important for the beginning of the American Revolution. It was also the year Adam Smith, the British writer, published the *Wealth of Nations.* In it, he defined most of the base principles that underlie international business even today. One of his most important observations was the contrary idea that countries that allow free trade are better off.

Free Trade Is Better

Adam Smith argued that countries should concentrate their production in something at which they are particularly good. If each country specializes they will be able to make more of a product with the same amount of labor than could another country. If countries then trade what they have produced the greatest amount of possible wealth will have been created. Adam Smith used many arguments to prove his point. It is best made by understanding absolute advantage.

Absolute Advantage Graph

Absolute advantage uses a simplified model with only two countries and two goods to show countries are better off trading.

To understand absolute advantage, consider two countries, Canada and Mexico. They both want bananas to eat and both need lumber to build. Each could grow both trees for lumber and bananas, but Mexico is far more efficient at growing bananas and Canada much better at growing the pine trees that make lumber.

Both Canada and Mexico have 100 units of labor to dedicate to making bananas and lumber. It costs Canada 2 labor units for each ton of lumber they produce but since it is very hard to grow bananas in Canada, it costs them 10 labor units for each ton of bananas. In warmer Mexico they can grow bananas for only 4 units of labor. Tall pine does not grow well in Mexico however so it takes Mexico 10 units of labor for each ton of lumber. That means Canada has an absolute advantage in producing lumber and Mexico has an absolute advantage in producing bananas. Table 8.1 sums up the situation.

Each country has 100 total labor units available.

Now let's consider the possibilities if Canada and Mexico decide to go it alone and produce their own lumber and bananas. Figure 8.1 shows the possibilities.

If Mexico uses all its labor to grow bananas, it can grow 100/4 = 25 tons of bananas. If Mexico instead uses all its labor to make lumber, it can get 100/10 = 10 tons of lumber. Mexico can decide to use any amount of its labor on either lumber or bananas. The line labelled Mexico on the graph shows all the possibilities for how many bananas Mexico can get depending on how much labor it chooses to spend on lumber.

The same approach works for Canada. If Canada uses all its labor to grow bananas it can grow 100/10 = 10 tons of bananas. If Canada instead uses all its labor to produce lumber, it can get 100/2 = 50 tons of lumber. Canada can decide to use any amount of its labor on either lumber or bananas. The line labelled Canada on the graph shows all the possibilities for how many bananas Canada can get depending on how much labor it chooses to spend on lumber.

Now, for sake of example, let's say Mexico and Canada each decides to spend half their labor on lumber and half on bananas. How many total goods would be produced?

To answer that question, let's start with Canada. If Canada used half its labor on bananas it would get to spend 50 units of labor at 10 units per ton to get 50/10 = 5 tons of bananas. It could then spend its other 50 units of labor to get 50/2 = 25 tons of lumber. The option for Canada to use 50% of its labor on bananas and lumber is illustrated as the dotted line in the graph.

If Mexico also equally divided its labor between lumber and bananas, it would get to spend 50 units of labor at 4 units per ton to get 50/4 = 12.5 tons of bananas. It could then spend its other 50 units of labor to get 50/10 = 5 tons of lumber. Table 8.2 shows the outcomes if we total Canada's and Mexico's production without trade.

If instead, Canada and Mexico decide to specialize in what they are best at and trade, Canada would spend all its labor on lumber and Mexico, all its labor on bananas. That would yield 100/2 = 50 tons of lumber from Canada and 100/4 = 25 tons of bananas from Mexico as shown in Table 8.3.

Because Mexico and Canada would only have 47.5 tons of goods without trade and 75 tons of goods with specialization and trade, they each would be better off specializing and trading.

Obviously, this example is contrived. Mexico and Canada produce many more goods than just two and we are ignoring transportation and other costs added by trade. This problem has been run through many different scenarios, however, and as long as each

TABLE 8.1	Units of Labor Needed to Produce Goods	
	Canada	Mexico
Bananas	10	4
Lumber	2	10

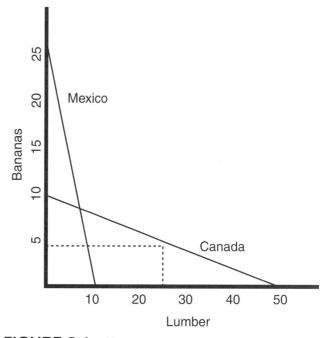

FIGURE 8.1   Absolute Advantage Production Frontiers

TABLE 8.2	Total Goods Produced without Trade		
	Canada	Mexico	Total
Bananas	5	12.5	17.5
Lumber	25	5	30
Total	30	17.5	47.5

TABLE 8.3	Total Goods Produced with Specialization and Trade		
	Canada	Mexico	Total
Bananas	0	25	25
Lumber	50	0	50
Total	50	25	75

country is significantly better at producing some good than the other country, the world is wealthier with specialization of trade. Under absolute advantage theory, each country has a specialty it is better at doing. By trading with each other, all the world is better off.

COMPARATIVE ADVANTAGE

Absolute advantage clearly shows that if you have two countries, each of which is better at producing one good, then it is far better for both countries if each specializes at what they are best at and trades. But what happens if one country is better at both goods?

The issue has been studied carefully. The math of comparative advantage is somewhat more complex than that of absolute advantage but the concepts are as easy to understand. If one country is better at making both goods then it might seem logical for that country to make both goods. That solution would make it impossible for poorer or less efficient countries to ever trade, however. Fortunately, careful analysis shows that most of the time, even when one country is better at both goods, both countries are still better off specializing and trading.

Consider again Canada and Mexico from the absolute advantage example. What if the goods we are considering are lumber and skis. Canada is likely to be better at producing both. Even though Canada would have an advantage at producing both goods the advantage they would have in producing lumber would be greater than the advantage in producing skis because lumber is less labor intensive and Mexico has a lower cost of labor. Let's look at the simple example in Table 8.4.

Each country has 100 total labor units available.

Table 8.5 shows that if Canada and Mexico do not trade and use half their labor for each good, they would produce.

Instead, in Table 8.6 see what would happen if Canada specialized in what it is most efficient at, lumber, and Mexico specialized in what Canada is less efficient at, skis.

As you can see from the example, total goods produced is greater due to specialization and trading even though one country is better at both goods so long as the country that is better at both goods is not equally better at both goods.

In the real world we are talking about thousands of goods and hundreds of countries, not just two. No matter how many variables you add, however, the same basic outcome is seen. The world is wealthier if each country specializes at the things it is best at and trades for other goods.

There are costs not considered in the absolute and comparative analysis. The biggest required cost is transportation. For heavy goods of little value, transportation costs can overwhelm the benefits of trade, so some heavy, low value goods are not often traded internationally. The thing that more frequently destroys trade is import and export taxes. A government with neomercantilist policies can always set import tax rates high enough that they are greater than the advantage of trade. In so doing the government hurts its own people but may make a small slice of the population richer. In reality, absolute

TABLE 8.4	Units of Labor Needed to Produce Goods	
	Canada	Mexico
Lumber	2	10
Skis	4	10

TABLE 8.5	Total Goods Produced without Trade		
	Canada	Mexico	Total
Lumber	25	5	30
Skis	12.5	5	17.5
Total	37.5	10	47.5

TABLE 8.6	Total Goods Produced with Specialization and Trade		
	Canada	Mexico	Total
Lumber	50	0	50
Skis	0	10	10
Total	50	10	60

and comparative advantage must include, in analysis, all factors of production. Costs of material, labor, transportation, etc. go into the costs of goods sold. All the complexities must be considered in order to determine trade advantages.

OTHER REASONS FOR TRADE

Beyond the increased wealth that comes from trade, there are other advantages to international trade that countries and companies pursue. Some of the more important are described here.

Product Lifecycle

Product lifecycle theory says that most goods live through a predictable lifecycle. At the earliest phases of new product introduction, sales of a good are low as customers learn that a new product exists. Sales grow as customers become accustomed to a product and as new companies enter the market with improvements in the price and features of the product. Eventually sales of the product mature and stabilize as customers become accustomed to the product and make it part of their regular purchasing cycle. Eventually, another new product comes along that better meets the same need as the existing product and decreases sales of the existing product as the new product replaces it in the market. The

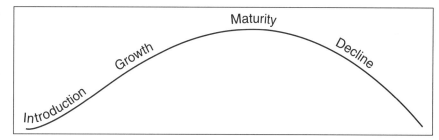

FIGURE 8.2 The Product Lifecycle

product lifecycle is often depicted by a curve similar to that in Figure 8.2.

International business will often try to extend the profitable mature phase by introducing a product in different countries at different times (Figure 8.3). Because the product lifecycle applies anew in each market, companies can keep existing factories and systems running profitably longer. The Internet and other rapid communication devices have made it more difficult to isolate markets. Thus, companies are being forced to introduce products much more rapidly around the world to avoid competitors developing before they arrive in new markets. The passage of time is a big factor in product lifecycle.

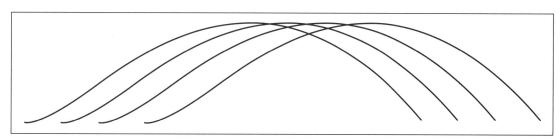

FIGURE 8.3 The Product Lifecycle Repeated across Several Countries

Economies of Scale

The economies of scale theory suggests there is cost advantages to building products in ever larger factories. Reaching most efficient economies of scale is another important reason for international trade in many industries. At some point diseconomies of scale eliminate the advantage of getting bigger. The question for every product is how large a factory works for the product before diseconomies of scale reduce profitability. For many industries today the most efficient economies of scale are bigger than the world market for the product. At that point it makes the best sense to build just one factory and serve the entire world from it. Obviously such an approach requires free trade to work.

Economic Diversification

Another important use of trade is to provide companies opportunities for economic diversification. Not all country economies are in sync. While some countries go into recession, others are experiencing boom cycles. Companies that have operations in many countries are able to concentrate sales in countries during their boom cycles then shift product to booming countries during recessionary cycles. This process has become more difficult as world economies have synchronized around the U.S. economy but even the economies that are most closely tied to the United States are not in perfect sync so there is still opportunity for diversification.

Technology Development Costs Shared

Many new technologies are extremely expensive to develop. A new drug usually costs more than $1 billion to produce. New cars, computer systems, other electronic devices, and major software systems require similar investments. It would be foolish for one country to spend all that is necessary to develop a new product and then require every other country to make similar investments for the same product. International trade allows countries to share the costs of technology development by allowing one country to make the investment and then sell new products that are developed to all the rest of the countries. Life expectancy in poorer countries would be much less if they had to rely on their own investment in new drugs and other lifesaving technologies.

COMPETITIVE ADVANTAGE

Even though most economic competition is between companies, countries have tried to figure out what they can do to make their companies more competitive. This idea goes beyond absolute and comparative advantage to include, in the more complete and complex analysis, whether the government's intervening will help the industry to go forth in international trade. The theory that best explains what makes a country competitive is Michael Porter's *Competitive Advantage* (1985). Porter theorizes that national competitive advantage is embedded in four determinants that must be favorable for a given national industry to attain global competitiveness. According to Porter, a country with only two or three of the determinants is not likely to be successful in supporting a given industry. Countries that try to become competitive by creating just one or two of the determinants are doomed to failure. The four determinants are:

> **Factor Endowments**—Factor endowments suggest countries must have both the natural resources that are base components and the skilled labor that goes into making the product. Most countries that tried to become competitive in a new industry have focused primarily on factor endowments and have failed.

> **Demand Conditions**—Demand conditions means that the product the country is trying to develop must be in high demand there. If there's little demand for the product in the country trying to develop it; people in the country will have very little natural understanding of the product. There will not be a substantial number of people in the country thinking about how to make the product better. People building the product will have little natural understanding of what the major defects in the product will be and will be less likely to catch them. In short, people who have little understanding of the product are not going to make it well.

> **Related and Supporting Industries**—Another requirement for a country to develop a successful industry is that it must have supporting industries as well.

Nearly all modern products are complex and built from many subcomponents. If a country tries to develop an industry without also developing the supply chain of industries needed for the subcomponents, the industry is likely to fail. Innovation and quality control of the subcomponents is just as important as in the final assembly. Interactions between the main product maker and subcomponent makers are critical to generating innovation and quality in the subcomponents. Countries with both the main product manufacturer and subcomponents manufacturers, therefore, have an advantage in creating more competitive products.

Firm Strategy Structure and Rivalry—Finally, Porter suggests that for a country to be competitive in a product it requires the country have several competitive companies that produce the product. A country with only one or two producers of a product will have companies acting in monopolistic ways. The companies will be less innovative and less willing to disrupt existing markets. Countries that have numerous competitors in an industry will have several companies constantly trying to outmaneuver one another. Companies in such a competitive industry will always be trying to be the first to market with a new product. They will always be trying to reduce manufacturing costs so they can be more price competitive. They will be paying far more attention to customers to better hone their product to customer demands. Companies in a more competitive industry will thus make better products and be more successful when they try to sell those products in overseas markets.

GLOBAL STRATEGIC RIVALRY THEORY

Global strategic rivalry theory takes what is learned from competitive analysis and applies it to how individual companies should compete to succeed internationally. The primary focus of the theory is to suggest that there are advantages to be gained by acquiring knowledge and then using that knowledge across world markets to build competitive advantage. This theory suggests that competitive advantage at the company level is gained primarily through having knowledge and skills that your competitors lack. According to global strategic rivalry theory there are four ways the company can gain sustainable advantage.

Owning Intellectual Property Rights

One way to gain sustainable advantage is to own intellectual property rights. The company that owns key patents, trademarks, or copyrights has legally defensible monopoly rights they can use to build products or services competitors cannot match.

Investing in Research and Development

Companies that invest heavily in research and development can also gain sustainable advantage. They can do so by making discoveries that lead to intellectual property rights but also by learning many new techniques and processes that are never turned into property rights. Much of what a company discovers in research and development is often tied to its own company culture, organizational structure, or other functions specific to the company that are difficult for other companies to copy. That makes those discoveries particularly valuable because they survive in the market for a longer period of time.

Achieving Economies of Scale or Scope

Companies can also gain competitive advantage by being the first to achieve important economies of scale or scope. The company that first achieves the size that is most efficient for its industry will have economy of scale cost advantages over competitors. Economy of scope is important too, however. Some industries can gain advantage by owning more or less of their own distribution system, or more or less of their own component suppliers. The company that best figures out the optimal mix of subcomponent manufacturing, product manufacturing, and distribution will have international advantages over competitors. They can use these advantages to defeat competitors.

Exploiting the Experience Curve

An often overlooked part of building competitive advantage is the experience curve. The experience curve says that employees become more efficient the more they work on a process. Some tasks are simple and employees become good at them quickly. Other tasks, like management, are more challenging and can take employees decades to really perfect. A company that can get its employees further along the experience curve will have cost and quality advantages over competitors. A company that employs all of a very specialized type of engineer or management group may be able to gain advantages that take competitors many years to copy. Investments in unique training can thus be an incredible advantage but only as long as employees are learning challenging tasks that add to profitability and the company is willing to pay what it takes to keep competitors from poaching those employees.

The complexities of global trade have evolved over centuries. It is imperative for success that a company have absolute or relative cost advantages as well as its government and its policies on its side.

SOURCES

Mahoney, D., M. Trigg, R. Griffin, and M. Pustay. 1998. *International Business: A Managerial Perspective*. Melbourne, Australia: Addison Wesley Longman.

Porter, Michael. 1985. *Competitive Advantage*. Free Press, New York, New York.

Smith, Adam. 1776. *The Wealth of Nations*.

 **NOTES**

Concept	Definition	Example
Mercantilism		
Pillaged the lands—did whatever it took to increase trade surplus.		
Used high import barriers and export subsidies.		
Increased national wealth but decreased consumer satisfaction.		
Neomercantilism The more recent strategy of countries that use protectionist trade policies in an attempt to run favorable balances of trade and/or accomplish particular social or political objectives.		
Absolute Advantage		
Adam Smith, 1776		
Free Trade Is Better—Countries should specialize production in something at which they are particularly good.		
Absolute Advantage Graph		
Comparative Advantage		
If one country is better at producing both goods, are you still better off trading? Often, yes.		
Comparative Advantage Graph		
Hecksher-Ohlin Theory of Factor Endowments		
Countries will tend to specialize in goods that utilize their abundant resources (labor, minerals, etc.)		

Concept	Definition	Example
The Leontief Paradox—The U.S. and other developed nations export many labor intensive goods, although they are capital intensive countries.		

Possible Explanation
   Productivity of resources
   Interaction of resources—
     labor absorbs capital
     through education and
     training		

Other Reasons for Trade		
Product Lifecycle		
Economies of Scale		
Diversification		
Costs of Technology Development		
Competitive Advantage		

Michael Porter theorizes that national competitive advantage is embedded in four determinants that must be favorable for a given national industry to attain global competitiveness.
   Factor Endowments
   Demand Conditions
   Related and Supporting
     Industries
   Firm Strategy Structure and
     Rivalry		

Global Strategic Rivalry Theory		

Gain Competitive Advantage through:
   Owning intellectual property
     rights
   Investing in research and
     development
   Achieving economies of scale
     or scope
   Exploiting the experience
     curve		

Governmental Effects on Trade

Chapter 8 showed how beneficial trade is to the world and to most people in each country. It also showed that governments can gain advantage for themselves by distorting trade. This chapter describes the arguments and approaches governments use in that distortion. Because companies generally benefit from trade, this chapter refutes those government distortions. Understanding those distortions and the arguments governments use for them is critical to the international business person who often has to counter those arguments to avoid bad policy and laws.

The fact that companies often have to counter governments on trade issues is not to say that government is corrupt. It simply recognizes that in a political system there will always be people trying to gain advantage. In a democracy, elected politicians need powerful supporters and those supporters will often request distortions in the system to favor themselves. In authoritarian governments, there are those willing to use government for personal gain. Businesses need to be able to counter government arguments. And let's not forget that those inducing government to distort trade are often businesses themselves. Businesses arguing against distortions are usually trying to prevent competitors or suppliers from gaining advantage through government manipulation.

WHY GOVERNMENTS INTERVENE— ECONOMIC ARGUMENTS

Governments rationalize protectionism with economic arguments. Governments will often claim that they're working to protect their economy when in fact they are protecting a small part of it at great cost to the rest. Following are three major economic arguments governments offer for protectionism.

Unemployment Argument

The most common argument is that they're trying to protect employment. It is a popular argument because employees in a threatened industry are usually vocal and motivated and thus gain the sympathy of people outside the industry who can identify with the stress. Frequently, attempts to protect employment in an industry will be made under great political pressure from the unions and management of the threatened industry. The unions and management will often use the press to demonstrate the plight of those whose jobs are at risk. An employment argument is, therefore, often successful.

A problem with the unemployment argument, like all protectionism, is that it favors a small group over the well being of the people in the country as a whole. Government protectionism can save jobs in one industry, but doing so may risk more jobs in other related industries throughout the economy. For example, consider one of the United States' more recent attempts at protectionism. The U.S. Steel industry has shed many thousands of jobs. Steel workers' unions and steel companies argued for, and received, tariff import tax protection for the steel industry from the U.S. government. The steel industry continued its employment decline in the United States but at a much slower rate. Many people considered it a victory for protectionism.

Those people, however, were not looking at the big picture. Steel is a base component in many products made in the United States. Cars, appliances, buildings, and a huge variety of other American-made goods are built from steel. The increased taxes on imported steel actually increased steel prices to the manufacturers of cars, appliances, and other products. Those manufacturers needed to increase prices to cover costs, resulting in sales decreasing in their industries. The number of jobs lost due to those sales decreases were greater than those jobs protected in the steel industry. The jobs lost in the steel-dependent industries were spread around the country so there wasn't any one large group to scream and yell about them. TV cameras never showed up to show the jobs lost at hundreds of companies. Thus, the political system protected a few steel jobs at the cost of losing more jobs in other industries. Most analyses show one protected job in a country usually costs somewhere between 1.5 and 3 jobs elsewhere in the economy. Unintended consequences.

Infant Industry Argument

In the infant industry argument the government says it is trying to develop a new industry or an industry in which it has not competed before. Because the country is new to the industry, the argument goes, it needs protections to allow its small companies to compete against larger international competitors. At first the process appears to work. If outside supplies of a good are blocked from a country, small competitors will develop within the country to produce it. The problem with the approach is long-term.

The infant industry approach to protectionism fails because the companies that grow up under protectionism are inherently flawed. They build management structures, distribution systems, salaries, and the entire rest of their business systems based on prices that are above international norms. If a country ever eliminates its protection, the companies that grew up under it are overpriced and unable to survive international competition. The only way the companies can live is to keep the protections. Consumers in the country end up paying a higher price for the good and get lower quality because small local companies can't afford the advances in technology or scale available to international firms. Thus, infant industry protections lead a country to protect the industry forever, damaging their own consumers, or the government eventually drops the protections which almost always kills the industry as it faces international competition in a weakened state. Think of the U.S. auto market in the 1970s and 1980s with its many protections from international competitors. Detroit was bloated with costs and hasn't been able to compete effectively since the protections were lifted.

Industrialization Argument

The industrialization argument is similar to the infant industry argument except on a grander scale. The industrialization argument is usually made by smaller or poorer countries. They argue that as a country they're not as sophisticated as big trading countries and so they must protect their economy so that it can catch up. Once the government protects its economy from outside competition it weakens its own companies. The companies that grow behind the protections are less efficient and less creative. They develop less skill at competing internationally.

The governments that have used the industrialization argument to justify broadranging protections and then kept those protections for a substantial period of time have generally destroyed their economies. The company's inside the protected economy become less efficient the longer the protections last. Eventually, the country that falls behind can do little more than sell natural resources to other countries. Countries with lots of oil, diamonds, or other valuable resources can survive as long as the resources hold out. For countries with few natural resources protectionism makes the future more bleak.

If high levels of protectionism are so destructive to an economy one might wonder why a government would ever consider them. Remember, however, that a few do usually gain through protectionism. Many of the world's richest people are often found in the poorest countries. The system of protectionism is there to make those rich people richer and the poor are made poorer as a consequence.

WHY GOVERNMENTS INTERVENE— NON-ECONOMIC ARGUMENTS

Beyond economic arguments there are occasionally non-economic arguments offered for protectionism. Because non-economic arguments are directed at non-economic goals, they are easier to justify as long as it is remembered that the non-economic goals are achieved at an economic price. Most countries use at least a few protectionist tactics for non-economic goals. Done in excess they can destroy an economy.

Maintenance of Essential Industries

Most countries define at least a couple of industries as essential. These industries are usually more heavily protected. For example, many countries define their military industry as essential. They protect military-related industries to assure that they will have their own production capacity for weapons in times of war. Other countries will defend essential food industries. For example, Japan very actively defends its rice producers even though they're very inefficient by world standards. Protecting at least a limited capacity in such truly essential industries is hard to argue against. A problem that frequently develops, however, is countries will often declare marginal industries to be essential and protecting them both weakens the industry argument and damages the economy of the country.

Prevention of Shipments to "Unfriendly" Countries

Countries of the world develop enemies, making it necessary to create protections to prevent militarily valuable goods from getting to their enemies. For example, the United States and a few other nuclear powers try very hard to prevent new nuclear weapons technologies from reaching unfriendly countries. The argument can go too far, however. The United States' embargo with Cuba for 46 years is probably a good example of a very powerful country using the argument well beyond the scope of the threat presented by its perceived enemies.

Maintenance of Sphere of Influence

Larger countries might also try to maintain a sphere of influence. A sphere of influence is a group of other countries usually surrounding the more powerful country over which the powerful country claims special rights. The powerful country will often develop special trade policies to maintain its friendly sphere. Thus, the powerful country will offer import tariff breaks on goods coming from countries within its sphere and subsidies on goods exported to those countries. All this is done to try to protect borders or traditional relationships and help the large country maintain its influence over the smaller countries around it.

Protecting National Identity

Countries often also protect goods that they consider to be an important part of their national identity. For example, France heavily protects its wine and cheese industries. It is not that the wine and cheese industries are of such great economic importance to France that they feel they must protect them. It is simply that French tradition holds wine and cheese in very great esteem, so the French are willing to pay a price in the rest of their economy to protect their wine and cheese interests. Music, dance, art, and traditional alcoholic beverages are often afforded such protections. As long as the number of goods and the size of markets are small, traditions can be maintained with little cost to the overall economy. As more goods are added, or the size of the markets grow, more and more damage is done to the country's overall economy by such protection.

WHY GOVERNMENTS INTERVENE— ECONOMIC RELATIONS

Sometimes protectionism, or the threat of protectionism, is used as an economic relations tool. Countries like the United States, and a few other powerful trading nations, will often threaten to close their markets to less powerful countries if they do not help the powerful country meet their economic goals. Trade protections in this sense work very much like possessing nuclear weapons. Sometimes good things can come out of threatening to use them but if anyone does use them everyone loses. The most common economic relations arguments follow.

Balance of Payment Adjustment

Quite often powerful countries of the world run a negative balance of payments. Those countries will often threaten to close their markets to weaker countries with large positive balance of payments. The assumption is that the large positive balance of payments is being generated by trade protectionism. The goal of the powerful countries is to remove that protectionism and give the powerful countries a fair shot at the weaker countryies' markets. If the threat works, as it often does, then trade is increased and the world's wealth is improved. That should be considered a good thing. We can't forget, however, that the richer, more powerful country is likely to get a bigger share of the increase in wealth. It is understandable that smaller and weaker countries do what they can to win advantage.

Comparable Access

The large and powerful countries of the world will often also use the comparable access argument. Because their markets are open to a particular country, that other country's markets must also be open to them. A large, powerful country making the argument usually wins, eventually increasing both its own wealth and the wealth of the weaker country. But, again, the new wealth is rarely shared equally.

Price Control Objectives

A rarer use of trade protectionism is an attempt to maintain a minimum or maximum price for a good in a country. A country that does not favor a product but does not feel it can ban it will often maintain a high minimum price on it. Most of the time this occurs because a more powerful nation has pressured the country not to ban the product. The weaker country will thus use trade protections to keep the supply low and price high to discourage consumption.

More often a country will try to maintain a maximum price for a good it considers important to its people. For example, many poorer Asian countries try to maintain a maximum price for rice. The maximum price keeps rice affordable so people in the country can eat but it can only be sustained by heavily subsidizing rice when world rice prices significantly exceed the maximum price set by the government. Those subsidies distort world markets, hurting other rice dependant countries, and distort farm production within the country. A common outcome is fields that would be much better suited for growing wheat or corn are used to produce low yields of rice, significantly reducing total food production in a country that desperately needs more of it.

TOOLS OF TRADE CONTROL

Governments have many arguments for why they attempt protectionism. Most tools they can use for protectionism are straightforward and easy to detect. But, other tools are well hidden and companies often don't know they exist until they run into them. There are basically two categories of tools governments use to control trade: tariffs and nontariff barriers. Each is described here.

Tariffs

Tariffs are the simplest and most straightforward tool governments use to control trade across their border. Tariffs are taxes charged on goods as they enter as imports or, less commonly, as they leave the country as exports.

Tariffs are easy to see and understand. A government may charge a general tariff on all goods of 1% for example. All goods are treated equally and companies rarely complain about such simple tariff systems because the companies understand that governments must pay for their customs services.

Sometimes governments will try to use tariffs to protect a particular good. If the country's general tariff is 1% they might charge 10%, 20%, 50% or sometimes even more than 100% tariff on a particular good. As that good enters the country the tariff becomes part of its base price in the country. So if there is a 50% tariff on a good that normally costs $100, the good ends up costing a $150.00 after it is imported. The simplicity of tariffs makes it easy to understand how much of a price effect a tariff will have on a good and what that price effect will have on demand.

The simplicity of a tariff actually makes it hard for countries to use them for protectionist purposes. Every country can view the tariffs of others and where they are prohibitively high, argue against them. Large trading nations like the United States constantly harass countries with high tariffs to reduce them. Few countries are able to resist the pressures to reduce tariffs over the long run. Because it is so difficult to support high tariffs, countries have turned to nontariff barriers for protectionism.

Nontariff Barriers

Nontariff barriers are tools other than specific taxes that countries use to influence their trade. All the nontariff barriers are more difficult to detect than are tariffs. Some of the nontariff barriers are so difficult to detect that they are popular in countries following strong neomercantilist policies. The most commonly used nontariff barriers are presented on the following pages.

Subsidies—While tariffs are the simplest tool for blocking goods from entering a country, subsidies are the simplest tool for aiding goods to be exported. With subsidies a government pays companies to help lower the price for export goods. For example, the United States heavily subsidizes its farming goods by paying farmers cash for certain export goods. The farmers are then able to sell those goods overseas for a lower price and capture more of the overseas market. The subsidies support higher farm prices in the United States by encouraging exporting. Farmers gain from the higher prices but all U.S. consumers must pay higher prices for foodstuffs.

Because subsidies show up on a country's budget, they are relatively easy to detect and to attack. There are still opportunities to hide subsidies, however. For example, another industry the United States strongly protects is its military industry. It subsidizes this industry in direct ways through purchases that are not always transparent due to aggregation under categories. It also subsidizes it in hidden ways. For example, a large portion of what the U.S. government spends on research and development in U.S. universities is geared towards military technologies. Those subsidies do not show up in the U.S. military budget so it can be hard for other countries trying to compete with the U.S. military industry to attack those subsidies.

Rich country subsidies can have a detrimental effect on poorer countries. Many poor countries try to survive on agricultural industries but have a very difficult time doing so because of rich countries' farm subsidies. Although the World Trade Organization has tried to level the playing field around the world, politics usually overrides these attempts in the richer countries.

Loans and Aid—Another indirect subsidy is in the form of aid or loans. A country will identify companies within the industry they want to support and then offer those companies loans at substantially reduced rates. Those reduced loan costs function exactly as a subsidy. For example, if a country wants to help out its corn farmers, it could see how much the typical corn farmer has to borrow to run the farm for the year. If the typical farmer has to borrow $100,000 at 10% interest, the government might offer a loan to the farmer at 1% interest. The farmer would have to pay $10,000 for interest with a 10% loan but instead would pay $1000 for the 1% loan. Thus, the government has hidden a $9000 subsidy in the form of a loan. Aid works similarly except the government, in effect, forgives the loan or a large part of it and thus not only eliminates interest payments but directly provides capital to the farmer. Aid and loans are thus more difficult to detect than is direct subsidy.

Customs Valuation—Customs valuation is a technique used by governments that want to increase tariffs on specific goods but find themselves unable to do so for political reasons. Instead of changing tariff rates directly, sometimes governments will simply change the reported value of goods entering the country.

One of the challenges with a tariff system is that it can be difficult to know the right price for a good as it enters a country. Often a company is selling the good from one of its subsidiaries to another. That allows the company 100% control over the price. Countries thus have no real way of knowing what the accurate price is. Countries usually trust the value they are told by the company importing the goods, but sometimes they change the reported value of the goods entering the country. So instead of adding a 10% increase to the tariff charged on a particular good, the country will keep the same tariff rate but increase the customs value of the good by 10%. The net effect is an identical 10% increase in the taxes the company pays to get the good into the country. Companies will complain when this happens but it is more difficult to prove than is a simple tariff increase so countries have an easier time getting away with it.

Quotas—Another way to protect trade is the quota. With a tariff, a country tries to reduce imports by increasing the price of imports with the expectation that domestically made goods will sell better against the higher priced imports. In the 1970s, the United States faced a dilemma. The U.S. government wanted to protect specific goods but had spent much of the previous two decades trying to convince other countries to reduce their tariffs. Not wanting to look hypocritical, the United States did not want to increase tariffs. They thus invented the quota as a more direct method for reducing foreign supply by setting a strict limit on how many of a foreign good are allowed to enter the United States. The idea was simple. The consequences were disastrous.

The reason quotas are such a disaster for a country is what quotas do with the extra money generated from reduced supply. With a tariff, the price difference is paid as a tax to the importing country's government. With a quota, foreign supply is reduced by law. That reduction in supply increases prices that are paid directly to the foreign company. In effect quotas set up monopolies for foreign companies that guarantee high profit margins. Most companies that received those high profits were smart enough to invest in research and development to gain further advantage in their products.

If, as a company, you feel your industry is about to be hit with trade protections by a country, argue for a quota. The competitive advantage you gain is the best thing that ever happened to companies hit with them.

"Buy Local" Legislation—Buy local legislation is a weaker form of trade protectionism. A country uses peer pressure and law to encourage or force consumers or businesses to purchase from domestic companies. In most countries, buy local legislation is a political ploy with mostly cosmetic effects. For example, goods sold in the United States must have a tag stating where the product was made. The hope was that Americans would pay more for American-made products. It hasn't worked out that way in America or many other countries. Some small countries are more influenced by local labels but generally the effect is weak.

Another approach to buy local legislation is requirements that government entities purchase domestic made products. Given the difficulty of determining what a domestically made product is today, this sort of legislation has again proven to be largely superficial. The one place buy local legislation has had an effect is in government operations in overseas locations. Those operations frequently must pay much higher prices to get home country goods. Most of that extra cost goes to distribution systems outside the home country.

Standards and Labels—As we reach standards and labels we're into forms of trade protectionism that are very difficult to identify and challenge. Therefore, they are popular tools for governments who wish to protect certain industries and product without appearing to do so. Companies are as guilty as governments in harming trade. Many companies lobby for standards or labels they can use to protect their products from competitors.

Using standards, a government sets requirements for a product in their country that are not common in other countries. This requires companies from other countries to modify their products, thereby increasing the costs for the product. It also provides a level of protection for domestically made goods. The standards rarely make the products any better so consumers still pay a higher price for no real benefits. For example, anyone who has travelled extensively will tell horror stories of dealing with all the world's different standards for electrical plugs. It would seem an easy enough problem to fix and it would be if governments really wanted to fix it. They don't, however, because having a different plug provides a level of protection to the domestic electronics industry.

Requiring specific labels serves the same function. Excess products produced in one country can't be shipped to another country if they don't include esoteric labels required in the other country. For example, most people have wondered what that stupid tag on your pillows and mattresses are all about. For the most part it serves one function. It makes it impossible for excess pillows or mattresses produced in Mexico or other countries to be shipped to the United States because they lack the appropriate tag.

Specific Permission Requirements—This technique allows a country to require some safety, environmental, or standards check of a product before it is permitted into the country. The country then makes it difficult, if not impossible, to get the checks done. The bureaucrats hired to do the checks will be allowed to hold limited hours and reject products for almost any reason. Countries can block products for years using this technique, and many do.

Administrative Delays—Administrative delays often go beyond specific permission requirements. Here a country will design complex paperwork to be completed to import a product. Any mistakes made in filling out the paperwork will get the product rejected. Even when the paperwork is done perfectly, bureaucrats will pass it from desk to desk making sure it takes a very long time to get completed. This process may not keep the product out but the importing company is financing the product the entire time it has been held up and their cost goes up commensurately. Some companies become so frustrated with the process they simply give up and go away. From the government's perspective that may be what they were trying to accomplish but consumers in the country are still hurt by the higher cost and reduced quality of constrained competition.

Reciprocal Requirements—A less common trade restriction is reciprocal requirements. Reciprocal requirements are usually only used by poorer countries with bad balance of trade problems. With reciprocal requirements a country will require that if a company is going to import $1,000,000 worth of goods it must also export $1,000,000 of goods. The reason most countries need to resort to such measures is because they have little of value to export. Companies are often required to figure out how to export goods for which they really have no need. Reciprocal requirements are rare because few companies are willing to deal with the challenges they present. Therefore, countries trying to use reciprocal requirements will see their international trade disappear. It is offered strictly as a measure of last resort.

Restrictions on Service Businesses—The last major trade restriction employed is restrictions on service businesses. Because most service businesses are large employers, many countries actively seek them out. Sometimes, however, a strong domestic company can push their government to defend their weak position. Unfortunately, it is fairly easy to block foreign service-oriented businesses because the primary import of a service business is skilled people and managers. The government can set visa requirements that make it difficult or impossible to bring skilled people into the country. By doing so, they effectively block the international service business. Unfortunately, the United States is the greatest practitioner of the strategy, making it nearly impossible for foreign companies to bring workers into the United States. That makes it difficult for the U.S. government to argue against other countries that do the same thing, so there is no one really fighting to prevent this strategy.

LEVELS OF REGIONAL INTEGRATION

Given so many readily available tools to block trade, countries find they end up doing significant damage to themselves. Protecting one or two small products is no problem for a large economy but the more that is protected the more damage is done to the country's economy. Because of self-inflicted damages, countries have decided they need tools to protect themselves against their own worst impulses. They have started forming regional groups which can overrule restrictions within an individual country. There are four levels of regional integration that are commonly seen.

Free Trade Area — No Tariffs between Members, Unrestricted Tariffs with Non-members

Within a free trade area, countries understand that restrictions on trade are damaging their countries. They agree to eliminate tariffs, and often other trade barriers, between all the countries involved in the free trade area. Eliminating tariffs between the countries substantially increases trade between the countries within the area. Countries outside the trade area are often hurt, however, because they're paying higher tariffs. But most outside countries quickly see the hole in free trade area logic. Because each country in the free trade area keeps its own tariffs with countries outside the trade area, a company that wants to import to a high tariff country can import their product to the country with the lowest tariffs in the free trade area and then export from there to the high tariff country. As this flaw is exploited, much of the trade within the defined trade area goes to the country with the lowest external tariffs.

Customs Union — No Internal Tariffs, Same External Tariffs

As countries in a trade area learn to trust each other more and discover the major flaws in their free trade areas, they will often decide to move to a customs union. In a customs union, what was a free trade area integrates their external tariffs so they're all the same. This process eliminates the ability of countries outside the area to exploit the lowest tariff country. It does not eliminate all the region's problems, however. Once a customs union is established, it begins to experience problems because factors of production are not free to move between countries. The availability of factors of production, such as labor and natural resources, dictates much of the costs of goods within a country. Because the factors of production cannot move freely between countries, distortions will begin to appear as outside companies seek the country in the customs union that has the lowest cost. Countries with large labor forces will start absorbing jobs that would have otherwise gone to better educated labor forces. Countries with abundant natural resources will find it difficult to afford labor to exploit the resource advantage. Imbalances in the countries of the customs union area begin to distort their economies.

Common Market — Custom Union Plus Factors of Production Free to Move

A few of the customs unions that have experienced the distortions that naturally develop in a customs union have moved to the next level of integration, i.e., a common market. In a common market, factors of production are freed to move between countries within the region. Most importantly, labor and people are freed to move and work in any of the countries of the common market. In theory, this eliminates the labor distortions that tear at a customs union. In practice, language differences, educational differences, and cultural differences leave some of the distortions intact but a common market does experience a more balanced economy. Common markets still allow some distortions. The biggest remaining distortions come from national laws that have differential effects on their economies. Most common markets will attempt to integrate laws, but some distortions remain.

Complete Economic Integration — Common Market Plus Policy and Money

The last step of economic integration is called complete economic integration. That includes integration of currency, policy, and law in the economic integration of a common market. Few regions have gone this far but it is worth remembering that complete economic integration between independent states is what the United States represents. Each of the states within the United States sets many of their own laws and their economic policy. They could have gone on as independent countries much as Europe did.

WORLD TRADE ORGANIZATION

The largest attempt to integrate trade rules and overcome protectionist instincts is the World Trade Organization. The World Trade Organization is a treaty signed by more than 140 countries. The treaty requires members to offer each other most favored nation trade status. What that status means is open to debate but theoretically it means you offer every country the same trade deal you offer the country that gets the best deal from you. In practice, the World Trade Organization is a negotiating body that helps forward three primary goals.

Promote Trade by Encouraging Non-discriminatory, Predictable Trade Policies

The World Trade Organization encourages countries to treat every country similarly in the belief that such actions will make all countries feel they're being treated fairly. They also try to enforce stability in trade practices so companies can predict trade practices and make long-term plans accordingly. The concept of fair is as challenging to the World Trade Organization as it is everywhere else in the world. Is it more fair to treat everyone the same or is it more fair to have tariffs that are lower for imports from poor countries? Such issues make it difficult for the World Trade Organization to create anything even approximating uniformity.

Reduce Trade Barriers through Multilateral Negotiations

Given the challenges of getting everyone to agree on what is fair, the World Trade Organization's primary benefit is providing a platform for multilateral negotiation. When those negotiations work, it is because the World Trade Organization provides a large enough platform that diverse issues can be negotiated together and tradeoffs can be made to meet diverse needs. All that diversity is a challenge, however, so negotiations in the World Trade Organization can often take a decade or more.

Establish Impartial Procedures for Resolving Trade Disputes

Finally the World Trade Organization treaty established the World Court. The World Court provides a forum for challenging countries that are believed to be engaging in unfair trade. When the World Trade Court agrees a country is being unfair, it can provide arbitration and even allow one round of retaliation against the offending country. In practice, the World Trade Court's power is really very limited because it has no real enforcement mechanisms. When the world trade court rules against a powerful trading country, the country often just ignores the ruling.

 NOTES

Concept	Definition	Example
Why Governments Intervene — Economic Arguments		
Unemployment		
Infant Industry Argument		
Industrialization Argument		
Why Governments Intervene — Economic Relations		
Balance of Payment Adjustment		
Comparable Access		
Restrictions as a Bargaining Tool		
Price Control Objectives		
Why Governments Intervene — Non-Economic Arguments		
Maintenance of Essential Industries		
Prevention of Shipments to "Unfriendly" Countries		
Maintenance of Sphere of Influence		
Protecting National Identity		
Tools of Trade Control		
Tariffs		

Nontariff Barriers
  Subsidies
  Aid and Loans
  Customs Valuation
  Quotas
  "Buy Local" Legislation
  Standards and Labels
  Specific Permissions
    Requirements
  Administrative Delays
  Reciprocal Requirements
  Restrictions on Services
    Businesses		

Concept	Definition	Example
Levels of Regional Integration		
Free Trade Area—No Tariffs between Members, Unrestricted Tariffs with Non-members		
Customs Union—No Internal Tariffs, Same External Tariffs		
Common Market—Custom Union Plus Factors of Production Free to Move		
Complete Economic Integration—Common Market Plus Policy and Money		
Effects of Integration		
Increases regional trade but decreases global trade		
Better environmental policies		
Better legal systems?		
Increases conflicts between regions		
World Trade Organization		
144 Member Countries		
World Trade Organization—4 Primary Goals		
Promote Trade by Encouraging Non-discriminatory, Predictable Trade Policies		
Reduce Trade Barriers through Multilateral Negotiations		
Establish impartial Procedures for Resolving Trade Disputes		
Enforcement through arbitration and allowing one round of retaliation		

Foreign Exchange

Most countries use a unique currency within their country, but trades between countries require agreement about how the different currencies will be used. The biggest question is how much country A's currency is worth in country B's currency. Exchange rate determination is a complex issue we take up in Chapter 11 but before that can be addressed, it helps to understand, at a practical level, how multiple currency markets work and how a company deals with them. That is taken up in this chapter.

EXCHANGE RATE TYPES

Not all currencies are traded in the same way. Although the exchange price between currencies is affected by many factors, the most important is how freely the currency can be exchanged. Four exchange rate types describe how the various currencies of the world trade.

Free Floating

Most of the major currencies of the world are free-floating currencies. A free-floating currency is traded in open markets. Participants are allowed to enter the market and negotiate their best price for their currency. The constant negotiation for the best price means currency prices are instantly updating and reflect an accurate market price. Markets for the world's major currencies are substantially larger and more dynamic than even the world's stock markets and commodity markets. Therefore, free-floating currency markets are the closest thing to "perfect markets" you can find.

Floating currencies challenge the governments that issue them because market forces determine the value of the currency against other currencies. As a country faces economic problems or bad government decisions the value of that currency will drop. A currency that drops significantly over time will increase the cost of imports, thereby increasing inflation and reducing the wealth of the country. Too strong a currency makes it difficult for a country to export goods because their goods are overpriced in comparison to countries with lower valued currencies. Even with these problems, allowing a currency to freely float is still the best way to keep a large economy stable because currency movements adjust prices around the world to more accurately reflect world economic conditions.

Pegged

Pegged currencies are currencies where the issuing government sets a fixed price for the currency. The currency is not allowed to vary from that fixed price. Countries with pegged currencies tend to be small countries that may not be able to succeed with a floating currency because 1) large country currencies could move easily to overwhelm them, or 2) a history of their own bad governmental decisions creates doubt about their own ability to support a floating currency. Most countries that peg their currency peg it to the U.S. dollar. For example, Panama pegs the Panamanian dollar to the U.S. dollar. For every two Panamanian dollars the Panamanian government issues they hold one U.S. dollar in their central bank. The currency exchange rate between the Panamanian dollar and the U.S. dollar therefore holds at 2 to 1. Physical gold is another peg standard.

Pegged exchange rates have problems. The biggest one is that many countries that peg their currency do not hold sufficient U.S. dollars, Euros, or gold in their central bank to support their peg rate. Those currencies are sometimes met with excessive supply or demand which can force the government to change the pegged rate. Substantial movements in a pegged rate can be damaging to the country's economy. Pegged countries that do hold enough foreign currency to support their peg rate can still run into the problem of effectively handing monetary control of their country over to the country with which they have pegged their currency. For example, if the United States has high inflation and sets high interest rates, Panama will have to follow the U.S. interest rates to keep its currency stable even if Panama is experiencing recession at the time. Doing that would make Panama's recession worse.

Banded Peg

Some mid-size countries have chosen currency policies that combine free-floating and pegged features. These countries specify a target price for their currency and then try to keep their currency within a defined range or band around that peg. For example, the Chinese won is by far the largest of the banded peg currencies. The Chinese government could define the desired won to dollar exchange rate to be 5 to 1 and the acceptable range for trading to be 1 won (see Figure 10.1). If they did so, China would allow markets to determine won to dollar rates as long as the market rate traded between 4.5 and 5.5 to 1. If the won dropped below 4.5 to 1 (point B in Figure 10.1), the Chinese government would use its existing dollars to buy won. Doing so would increase the supply of dollars in the market and decrease the supply of won. That would increase the value of the dollar to the won and move the exchange rate back toward 5 to 1. If the won climbed above 5.5 to 1 (point A in Figure 10.1) the Chinese government would use its existing supply of won to buy dollars. Doing so would decrease the supply of dollars in the market and increase the supply of won. That would decrease the value of the dollar to the won and move the exchange rate back towards 5 to 1.

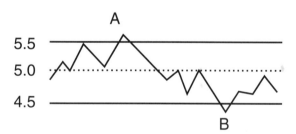

FIGURE 10.1   Model of Banded Peg Currency Movements

The problem with a banded peg is a government may need to regularly intercede in the market to maintain their peg if the market thinks the exchange rate should be substantially different. The government can intercede for a time but if it's trying to support an exchange rate lower than the market considers appropriate (5:1 instead of 5.5:1) eventually the government will run out of foreign currencies to buy their own currency. When that happens, currency exchange rates will change quickly, badly damaging the country's currency and economy.

Non-convertible

A small number of countries have non-convertible currencies. Their governments simply declare it illegal to exchange their currency with any other. Such restrictions make it extremely difficult to trade with the country because all trade must be done as barter. Only the most severely damaged economies will attempt non-convertibility and they usually only keep it for a brief period.

FOREIGN EXCHANGE MARKETS

All but non-convertible currencies require markets to enable international trade through exchanges. Many markets are available for currency exchange. Major markets are listed below.

Types of Currency Markets

There are many kinds of currency markets. In some countries they are little more than people standing on a street corner with pockets full of various currencies. Most countries have substantially more sophisticated markets. Unlike stocks, where there's one major market as the register of the stock and the major trader, currency markets are open to everyone for access to world currencies. Therefore, there are usually many markets trading the same currencies at the same time. These markets stay more or less in sync with each other. Lesser markets can, at times, get substantially out of sync with the major markets and therefore usually charge a substantial risk premium. The two major types of currency markets are described below:

> **Over the Counter (OTC)**—Over the counter currency markets include a wide variety of currency exchanges. The currency exchange windows you see in most tourist destinations are part of the over the counter market, however, most of the over the counter market occurs in large trading banks. Large international banks have created over the counter trading desks that allow client corporations and individual traders to exchange currencies and currency-related financial instruments. Close to a trillion dollars a day are traded in the world's major over the counter markets.

> **Exchange Traded**—A significant portion of currencies traded each day are traded on exchanges. Exchanges establish set contracts for fixed amounts of currencies that are traded much like stocks. There are several large currency exchanges around the world with the largest being in London. The largest in the United States is the Chicago Mercantile Exchange. There are other major exchanges in Tokyo, Frankfurt, and other financial centers. The huge amount of currency exchange completed in the major currencies on the exchanges each day assures incredibly competitive markets with exceptional information.

Trade Time Frames

Both over the counter and exchange traded currencies can be traded in different time frames that range from now to set times into the future. They are described here.

> **Spot**—In some currency transactions people or companies simply want to exchange a currency they have for one they need for immediate use. Those are called spot transaction. On exchanges, spot transactions are expected to be closed within two days of a contract.

> **Forward**—Forward transactions are used to hedge currency risks over time. Any transaction that is not expected to conclude within two days is considered a forward transaction.

> > **Outright Forward Contract—Currency at a Specified Rate on a Specified Date at Least Three Days Out.** Outright forward contracts allow you

to hedge risk by allowing you to buy a currency at a future time for a price agreed upon today. That means a company that normally works in U.S. dollars but knows it will get paid a sum in Euros six months from now can lock in an exchange rate by buying a forward contract. That eliminates the risk that Euros will be worth less in six months than they are now thereby allowing the U.S. company to write budgets on an overseas transaction and determine profits without worrying about future currency exchange rates. By locking in the rate, the U.S. company also foregoes the opportunity to profit from a favorable exchange rate six months from now.

FX Swap—Simultaneous Spot and Forward Transaction. The foreign exchange (FX) swap is a special currency contract that effectively combines a spot and forward contract. Many companies that do business overseas do it on a short term basis. They go into a country, do a project, and leave the country. In such a situation, a company needs to borrow money in the foreign country to purchase components or establish operation. They use the foreign money for a time but then sell the product or service, receive payment in the foreign currency and need to bring it home in their own currency. An FX swap makes the process easier. The company can fix their exchange rate for both entering and leaving the country at once, eliminating currency risk without the cost of two separate transactions.

Currency Swap—Swap of Currency and Interest at a Specified Date. Another common type of forward contract is a currency swap. In a currency swap, two companies exchange currencies at a given time but also exchange interest payments on those currencies. Effectively what a currency swap does is allow companies to trade a loan. The ability to trade loans is important because large companies can usually get better interest rates in their own home country. When a company borrows money in a foreign country, they pay a premium for the risk to the host associated with their being foreign. Large companies have discovered they can borrow money in their home market and then set up a currency swap with other companies in markets they want to enter. Those other companies can use their power in their home market to get the best interest rates and profit by trading those interest rates with companies in markets they wish to enter.

Options

With forward contracts a company promises to exchange a set amount of currency at a specific time. Sometimes, however, a company wants to protect itself from risks if it might need to exchange currency but doesn't know for sure. If it bought a forward contract and didn't need to make the exchange, it would have to sell the contract and lose or gain whatever the difference was in currency prices between when bought and sold. For most companies that is unacceptable. Options give companies an alternative. Options are not a promise to buy or sell a currency, they are a right to buy or sell a currency.

Consider an English construction company that is bidding for a contract to build an office tower in Germany. The construction company needs to make an offer for building the tower in Euros but the company usually works in British pounds. They want to fix the exchange rate they would get on the Euros if they win the contract now so they can price the contract appropriately. They don't want to get stuck with currency losses if they don't win the contract, however. By buying an option they set the price at which they're allowed to buy Euros if they win the contract. If they do not win the contract all they lose is the cost of the option.

Call—Right to Buy at Specified Price by Specified Date. A call option is an option that gives the purchaser the right to buy (call) a specific amount of a currency by a specific day for a set exchange rate. It is used by companies that think they will need a currency in the future but are not sure. A call option is a popular speculative instrument for people who want to trade currencies in a highly leveraged fashion.

Put—Right to Sell at Specified Price by Specified Date. A put option is an option that gives the purchaser the right to sell a specific amount of a currency by a specific day for a set exchange rate. It is used by companies that think they will need to sell a currency in the future but are not sure. A put option is also a popular speculative instrument for people who want to trade currencies in a highly leveraged fashion.

CURRENCY ARBITRAGE

Arbitrage is the ability to make money with limited risk from market anomalies. Currency arbitrage develops in currency exchange markets. Because there are multiple currency exchange markets trading the same currencies at the same time, market anomalies develop more frequently than in most other markets. Currency arbitrage opportunity means that more companies and individuals are involved in trying to discover and profit from currency arbitrage. Arbitrage opportunities are usually difficult to find and short lived when they appear, but many of the world's wealthiest people (George Soros, for example) made their money in currency trading. For those with the intelligence, skill, and diligence seeking currency arbitrage can be a very lucrative experience. Following are two simplified examples of common arbitrage opportunities. In real life, the opportunities are smaller than the examples but understanding the examples can help you understand currency arbitrage and, more importantly, understand why currency markets are the closest thing to perfect markets available.

Geographic Arbitrage

Geographic arbitrage opportunities are anomalies that develop because the same currencies are being traded in more than one market at the same time. For example, the U.S. dollar and Japanese yen are traded simultaneously in both Tokyo and Chicago for several hours each day. It is quite possible for a news announcement or some other information to enter the Chicago market and begin to affect the exchange rate between the dollar and the Yen before the news is translated into Japanese and begins to affect the Tokyo market. For a brief time the exchange rates between the dollar and the yen will be different in the two markets, creating an arbitrage opportunity.

If the yen to dollar rate in Chicago becomes 100 to 1 and the yen to dollar rate in Tokyo stays at 90 to 1 for a while, a trader working at a terminal in Seattle might see the difference and simultaneously buy 100,000 yen at 100,000/100 = $1000 in Chicago and sell 100,000 yen in Tokyo for 100,000/90 = $1,111, letting the trader turn $1000 into $1,111 dollars with no risk. In real life examples, the gaps between Chicago and Tokyo are almost never that big but traders usually are trading with sums much larger than $1000. The cost of the two transactions and the taxes must also be considered. The time windows for these gaps are often seconds or less so trades must be made very quickly and the technology used must be reliably faster than that used by others who might discover the arbitrage.

Cross Rate Arbitrage—Pound, Dollar, Yen

Cross rate arbitrage works similarly to geographic arbitrage but it can occur in just a single market. Because currencies are perfect commodities, at any specific time all currencies within a market are interchangeable at the current price. Each currency's price moves more or less independently, however. Multiple interchangeable currencies all pricing independently against each other allows small errors to develop in pricing. Astute traders can use those errors for arbitrage opportunities. Cross rate arbitrage occurs when the price of three or more currencies go out of alignment with one another. For example, a trader might discover that the British pound to U.S. dollar rate is 0.5 to 1, the U.S. dollar to Japanese yen rate is 120 to 1 and the British pound to Japanese yen rate is 200 to one. That presents an arbitrage opportunity.

An astute trader could see the exchange rates and simultaneously take £500 and trade it for 500*2 = $1000, take $1000 and trade it for 1000*120 = ¥120,000 and take ¥120,000 and trade it for 120,000/200 = £600. This would turn £500 into £600 for a £100 or $200 profit with no risk. As with geographic arbitrage the difference in cross currency rates are almost always much smaller than shown in this example and very short lived, but they do frequently arise and provide large trading profits for those companies and individuals who can set up systems fast enough to catch them.

EUROCURRENCIES

As you begin to become familiar with how currency operates in world markets, you discover that a currency outside your home country behaves slightly differently than that same currency within your own country. Within its home country people think of a currency as if it were a fixed good. To quote a common American phrase "a dollar is a dollar." Outside its home country, however, currencies are seen differently. Because most people holding foreign currencies in another country expect to convert that currency back to their home currency someday the frequent changes in value of the foreign currency make people think about it differently. To reflect those differences, unique names are applied to currencies outside their home country.

Eurodollars—U.S. Dollars Held Outside the United States

By far the most commonly held currency outside of its own country is the U.S. dollar. In Chapter 11 the Bretton Woods Agreement will be described in greater detail, but to understand the names given currencies outside their own countries you need to know now that during World War II Europe was largely destroyed. The governments of Europe were unstable at the end of WWII and they had nowhere near enough money to rebuild. The United States wanted to help so it sent massive amounts of dollars to Europe. For a time the most destroyed European countries used the dollar for most transactions in their country. During this time, the name Eurodollar developed for U.S. dollars circulating in Europe. The name stuck and now any U.S. dollar outside the United States is called a Eurodollar even if it is in Japan or China.

Eurocurrencies—Other Currencies Held Outside Their Home Country

As the Eurodollar name took hold, other currencies strengthened. As the market was familiar with the term Eurodollar, they started calling any other currency that is outside its home country a Eurocurrency. Thus today, even Japanese yen held in China are called Eurocurrency.

Foreign Bonds—Bonds Sold Outside the Country of the Currency in Which They Are Denominated

As we develop a deeper understanding of what a currency is in Chapter 11, you'll see that bonds and currencies are almost identical. In a sense, a currency is a bond with a 0% interest rate. Thus, naming conventions for currencies passed over into bonds. Foreign bonds are so named when a bond is sold outside of its country of origin. For example U.S. government bonds owned by the Japanese, Chinese, Saudi Arabian, and numerous other governments are all considered foreign bonds to the owners.

Eurobonds—Bonds Sold by a Country or Entity Using a Different Currency than Their Home Currency

Sometimes a small country or a country with a weak currency will find it very hard to sell bonds denominated in their own currency. Those countries might choose to issue bonds in another country's currency. Thus, you might see Argentina issuing bonds paid in U.S. dollars. Bonds denominated in another country's currency are called Eurobonds. Eurobonds carry two distinct risks. One risk is that the government issuing the bond will not be able to pay it back with interest. The other risk is that the currency in which the bond is denominated will devalue. Eurobonds are usually issued because markets believe the currency risk is lower with the denominated currency then with the home currency. That should lower the interest rate the country must pay. It should be remembered, however, that although currency risk decreases with a strong currency the default risk increases. A government that issues bonds in a foreign currency can't print money to pay off the debt if their economy goes horribly wrong. That significantly increases the chances they will need to default on the debt.

$US AS A WORLD CURRENCY

There is no official world currency. Each major currency is issued by a government and is dependent on that government for survival. Because of the dollar's history after World War II, however, it has come to function much like a world currency. That provides U.S. businesses with an incredible advantage. The processes that support and create the advantage of the dollar as a world currency are described here.

Eighty-five Percent of All Currency Exchanges Have the $US as Half the Transaction

Trillions of dollars worth of currency exchanges occur every week. Many of the currency exchanges are between small country currencies. It would be truly difficult to have independent markets that accurately priced every currency pair. Trades between Czech Koruna and Thai baht do occur but not often enough to keep an accurate market flowing. Thus, currency markets have settled on a dollar-centric approach. Trades between all but the largest currencies are done in a two step process. If someone wants to trade Czech Koruna for Thai baht they trade Czech Koruna for U.S. dollars and then trade U.S. dollars for Thai baht. That leaves most other countries at a disadvantage because they must pay for two currency transactions for each currency movement while U.S. companies or companies trading with the United States only pay for one transaction.

The Dollar Is Investment Currency in Many Capital Markets

Because the U.S. dollar is the center of most currency transactions, many countries base international capital market transactions on dollars as well. By basing their capital markets on dollars, countries can ensure that anyone from any country can price capital goods in a single step. It is more efficient for the capital markets and purchasers from outside it but again, it hands substantial advantage to American businesses already based in dollars.

The Dollar Is a Reserve Currency Held by Many Central Banks

Countries need reserves of valuable assets they can use to support their own currencies. Because most valuable commodities are priced in dollars anyway, most countries have settled on holding dollars as their main central bank deposits. Since currency works exactly the same as a bond with a 0% interest rate and with central banks holding literally trillions of U.S. dollars, the U.S. government is, in effect, being given an interest free loan for trillions of dollars.

The Dollar Is a Transaction Currency in Many International Commodity Markets

With the dollar's dominance in so many other areas, most world commodity markets price in U.S. dollars. That means commodity goods like oil, coffee, and wheat are priced in dollars wherever they are sold in the world. This, again, gives American companies a great advantage because they do not face currency risks that other countries do when purchasing commodities. This advantage is so great that many of the countries whose economies are largely tied to commodities have tied their currencies to the dollar also. Many South American and Middle Eastern countries that do not necessarily consider the United States a friend still peg their currency to the U.S. dollar because most of their goods are sold in commodity markets and a dollar base stabilizes their economy.

The Dollar Is an Invoice Currency in Many Contracts

Because of the U.S. dollar's dominance in so many other areas, most countries have shifted to invoice pricing in dollars for all international business. That means when a Polish company writes a contract with a company from Malaysia the contract usually specifies price in U.S. dollars. That, yet again, gives U.S. companies an advantage because they do not need to price in risky currency.

The Dollar Is the Major Intervention Currency Employed by Monetary Authorities in Market Operations to Influence Their Own Exchange Rates

When other countries try to manipulate their currency, it is almost always against the U.S. dollar. That provides a natural stability to the U.S. dollar that other countries do not get with their currencies. That, again, provides a substantial benefit to American companies because they do not need to price in nearly as high a level of currency risk.

 **NOTES**

Concept	Definition	Example
Exchange Rate Types		
Free Floating		
Pegged		
Banded Peg		
Non-convertible		
Foreign Exchange Markets		

Types of Markets
   Over the Counter (OTC)
   Exchange Traded		

Trade Time Frames—Spot		

Trade Time Frames—Forward
   Outright Forward Contract—
     Currency at a Specified
     Rate on a Specified Date
     at Least Three Days Out
   FX Swap—Simultaneous
     Spot and Forward
     Transaction
   Currency Swap—Swap of
     Currency and Interest at
     a Specified Date		

Options
   Call—Right to Buy at
     Specified Price by
     Specified Date
   Put—Right to Sell at
     Specified Price by
     Specified Date		

Exchange Rate Tables		
Currency Arbitrage		
Geographic Arbitrage— London, Chicago		
Cross Rate Arbitrage—Pound, Dollar, Yen		

Concept	Definition	Example
Eurocurrencies		
Eurodollars—U.S. Dollars Held Outside the United States		
Eurocurrencies—Other Currencies Held Outside Their Home Country		
Foreign Bonds—Bonds Sold Outside the Country of the Currency in Which They Are Denominated		
Eurobonds—Bonds Sold by a Country or Entity Using a Different Currency than Their Home Currency		
$US as a World Currency		
Eighty-five Percent of All Currency Exchanges Have the $US as Half the Transaction		
The Dollar Is Investment Currency in Many Capital Markets		
The Dollar Is a Reserve Currency Held by Many Central Banks		
The Dollar Is a Transaction Currency in Many International Commodity Markets		
The Dollar Is an Invoice Currency in Many Contracts		
The Dollar Is an Intervention Currency Employed by Monetary Authorities in Market Operations to Influence Their Own Exchange Rates		
Global Equity Markets		
Foreign Stocks		
Euro Equity Offering		
Global Equity Offering		
World Market Capitalization		

Exchange Rate Determination

Chapter 10 showed how to find and use different currency exchange rates. Currency rates are so important to international business that you cannot afford to wait to see what currency exchange rates are like when you need to do a transaction. Businesses need at least rudimentary skills at predicting currency rates in order to hedge risks or lock in rates in advance of a transaction. This chapter does not provide enough detail for you to expect to make accurate currency predictions based on it. It should provide you the foundation to understand how and why currencies move against each other and what factors you'll need to take into account as you try to predict your international business' currency risks.

WHAT'S DIFFERENT ABOUT INTERNATIONAL MONEY?

The money used in international business must be viewed slightly differently than money used within one country. In one country, everyone uses the same currency. In the United States you can drive from Miami to Seattle using the same currency with similar purchasing power all along the way. In the international scene most nations have unique currencies. That means trades made between countries have to be valued in someone's money. Choosing whose money to use is a challenge because the value of different nation's money changes in relation to each other. The changes in the value of the currency can drastically affect the profitability of a deal. If you built a 10% profit margin into a deal but your currency price drops 15% against the other currency, you could end up losing money. That makes understanding currency movements absolutely critical to understanding international business.

MONEY

Most people think about where to get and how to use money. Very few people think about what money itself is. If you're to understand how currencies move against each other, first you need to have a clear understanding of what money is.

What Is Money?

When asked what money is many people stare at you with a blank face. After a bit of thought some will pull out a bill from their pocket and read "This note is legal tender for all debts, public and private." Those who have had a few economics courses might answer "it is a storehouse of value." Very literal people might answer "it is printed paper or a stamped piece of metal." All are elements of the truth but none get to the core of what money is. **It is a storehouse of trust.**

Calling money a storehouse of trust breaks somewhat with traditional definitions seen in economics textbooks. Traditional economic texts describe money as a medium of exchange, a unit of account, and a store of value. That definition works fine when considering one currency. When different currency values change against each other minute by minute or even split second by split second the classical definition becomes problematic. In an international setting, money is a medium of exchange only if people trust they will be able to exchange a currency received at a later date for similarly valued goods. In an international setting, money is only a unit of account if people trust the currency to hold value against other currencies. In an international setting, money is only a store of value if people trust the currency value to remain stable against other currencies over time. In sum, money is nothing more than a storage system of people's trust in the government issuing a currency and the economy supporting that government.

Do You Have To Accept It?

An easy way to understand how dependent money is upon trust is to consider the question "do you have to accept as payment the money someone else offers?" For example, if you are walking in a busy downtown and a stranger walked up and offered to sell you a $100 bill for $20.00 would you accept? Most people would not because they wouldn't trust the $100 bill to be "real" and worth $100. If they did believe it was truly worth $100 they would have no trouble trading $20.00 for it. A similar question of trust and value occurs anytime people exchange different currencies. There's always a question of how much one trusts the government that issued the currency to continue supporting it and whether the economy of that country can support the government's claim of value.

Consider the confederate dollar. During the U.S. Civil War the southern states printed and used a confederate dollar. When the south lost the war the money became worthless other than as a collector's item. The same could happen to any other currency and part of your willingness to accept a currency is your belief that that will not happen. When betting on U.S. currency most people have enough trust in the U.S. government's stability that they don't worry about the currency becoming worthless. When taking Zimbabwe's currency people are nowhere near as sure and many won't accept it.

Who Backs Electronic Money?

Another way to understand the link between money and trust is to consider "electronic" money. Now most large transactions in developed economies don't rely on paper currency. All that is transferred are digital codes intended to convey a value. What would happen if someone destroyed the digital systems where your bank account, brokerage accounts and pretty much all records of your wealth are stored? Would you and the others affected still own anything? If so, who would back your claim?

Understanding that any money is a storage house of trust is critical to understanding international money. Once you understand that, then understanding how currencies move against one another clearly becomes a task of understanding how much trust there is in the government that issued the currency and the economy that supports it.

WHAT LEAD US HERE?

Money as nothing more than a storage system of trust is an unusual concept. The only way the current situation can be understood is to understand how we got here. A very brief history of money therefore follows.

Gold Coin and Gold Bullion Standards

Throughout mankind's history, rare commodities have been used as money. Items such as rare sea shells and other precious metals have been used for money but gold has long been the most common coin. Gold has the advantages that it is rare, it is easy to carry in small quantities, it doesn't rust or deteriorate and until recently it couldn't be made or duplicated. Thus through most of man's history, gold coin was money. Less valuable metals were made into coins and given a fixed relationship to gold. As people looked to expand the amount of money available and the ease with which it could be carried, they turned to printed paper money with a fixed value to gold. That system survived throughout most of the world right up until World War II. After World War II, Europe and the rest of the world had a problem resulting from wild currency fluctuations. Europe and parts of Asia needed to be completely rebuilt but there was not enough gold in the world to pay for all the reconstruction. The United States and Europe, actually 44 Allied countries, came together in 1944 in Bretton Woods, New Hampshire, to solve the problem with the Bretton Woods Agreement.

Bretton Woods System

Following World War II in 1945, the ratified Bretton Woods Agreement established the monetary system that allowed the world to create far more money than would have been possible with a strict tie to gold. It did so through three mechanisms.

U.S. Dollar Fixed to Gold—To make the Bretton Woods Agreement work, the U.S. dollar was tied to gold with a set exchange rate. The U.S. government horded huge stores of gold to back the value of its currency.

Other Nations' Currency Fixed to U.S. Dollar—The second step in the Bretton Woods Agreement was to tie the European currencies to the U.S. dollar with pegged exchange rates. Because European currencies were tied to the dollar and the dollar was tied to gold, then by deduction, the European currencies were tied to gold but with a major advantage. To create more European money for reconstruction all they needed to do was change the pegged rate between the European currency and the dollar. The system worked well, providing money for reconstruction while preventing runaway inflation that might have developed if the European currencies were not pegged to a fixed commodity.

Set up IMF and IBRD (Now World Bank) to Hold Currencies, Maintain Ratios and Make Loans—Finally, the Bretton Woods Agreement established the International Monetary Fund and IBRD (now the World Bank) to help maintain trust between countries and the currencies of the members of the Bretton Woods Agreement. The Bretton Woods Agreement maintained decent currency stability for the United States, Europe, and many other regions of the world for twenty-five years.

Nixon Eliminates U.S. Gold Standard

In 1971 the Nixon administration faced a severe financial problem. The Vietnam War was immensely expensive as were many new social programs created during the sixties and seventies, resulting in inflation. For the first time in the twentieth century, the United States had a trade deficit. The United States didn't have enough gold to support all the costs it faced. Nixon solved the dilemma by taking the country off the gold standard. That move allowed the United States to print more money and solved some problems but, because most of the world's tie to a gold standard was through the U.S. dollar, most of the world was taken off the gold standard with us and the dollar, the most trusted currency, became the reserve currency of the world.

Without a gold standard, the world's currencies were clearly nothing more than printed paper and the trust vested in that paper. But if you think about it, what is the value of gold? Is gold really any different? Is its value any different than the trust people have in it because people have trusted it for so long. In a sense going off the gold standard just proved how much money has always been nothing more than a system of trust.

PURPOSE OF IMF

After the U.S. gold standard ended, it became incredibly clear that money was nothing more than a system of trust. It became even more important that there be institutions to support that trust. The primary institution that supports trust in currencies is the International Monetary Fund (IMF). The way the IMF tries to develop trust in currencies is through promoting five goals.

To Promote Exchange Rate Stability

The major purpose of the IMF is to support exchange rate stability. The IMF, therefore, constantly endeavors to make currency value movements a slow and steady process. To keep movements steady the IMF helps support free exchange of information that affects currencies and uses it for other goals to further create stability.

To Facilitate the Flow of Currencies and the Balanced Growth of International Trade

If people only encounter foreign currency on rare occasions, they are less likely to trust it. If they encounter it regularly in day to day operations it becomes a normal part of their life and they are more likely to trust it. The IMF, therefore, tries to make international currency flows a normal, everyday operation so people learn to trust it. The IMF constantly pushes to help increase international trade because that trade is the mechanism through which most people come in contact with foreign currencies and where they learn to trust those currencies.

To Promote International Monetary Cooperation

When governments and central banks cooperate they are less likely to attack one another's currency. Therefore, the IMF attempts to help governments and central banks work together to keep their currencies stable. The IMF regularly promotes meetings and planning sessions for those most highly involved in maintaining the world's currencies.

To Establish a Multilateral System of Payments

For currencies to remain strong countries need to have an easy system for dealing with other currencies. The IMF, therefore, has built an almost worldwide system through which countries can make payments to one another in designated currencies. By maintaining the system, the IMF provides countries with a confidence that they will be able to use their foreign currency holdings to pay their obligations and thus increases their willingness to hold and trust those foreign currencies.

To Make Resources (SDRs Plus Technical Help) Available to Member Nations Experiencing Balance-of-Payments Difficulties

Perhaps the most useful, but surely the most controversial, goal of the IMF is to help out member countries when they have serious balance of payment difficulties. It is important that countries with serious balance of payment difficulties have some sort of support. Without trust in their currency, its value would severely drop, other countries would stop being willing to accept the weakened currency and its value would drop even further. Without some form of support a currency could easily end up in a downward spiral that would leave it worthless. The IMF tries to prevent that downward spiral by providing special drawing rights (SDRs) which function somewhat like a world currency for banks. The country in trouble can use the SDRs to buy their own currency and support its value.

The reason this process is so controversial is that the IMF does not just give countries special drawing rights. Countries whose currency is in trouble must apply for them. Before giving the SDRs the IMF requires the country in trouble to fix whatever put them in trouble. Most often what put the country in trouble is excessive government spending. The IMF thus forces the government to significantly reduce spending before getting SDRs. Requiring faltering governments to significantly reduce spending is almost never popular. The governments involved almost always spin it as the rich governments of the world using their power to force the poorest countries of the world to do things their way.

Special Drawing Rights

The value of the SDR is based upon the weighted average of a basket of four currencies.

Weights as of Oct 2008

U.S. dollar	41%
Euro	38%
Japanese yen	11%
British pound	10%

CENTRAL BANKS

While the IMF attempts to support trust in currencies around the world, it is usually left to each country's central bank to support its own currency and sometimes provide secondary support for major trading partners' currencies. Next we explain the processes most countries' central banks use to support their currencies.

Set Policies for Currency Manipulation

Most central banks set a specific policy for when they are permitted, and expected, to attempt currency manipulation. They define expected values of their currency in relation to other major currencies of the world and either automatically begin manipulation attempts if those relationships are out of line with pegged currencies or review whether manipulation attempts are appropriate for free-floating currencies.

Buy and Sell Currencies to Try to Affect Value

As a central bank determines its currency is too far out of line with expectations, it may decide to buy or sell its currency to affect its price. If a country feels its currency is overvalued it will use its own currency to buy usually U.S. dollars but sometimes euros, yen, or other major currencies. By buying dollars with their own currency the country increases the supply of their own currency in the market and hopefully decreases its price. When a country feels its currency is undervalued in the market it can use its stores of dollars or other major currencies to buy its own currency, reducing its supply in the market and increasing its price. This can work as long as the country has substantial stores of foreign currencies, but if it ever runs out because of prolonged efforts to support a currency above its natural level the end result is usually disastrous.

Hold Reserves in Gold, SDRs, or Other Currencies

To support their ability to buy their own currency when needed, most central banks hold large reserves of gold, SDRs and, for most countries, U.S. dollars. These reserves serve two purposes. First, they allow the central banks to buy their own currency to support its price. Maybe more importantly, large reserves show currency markets that this government can support its currency if needed. That increases trust in the currency and promotes stability in price. Countries with small or shrinking reserves send the opposite message. They are currencies at risk and encourage some currency market traders to attack.

PURCHASING POWER PARITY

The world's major currencies are traded in open markets with those markets determining appropriate exchange rates. Now that you understand that currencies are a storehouse of trust and the world system for supporting that trust, you are ready to understand the major theories that describe how currency prices are predicted. By far the most frequently used theory for currency rate prediction is purchasing power parity (PPP).

PPP Definition: the number of units of a country's currency required to buy the same amount of goods and services in the domestic market that one unit of income would buy in another country.

According to purchasing power parity, the price of tradable goods should be the same in every country. The logic behind that statement is fairly simple. If a good like a car, a television set, or food is tradable it could be sold in any country. If a seller could get a substantially higher price for a good in another country they would simply sell the product in the country with a higher price. That may not happen with any individual product but over the long term companies would divert more of their goods to the country that has the highest price. That will increase the supply of the product in the country and decrease its price. As the system plays out over time prices for any tradable good should reset so that they end up the same in every country.

If products all adjust to the same price in every country then all one need do is compare the price of products in two countries in their local currencies and you can figure out what the exchange rate for the two countries should be. For example, if a TV set in the United States costs $100 and in the UK costs £50 then the exchange rate between the dollar and pound should be (100/50 = 2 dollars to 1 pound) or pound to dollar of (50/100 = 0.5 pounds to 1 dollar) depending on which direction you want to do the transaction. If the currency rate is anything other than 2 to 1 then the price of the good would be higher in one of the countries and manufacturers of TV sets would send them to that country to make greater profits. The increased supply would lower the price in that country until it equalled that of the other country again.

Purchasing power parity doesn't predict that the price of each individual good will be the same in every country. It does predict that a large basket of tradable goods like those used to define inflation rates in most countries will be the same.

Purchasing power parity, therefore, predicts that as relative prices in countries change then exchange rates must change to reflect the difference. As a predictive tool then, one could look at relative prices in a country and look at the currency exchange rate between the countries. Anytime the exchange rate does not accurately reflect the relative prices between the countries one can predict that over time the exchange rate will move to where relative prices predict it should be.

Because changes in prices is what the inflation rate of each country measures, change in the comparative rates of inflation in two countries, according to purchasing power parity, necessarily causes a change in their relative exchange rates in order to keep prices fairly similar. That means inflation rates should be a good predictor of future currency exchange rates.

INTERNATIONAL FISCHER EFFECT

As purchasing power parity has become broadly accepted, a derivative of it has developed that is easier to measure and, therefore, use. It is called the International Fischer Effect.

To understand the International Fischer Effect first you must know or be reminded of the Fischer Effect you probably learned about if you have taken a finance course. The Fischer Effect says that:

A country's nominal interest rate (r) is determined by the real interest rate (R) and the inflation rate (i) as follows:

$$r = R + i.$$

where

- r: the nominal interest rate, i.e., the named or actual rate of interest earned on an investment
- R: the real interest rate, i.e., the nominal interest rate less inflation
- i: the real inflation rate

Thus, although it may be hard to know a country's inflation rate at any given time, changes in it are reflected in the country's nominal interest rate as long as the real interest rate is steady or known. The nominal interest rate is easy to find.

The International Fischer Effect uses the Fischer Effect to link interest rates and exchange rates.

The International Fischer Effect says according to purchasing power parity real interest rates (R) must be equal all around the world because money is a tradable good. Therefore, given the Fischer Effect if you know the countries nominal interest rate you'll have a good predictor of its inflation rate and thus a good predictor of its future currency exchange rate.

According to the Fischer Effect, the currency of the country with the lower interest rate will have the lower inflation rate. The goods in the country with the lower inflation rate will decrease compared to the prices in the country with the higher inflation rate. That will lead the currency from the country with the lower inflation rate to strengthen in the future against the country with the higher inflation rate.

EFFECTIVENESS

In many long-term studies of both PPP and International Fischer Effect, both are found to be useful long-term predictors of future currency exchange rates. The definition for long-term, however, changes from country to country. In aggregate it appears that PPP and the International Fischer Effect are very useful predictors for three to five years. Unfortunately, PPP and the International Fischer Effect have proven much less useful for shorter time windows. For predicting day to day movements in currency the two theories are almost useless beyond predicting the long-term trend.

Governments Can Have Significant Short-Term Effects

It is also important to remember that governments and their central banks will frequently intercede in currency markets. Anything they do which substantially affects trust in their currency will substantially affect its price. Thus, even though PPP or the International Fischer Effect may predict the long-term direction for a currency, government policy changes or currency market interventions can substantially change the trust and therefore value of a country's currency.

You Must Always Look Out for the Unexpected

When trying to predict currency market directions it is also important to remember you must always be ready for the unexpected. So many factors affect the trust in a government and its currency that no one will ever be able to perfectly predict a currency's future. Thus, even though it is wise to make limited predictions about currency directions so your company can better plan, it is also important to have contingency plans for all the many times your predictions will prove wrong.

SOURCES

Krugman, P. 1984. *The International Role of the Dollar: Theory and Prospect-Exchange Rate Theory and Practice*. Chicago, IL: University Of Chicago Press.

 **NOTES**

Concept	Definition	Example
Money		
What Is Money?		
Do You Have To Accept It?		
Who Backs Electronic Money?		
What's Different about International Money?		
Most nations have unique currencies		
Trades between nations must be valued in someone's money		
Value of different nations' money change in relation to one another		
What Lead Us Here?		
Gold Coin and Gold Bullion Standards		

Bretton Woods System
  U.S. Dollar Fixed to Gold
  Other Nations Currency Fixed
    to U.S. Dollar
  Set up IMF and IBRD
    (Now World Bank) to Hold
    Currencies, Maintain Ratios
    and Make Loans		

Nixon Eliminates U.S. Gold Standard		
Purpose of IMF		
To Promote Exchange Rate Stability		
To Facilitate the International Flow of Currencies and the Balanced Growth of International Trade		
To Promote International Monetary Cooperation		
To Establish a Multilateral System of Payments		

Concept	Definition	Example
To Make Resources (SDRs Plus Technical Help) Available to Member Nations Experiencing Balance-of-Payments Difficulties		

Special Drawing Rights
   The value of the SDR is based upon the weighted average of a basket of four currencies.
   Weights as of Oct 2008
   U.S. dollar   41%
   Euro   38%
   Japanese yen   11%
   British pound 10%		

Central Banks		
Set Policies for Currency Manipulation		
Buy and Sell Currencies to Try and Affect Value		
Hold Reserves in Gold, SDRs, or Other Currencies		
Purchasing Power Parity		
Definition: the number of units of a country's currency required to buy the same amount of goods and services in the domestic market that one unit of income would buy in another country.		
Purchasing power parity predicts that the exchange rate will change if relative prices change.		
A change in the comparative rates of inflation in two countries necessarily causes a change in their relative exchange rates in order to keep prices fairly similar.		
Big Mac Index		

Concept	Definition	Example
International Fischer Effect		

Fisher Effect Theory: links interest rates and inflation
   r: the nominal interest rate, i.e., the actual rate of interest earned on an investment
   R: the real interest rate, i.e., the nominal interest rate less inflation
   A country's nominal interest rate (r) is determined by the real interest rate (R) and the inflation rate (i) as follows:
     $r = R + i.$		

International Fisher Effect Theory (IFE): links interest rates and exchange rates		
The currency of the country with the lower interest rate will strengthen in the future because the interest rate differential is an unbiased predictor of future changes in the spot exchange rate.		
Effectiveness		
Both PPP and International Fischer are useful long-term predictors but neither is very effective in short-term.		
Governments can have significant short-term effects		
You must always look out for the unexpected		
Constructed Approach		

International Business Strategy

Chapters thus far have focused on how international business is different from business done in just one country. Given that background, you should now be ready to understand how the traditional functions of business differ when they are performed on an international scale. This chapter begins an international review of the traditional business functions and starts with the highest level function—business strategy. Most educational programs in business leave strategy as the last course. Because no previous knowledge of business strategy is assumed, this discussion of international business strategy includes more details of strategic theory itself than will the chapters on marketing, finance, and other business functions in which you are likely to have more foundation.

STRATEGY PRIMER

Because it is assumed that you have not yet been exposed to business strategy, it is important to explain the basic concepts of strategy. Strategic theory is built upon three basic understandings. They are described here.

Strategy Is the Tools for Devising How You Gain Monopoly for Real Profits

Economic and business theory clearly demonstrates that the only way to generate real profits in this world is to create and maintain a monopoly position. Without some form of imperfect monopoly a company cannot constrain supply and increase prices beyond that which is required to repay their cost of capital. That means the company cannot generate real profits. Because real profits require a monopoly position, strategy is the field in which companies learn to create and maintain a monopoly position.

You Win by Beating Others

If monopoly is the goal, then the question becomes, How does a company generate a monopoly?. The answer is fairly simple. A company generates a monopoly by beating all the other companies in its industry.

A company that does everything right but is not able to beat even stronger companies within its industry will find it impossible to constrain supply and gain sufficient profits. Any constraints in a weaker company's supply will simply shift market share to the stronger companies in the industry. Thus, a company that does everything right but is not able to beat competitors finds itself unable to generate monopoly and real profits. Take, for example, RC Cola. Most people who have analyzed RC Cola would say it is a very well run company. RC Cola, unfortunately, is in an industry with Coke and Pepsi which are even better run. That has left RC Cola as a perennial also ran with a small market share.

A company that does everything wrong but is faced with even weaker competitors can still generate profits because it has found a way to protect some level of monopoly positioning. Consider, for example, the typical cable TV company. Most are not very well run and provide poor service. They can still be profitable, however, because government mandates local monopolies. The cable companies may not do anything right but they are still profitable because they have defeated competitors by eliminating them from the game.

There Are Usually Only Two or Three Winners in an Industry

If success is defined by beating competitors then it should be reasonably obvious that there's only room for two or three winners in most industries. There are very few defendable monopolies in most industries. The companies that gain and hold those positions are the only companies generating real profits in the industry. That is why most industries, over time, filter down to a small number of companies. It is also one of the reasons why international businesses are coming to dominate the world. It is very hard for a small local competitor to stand up against the technological and cost advantages of a large international business. Thus, international businesses are replacing most small and local companies. It is important to remember that these international businesses are winning because they can offer a better product at a lower price. Local businesses may be disappearing but consumers are gaining through lower cost, better quality products and services.

THREE GENERIC STRATEGIES

As researchers and companies looked to discover how a company could be one of the successes in their industry, they discovered there are limited possibilities. Those possibilities were very well summarized in Michael Porter's three generic strategies. According to Porter there are really only three ways to gain competitive advantage.

Low Cost

The low-cost strategy suggests that one way for companies to beat their competitors is to make sure they have the lowest costs in their industry. To become that lowest costs company is no easy task. All extra costs must be wrung out of research and development, product design, production, distribution, advertising, finance, management, and all other systems of the company.

Discipline and requisite expert knowledge of the industry makes the low-cost position difficult to gain and hold. The low-cost position offers great advantage to the company that holds it, however. The company with a low cost position can charge prices similar to competitors and gain better profit margins. More commonly, they can start strategic price wars with competitors that the competitors cannot win. Because competitors have a higher cost of production the low-cost producer can set a price below competitors' costs and drive them out of business.

Low-cost competitors are usually the biggest companies in an industry. That means they're almost always an international firm. Only by spreading research and production costs across several countries can a company maintain the lowest cost in most industries. It should also be noted that there is exactly one lowest-cost producer in any industry. The company that gets the second lowest cost in its industry without any other advantage is easy prey for the low-cost leader and quickly destroyed. Witness what happened to Kmart when Wal-Mart became the retail industry's clear low-cost leader.

Differentiation

If a company can't win its industry by being the low-cost leader, there's really only one alternative that is available to convince customers to pay more for your product. You have to convince them that your product is somehow better. You end up marketing how your product is different, hence the term differentiation. The trick to a successful differentiation strategy is to get customers to pay a higher premium for your product than it costs you to differentiate your product. For many product categories that proves impossible. People are often unwilling to pay enough for the differentiation than it costs you to produce it. In that case, the industry ends up with commodity goods dominated by the low-cost producer.

There are several ways a company can differentiate their product and thus profitably defend. Those differentiation types are listed here

High Quality—The most commonly discussed type of differentiation is the high quality strategy. Many companies profess to offer a higher quality product and try to convince consumers to pay for the improved quality. In many industries a true high quality strategy can work but in other industries customers are unwilling to pay enough more to cover the costs to produce a truly higher quality product. For example an average toaster may last 20 years. A company that tries to produce and sell a toaster that lasts 30 years will probably find customers unwilling to pay a premium price. Therefore, a true high quality strategy is unlikely to work in toasters.

Perceived High Quality—Because the true high quality strategy is difficult to use in many industries, the perceived high quality strategy has replaced it in many cases. Here a company tries to convince customers that a product is higher quality without adding substantial differences to the product.

For example, few people know what makes a higher quality television. Companies use this to their advantage by offering identical televisions under two or three different brands. When a customer arrives at the store they see what look to be identical televisions but with different brands and prices. Many people assume the more recognizable brand with a higher price is the higher quality product and purchase it, even though the two brands came off the exact same assembly line. Companies use heavy advertising, nicer packaging, higher pricing, and other non-product related tools to support a quality image that has nothing to do with the durability or usability of the product.

The perceived high quality strategy can be more difficult to use in international markets because each culture will have different clues that indicate quality. The international company trying to use a perceived high quality strategy must adapt its perceptual manipulations to each market.

Technical Leadership—In the technical leadership approach to differentiation the company tells prospective purchasers that it offers the most technically advanced product. There are consumers who are happy to pay a significant premium for having the latest technology. These first adopters are the main targets of technical leadership companies. Technical leadership often requires extensive research and development costs and the company is usually selling to a small market so price premiums must be large. International companies using a technical leadership strategy, therefore, usually focus their efforts on large wealthy countries. The United States, Japan, and a few European or other Asian countries are almost always targeted with technical leadership strategies.

Special Features—There are also consumers willing to pay a substantial price premium for special features that are not offered on the lowest cost products. Many of these features are bells and whistles that offer little added value to the product but may be important customizations for special groups. People with disabilities or other special concerns often rely on these special features to make a product usable. In international markets, special features like adaptations to less popular languages or adjustments to other cultural traits can often generate substantial price premiums.

Prestige—Another differentiation strategy is to claim higher prestige for a particular brand. One of the easiest ways is to tie a brand to a country that already carries prestige in the industry. For example, most blue jeans sold around the world use American images to bring with them American prestige. Similarly, most electronics use American or Japanese images to borrow their cache. Wines and cheeses are sold as French, clothes as Italian. Cars are sold as German or Japanese usually, regardless of where the good is produced. National branding adds little to the cost of most goods but can generate significantly higher prices at times. For example, most Americans are shocked to see Levi jeans are regularly sold for $100 a pair or more throughout most of Europe.

Better Service—Finally, many companies attempt to generate higher prices for their goods not by claiming their goods are better but that the services they offer along with the product are better. By offering better warranties, installation, or adaptations, some companies are able to generate significant premium pricing for their products. An excellent example of this came when Hyundai Motors offered a 10 year warranty with what, at the time, was a fairly unpopular car line. Many people bought the cars not because they wanted them but because with a 10 year warranty they wouldn't have to pay for any problems.

What would be considered premium services in America are often required in many overseas markets. Where Americans have become used to a do-it-yourself attitude, many other countries have not. Installation services, sales support, and delivery, even for midsize products like televisions, are often expected in other countries and a good source of differentiation for companies that can do it better.

Niche

According to Porter, the third generic strategy is niche markets. Other theorists have suggested niche markets are just another type of differentiation. Regardless, niche markets are small sub-segments of larger markets that are not well served. In international business niche markets are common. There are small countries, poor countries, or countries with languages that have few native speakers. Each offers a potential niche market. The company that can devise or deliver products for these niche markets can often charge significant premiums.

One must be careful in using the niche strategy. Niche companies survive at the good graces of the large companies in their industry. Most of the time it would be easy for a large industry player to enter and wipe out any niche player. They usually do not because they do not consider the markets large enough to be worth their effort. If the market or premiums in the niche market ever grow attractive enough, however, the large companies usually can and will take over the niche player's market.

TRANSNATIONAL STRATEGIES

Chapter one introduced three international perspectives: the multinational perspective, the multidomestic perspective, and the global perspective. Each perspective functions as an overall approach to strategy as well. A multinational company tries to use what it learned in its home market to conquer the world. A multidomestic company attempts to adjust its strategy to every market. A global company tries to choose the best answers from all around the world and then implement them all around the world. Each approach has substantial limitations. Transnational strategies are a new approach being used to get around the weaknesses of the three dominant perspectives.

Transnational Strategy—Simultaneously Exploits Location Economies, Core Competencies, and Pays Attention to Regional Responsiveness

A company that tries to use a transnational strategy will exploit location economies. It will look to find which countries are best at which tasks and try to divide its work so that each task is done in the country whose culture, political systems, economy, and other factors best support the task. At the same time, the company tries to focus all its activities around the things it does best, its core competencies. A company using a transnational strategy will outsource anything at which it isn't exceptionally good. That requires a great deal of understanding of one's own corporation. Finally, a company using a transnational strategy pays attention to regional responsiveness. It understands the product traits for which customers are willing to accept a world standard and which traits they expect to be adapted to their culture. The company modifies their products to meet each important cultural expectation.

It should seem obvious that exploiting location economies, core competencies, and regional responsiveness all at the same time should create an unbeatable package. So, why doesn't every company do it? The answer is simple. It is extremely hard to pull off. Very few companies can pull together all three of the required skill sets.

Requires Excellent Understanding of Each National/ Local Market

Implementing a transnational strategy requires a company to have an excellent understanding of each national and local market where it operates. It is difficult enough for one person to understand the one country where they grew up. There are so many variations and subcultures even within just one country that it can be hard to predict how a culture will respond to a product, product promotion, production process, or any of the many other tasks a company must implement to make a business run. Trying to understand how hundreds of countries will respond is next to impossible. The information technology and information integration capacity needed can be overwhelming and costly so few companies have even tried and far fewer have succeeded.

Requires Expert Knowledge of What Your Company Can Bring to the Table

Along with understanding the market, a company has to understand what value it can uniquely add to the market. Most developed countries have several competitors in any industry. A company must know what it alone can do that others cannot. It must understand its own expertise so well that it can see how it applies to many different situations. In short, the company must understand itself. Again, that sounds simple enough but in practice is difficult. Few people or companies are willing to admit their own weaknesses and are thus blinded to their true strengths.

Requires Integration of Company Skills with Local Market Needs to Better Fulfill Them Efficiently

Finally, a successful transnational strategy requires a company be able to fully integrate its local market knowledge with its company's skills. Integration is a task that is still only accomplished well by human beings. That means a transnational company must be able to train people who can understand multiple countries and company skill sets. That is not an easy task and one where few companies succeed even though most try. The companies that do succeed are widely recognized as the world's best management training grounds.

INTERNATIONAL STRATEGY PROCESS

Beyond devising the overarching approach to competitiveness in a company, strategy is primarily a process. Because strategy is competitive, doing the same things as your competitors virtually guarantees you cannot win. Thus, strategy can never find the "magic trick" that will always allow a company to win. If such a magic trick were ever found, everyone would use it and no one could gain advantage by it any longer. So strategy focuses on the process a company needs to understand its environment, itself, its competitors, and what it needs to do to win in its market place. The strategic process is usually described using between five and ten steps. The eight step process described here is one commonly used in the international environment.

International Mission—The first step is to form an international mission. A company that doesn't know where it's headed might get somewhere but where they end up randomly is rarely a good place. Companies that consistently succeed do so by setting a direction and moving forward with determination. For a company that wants to go international, knowing why is particularly important. Being international significantly increases the company's chance of long-term survival. But moving from being a one country company to an international one frequently bankrupts companies. If a company is going to move internationally it needs to be very specific in what it is trying to accomplish and why.

International Environmental Assessment—Next, a company must do a careful analysis of business environment. It has to understand the culture, politics, and existing business systems within a country before trying to do business there. It also must understand the competitors who are there as well as predict those competitors' reactions when it tries to move in. Finally, the company must understand that if it sees an opportunity in the country others will too, so it must predict which new competitors will arise once it is there.

Multinational Corporation Organization Analysis—While the company is doing its analysis of its external environment it must also carry out a careful analysis of its own capabilities. A company must go through all of its own functions to get a realistic picture of strengths and weaknesses. Careful analyses of marketing, finance, production operations, human resources, and all the other critical elements within the company must be made. While this is being assessed, higher level managers need to understand that everyone below them is lying to them or shading the reality. It would be rare for a manager to ask his subordinates what they are bad at and have those subordinates answer they are very bad at their own jobs. Managers must, therefore, learn to get independent analyses that are more realistic.

International Objective Formulation—Once a company knows its overall direction, what its environment looks like, and its own strengths and weaknesses, it is time to formulate specific objectives it wants to meet through defining specific goals. For example, the company might say it wants a 40% market share in

Germany and a 30% share in Spain for its primary product line. It would define similar specific goals for each country and product line.

International Alternatives—With specific goals the company is now ready to develop alternatives for how it might meet its goals. There are numerous ways any goal can be met. For example, a company might lower its price to gain market share or increase its advertising budget. Each option will have other effects on the company that it must consider. The more common international options are described later in the "Gaining Opportunities" section.

Choice of International Strategy—After defining strategic alternatives, a company must make choices. Many strategies do not work well together. For example, promoting a product's quality image while lowering its price rarely works. Therefore, a company must carefully consider what steps will help it outmaneuver its competitors and win customer loyalty. It will try to choose a set of alternatives that can be integrated into a winning package.

International Strategy Implementation—Finally, after completing the first six steps, the company is ready to actually begin its core work. The first six steps of this process are all planning, but all the planning in the world won't help a bit if the company does not implement its plans well and adjust its plans where needed. That makes strategy implementation the most difficult and, in many ways, most important step in the strategy process. Details of the strategy implementation process as it is carried out in local subsidiaries is described later in the "International Strategy Implementation" section.

Evaluation and Control—Things never go exactly as expected. Some things go much better than expected others much worse. A company needs to know which of its strategies are working and which aren't. That means a company must build an evaluation system into its strategy process. The evaluation system should measure activities in as close to real time as possible so that the mistakes can be seen early and corrected. Many companies try and skimp on the evaluation process and then pay a high price. As competitors respond to their strategic moves, it changes the company's outcomes. If a company fails to see the spiraling effects early, competitors will outmaneuver them.

GAINING OPPORTUNITIES

As a company searches for strategic alternatives it can use to defeat competitors, it finds that there are literally thousands of options. Unfortunately, most of those options have little to no chance of succeeding in any specific case. A small number of possibilities exist that could work if competitors actions don't eliminate the alternatives' effectiveness. International business offers some alternatives that are difficult for competitors in a single country to use. Therefore, they often offer strategic advantage to international businesses. Some of those effective strategy alternatives are described here.

Host Government Policies

International businesses have a unique opportunity to choose host government policies. With more than 200 countries on the planet a company can usually find a country with policies that specifically help it. For example, some industries have inherently high injury rates. Companies in those industries are better off working in countries with nationalized medicine. Similarly, companies that require many well-educated workers are better off in countries with strong educational systems. An international company that understands its own needs can choose where to operate to fulfill those needs.

Overcoming Operational Obstacles

Many markets offer substantial obstacles to efficient operations. For example, agriculture in a desert country can be very difficult due to a lack of water. Companies that have expertise in overcoming specific obstacles can find profitable opportunities in helping countries overcome their problems. Old or narrow roads, poor electrical infrastructure, limited education in the populace, and other problems prevent most companies from succeeding in those markets. Companies that know how to overcome such problems can quickly develop monopoly positions.

Efficiencies of Standardization

Because of their size, international firms often have an advantage in creating standardization. If a company can create a product standard around its own designs, the company will have a natural advantage. That standard will drive activities of supporting companies and make it hard for new competitors to develop. Witness what Microsoft has done with Windows and Apple has done with the ipod. By making their products standard every other company must respond to them.

Production Shifting

Another strategy available only to international companies is production shifting, where a company moves its factory from country to country always looking for new competitive advantages. For example, consider a t-shirt company. The skills needed to sew a t-shirt are minimal. T-shirt sewing factories are nothing but an empty building and lots of sewing machines. T-shirt companies will constantly seek the lowest cost labor available. When they move into a poor country they will quickly train workers and pay low wages. As other companies move in and increase local wages, the t-shirt companies move on to the next low-priced country. Even more complex companies can carry out similar strategies over longer periods. Many governments offer substantial benefits to new large employers. Companies will move in to gain those benefits, but then move on when the government becomes less generous.

Tax Minimization

A number of strategies can be followed to minimize taxes when a company is operating internationally. Tax minimization itself can become a competitive strategy in industries facing high tax rates. If an industry typically faces 10 to 20% tax rates and a company can eliminate those taxes, the company will have a 10 to 20% cost advantage over competitors. If some companies in an industry try to minimize taxes, all companies must follow suit or find themselves at great strategic disadvantage. More detailed international tax minimalization strategies are presented in the chapter on international financial management.

Financial and Information Arbitrage

Strategies uniquely available to international firms are financial and information arbitrage strategies. As a large international business, some companies have very unique access to country information. For example, Wal-Mart knows what is happening in America's retail sector long before anyone else. Such information can be used to predict currency flows between countries and other future market rates. Some companies trade on such information and make substantial profits. There are a number of large trading companies that make almost no profit from their operations. Their operations, however, are run primarily for the market data they generate and profits instead are all made through trading currencies or other financial instruments.

Leveraged Resources

Large international companies can often increase profits by leveraging combined resources. For example, Pepsi could have trouble gaining grocery store display space in countries where Coke is dominant. But because Pepsi owns Frito-Lays which has a near global monopoly on potato chips, Pepsi can use its strength in potato chips to pressure grocers for more space for its soda. Many large international companies have several related operating divisions they can use to leverage advantage for their other operating divisions making it difficult for small local companies to compete.

Unique Markets

Unique markets offer two types of strategic advantage. First, a company can develop expertise in a unique market that is difficult for other companies to match. For example, a company could devise systems for delivering fresh fruit in markets with poor roads. If the company is uniquely able to get fresh fruit to such markets undamaged then it is likely to have the market to itself.

Second, unique markets can present strategic opportunities by allowing a company to learn things it otherwise might not. For example, the market for consumer electronics in Tokyo is very unique. People in Tokyo will often pay a high premium for having the most unique gadgets. Companies can learn what does and does not work in the Tokyo market and then sell those ideas around the world.

Political Control

One final strategy available uniquely to large international firms is the opportunity for political control. Many large international firms are bigger and wealthier than some of the countries where they operate. That wealth can often buy a large degree of political control over the country and allow the company to dictate what laws they operate under. Companies can use that political control much to the country's benefit. Some companies have helped countries become more humanitarian and have eliminated trade barriers that were hurting them. Other companies have used political control far more negatively. There is a fine line companies must closely watch.

INTERNATIONAL STRATEGY IMPLEMENTATION

For the overall strategy to work numerous steps are taken. Strategic work is often done at the corporate level far away from individual country offices. The following steps need to be observed if there's going to be any chance the strategy will be implemented as desired.

Consider Procedural Justice

Procedural justice suggests that regardless of how good a strategy is, if the people who have to implement it don't feel the process for developing the strategy was fair, they won't follow it. Because strategy is usually developed in corporate offices, international offices are often left out of the process. Even if the corporate strategy is brilliant it probably still won't work because the people in the international offices who have to implement it are angry that they were not consulted and so they refuse to follow it or may even sabotage it. Particularly when there are large cultural differences between international management and local workers, a company must be very careful to listen to what local workers have to say. If they do not, local workers will decide that the international managers don't understand the local market and they won't feel bound to follow the strategies.

Localize International Strategy to Take into Account Local Market Idiosyncrasies

During the strategy implementation phase, an international manager's major task is to make sure the strategy process takes into account the local market differences the manager faces. Because the overall corporate strategy can't possibly address every country, it is up to the local managers to take the overall strategy and adjust it to fit that local market. The balance is always tricky as a manager tries to keep his or her unit consistent with the overall strategy but also adapt the overall strategy to local market conditions.

Maximize the Subsidiary's Contribution to Its Parent Corporation

Country managers also need to pay careful attention to make sure their subsidiary is maximizing its contribution to its parent corporation. Local workers will naturally want to optimize a subsidiary's performance. What is best for the subsidiary is often not best for the parent corporation, however. The local manager must understand what the parent corporation's goal is for the subsidiary and make sure to meet it even if that damages the subsidiary.

Plan and Manage Subsidiary in a Manner Consistent with Company Mission

In implementing a company strategy it is also important for a subsidiary manager to make sure to manage in a manner consistent with the company's mission. Local culture sometimes will conflict with the company mission. A country manager needs to take local concerns to heart and understand them. At times, it may be necessary to overrule local needs to meet the company mission. The hard part for a country manager is to figure out what are important company values and what are important country values and how to make the two work together.

Promote Trust and Confidence in Local Management

Another important task of the country manager is getting corporate managers to trust local management decisions. Because local managers are usually from a different culture than corporate managers, corporate managers often won't understand local manager's decisions. As local managers are constantly overruled, they stop trusting corporate managers' understanding of their market. The combination frequently leads to a stalemate in which nothing gets done. To prevent this, a country manager must help corporate managers understand and trust their local management. Frequent travel and other direct interaction is often necessary to make this work. Trust is most efficiently and effectively built through personal contact.

Align Plans, Goals, and Activities within the Subsidiary

Finally, the country manager's job is to align two or more disparate cultures. To get a strategy implemented well, the country manager must help corporate managers understand local needs and must help local workers understand corporate needs. If they can succeed, local decisions will be made consistent with corporate goals. If they fail, local decisions will not align with corporate goals and other activities within the corporation will cancel whatever efforts are made. Ultimately, a well aligned strategy will keep all pieces of a company working together. Where a company is not working together, bureaucracy, inaction, sabotage, and, at times, vandalism will damage corporate efficiency and effectiveness.

SOURCE

Porter, Michael E. 1985. *Competitive Advantage*. New York: The Free Press.

NOTES

Concept	Definition	Example
Strategy Primer		
Strategy Is the Tools for Devising How You Gain Monopoly for Real Profits		
You Win by Beating Others		
There Are Usually Only Two or Three Winners in an Industry		
Three Generic Strategies		
Low Cost		

Differentiation
  High Quality
  Perceived High Quality
  Technical Leadership
  Special Features
  Better Service		

Niche		
Four International Perspectives		
International—Home Country Oriented		
Multidomestic—Host Country Oriented		
Global—World Domination Oriented		
Transnational—Weave Together the Best of All Countries		
Transnational Strategies		
Transnational Strategy—Simultaneously Exploits Location Economies, Core Competencies, and Pays Attention to Regional Responsiveness		
Requires Excellent Understanding of Each National/Local Market		
Requires Expert Knowledge of What Your Company Can Bring to the Table		

Concept	Definition	Example
Requires Integration of Company Skills with Local Market Needs to Better Fulfill Them Efficiently		
International Strategy Process 1. International Mission 2. International Environmental Assessment 3. MNC Organization Analysis 4. International Objective Formulation 5. International Alternatives 6. Choice of International Strategy 7. International Strategy Implementation 8. Evaluation and Control		
International Environmental Analysis		
Considers all the things covered in this class including: Culture Markets Laws Finance Technology Human Resources Operations		
Plus Analysis of Major Competitors Suppliers Customers Potential New Market Entries		
Develop Threats and Opportunities Profile		

Concept	Definition	Example
MNC Internal Analysis		

Determine Strengths and Weaknesses of Firm in Relation to Global Competitors
  Market Understanding
  Marketing Capabilities
  Production Skills in
    Multinational Setting
  International Finance Skills
  International HR Capabilities
  International Law Capacity
  International Logistics
  Technology Adaptability
  International Service		

Gaining Opportunities		
Host Government Policies		
Overcoming Operational Obstacles		
Efficiencies of Standardization		
Production Shifting		
Tax Minimization		
Financial and Information Arbitrage		
Leveraged Resources		
Unique Markets		
Political Control		
International Strategy Implementation		
Must Consider Procedural Justice		
Localize International Strategy to Take into Account Local Market Idiosyncrasies		
Maximize the Subsidiary's Contribution to Its Parent Corporation		

Concept	Definition	Example
Plan and Manage Subsidiary in a Manner Consistent with Company Mission		
Promote Trust and Confidence in Local Management		
Align Plans, Goals, and Activities within the Subsidiary		

International Organizational Structure

Chapter 12 described how organizations build their overall strategies. One important step in making a strategy work is to build a structure that supports it. Organizational structure defines who reports to whom within the organization and is represented by a diagram showing the relationships. It also defines the natural flow of information within an organization. Many people make the mistake of thinking that organizational structure is unimportant. They make the mistake because they forget that corporations are political systems and the politics matter.

The organizational structure of a company formally defines the power relationships within it. Failure to understand the organizational structure leaves one unable to work the levers of power within the organization. Many employees find themselves frustrated because they are working for companies whose organizational structure will stymie their careers. Different organizational structures favor different skill sets. Someone who hopes to move to the top of their organization will need the appropriate skills for that organizational structure.

FACTORS THAT INFLUENCE STRUCTURE

Companies have surprisingly little freedom to choose an organizational structure because there are factors that affect what organizational structure will work best for a particular firm. A company that tries to operate under an organizational structure not optimized to those factors will have a difficult time succeeding. There are five primary factors that influence organizational structure.

Number of Lines of Business

One factor that influences organizational structure is the number of lines of business within the company. Some companies run many different product divisions. For example, GE makes a huge variety of products such as appliances, jet engines, light bulbs, wind turbine blades, and electrical power generation equipment and it has a major finance division. With such a wide variety of products no one person could be expected to understand all of GE's markets. A manager who understands the jet engines market is going to be of little use in the light bulb market. Therefore, companies who have highly diverse products tend to manage their products in multiple divisions or product lines. Each division operates largely as an independent company. They often share financial resources, top management, and a Board of Directors, but little else.

Other companies maintain a tighter focus on what products they offer. Those companies may offer several closely-related products. Management, marketing, and product knowledge gained in one of the products can help the company in its other markets. Individual managers can understand most, if not all, of the products the company offers. The focus of a single division company allows a simpler organizational structure.

Product Diversity

Even in companies that have only a single product line, products within the line can be similar or diverse. For example, GE Appliances makes dishwashers, refrigerators, ovens, and clothing washers and dryers. Although all the products are similar enough to be in a single product line, they are different enough from each other that they are probably not built in the same factories or designed by the same engineers. A company like Dell, however, may make many different lines of computers but all rely on very similar components and could be handled with a single set of engineers and factories. More product diversity requires more complexity in the company's organizational structure.

Customer Differences in Tastes

Another factor that affects company structure is how differences in customers' tastes in a product determine production decisions. With a product like the iPod there is no long history of similar devices so that a nearly identical iPod can be sold to customers all around the world. That simplicity allows the company to focus on efficiency. Some products, like soup, have been in almost all the countries of the world for centuries. Each country, therefore, has developed unique expectations for soup. If a company like Campbell's wants to sell soup all around the world it has to modify the soups to each country's unique expectations for flavor. Tomato soup sold in Norway may be very creamy and bland while tomato soup sold in Mexico would be much more watery and spicy. When customer differences in taste are high, a company needs a structure that adapts to regional differences.

Geographic Breadth

A company's geographic breadth is a measure of the number of countries of the world in which a company is trying to do business. A company doing business in only two or three countries has a fairly narrow breadth and will tend to focus on other issues in making its structural decisions. A company operating in 100 or more countries has a very wide geographic breadth and will have to focus more on geographic issues if there is customer difference in taste for its products.

Specialized Skills Involved in the Production of Products

The final factor that has a substantial affect on organizational structure is the specialization of skills needed to create a product. Some companies, like McDonald's, have simple products. Employees can be trained to make hamburgers or french fries in a short time. Because the skills involved in the product are easy to learn, McDonalds doesn't need to organize around them. Other companies, like iRobot, require very specialized skills in the production of their goods. Very few people know how to produce a robot. Marketing and designing robots are equally complex skills. Because the skills for such a company are so complex, that company tends to organize around the skill sets so employees have a better opportunity to acquire further skills.

INTERNATIONAL ORGANIZATIONAL STRUCTURES

The five factors that influence organizational structure work together to dictate the type of structure a company can implement. The number of lines of business and product diversity work together to dictate whether a company can operate as a single entity or if it needs to be broken into several more or less independent operating divisions. Customer differences in taste and geographic breadth define how much a company must focus its structure on regional differences. The specialized skills involved in producing a product define how much a company must focus its structure on developing employees' functional skills. Combined, these three sets of factors create the six or seven organizational structures that are most common in international business.

Virtually all the structures have a corporate headquarters. Corporate headquarters is the ultimate decision-making body. Corporate headquarters is usually headed by someone with a title of Chief Executive Officer (CEO) or something similar. There is a Board of Directors who oversees the CEO's work but does not directly manage it. Depending on the size of the corporation, the CEO will have a support staff of anywhere from a couple to a couple hundred employees.

Reporting upward to the CEO are the top level managers of an organization. Who sits in these top level seats is critical to how a corporation operates. These top level managers are the ones who make the most important decisions for the corporation. Those in these positions are the people competing to become the next CEO.

The global functional model, geographical model, and single matrix model are simplified models that work well for companies that are focused enough to operate under a single product division. The multi-business global product division model, multi-business geographical model, and the multi-business matrix model are models that add the complexity of a multi-division structure to the three single product division models. Hybrid models are complex organizational models that mix and match components from all six models to meet a company's unique needs. All seven models are defined in greater detail below.

GLOBAL FUNCTIONAL MODEL

The global functional model is the simplest model for multinational firms.

For corporations using the global functional model, the people in the top management positions are functional experts. They're usually people who have spent their entire careers in one of the functional areas of the corporation. Those functional areas tend to match the majors one can earn in college. There are heads of marketing, finance (with accounting reporting to them), information systems, research and development, and operations management. In a global functional model, all the people who report to the functional level managers are people with the same functional expertise.

The global functional model works especially well for companies where there are few customer differences in taste but there are highly specialized skills used in creating the product. With a global functional model, new employees can be hired into the marketing function and placed in a small country subsidiary. These people can learn marketing in the subsidiary and, as they gain experience, move up to a larger subsidiary. Because everyone they work for and with also worked for the marketing department, it is easy for skills to transfer and employees to understand how they move up the corporate ladder.

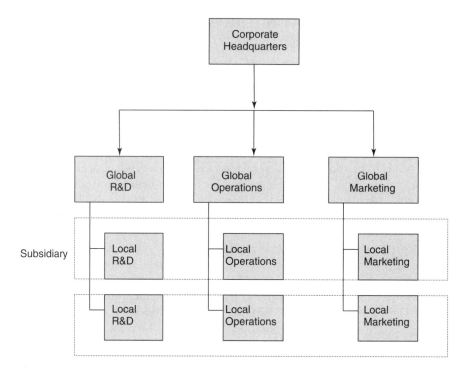

FIGURE 13.1   Global Functional Model

The global functional model is an excellent model for those who are technically oriented. If one person understands the rules of a profession better than others that person tends to be able to move up in a global functional model quickly.

The lines for the subsidiaries in Figure 13.1 show that even companies using a global functional model usually need someone to oversee country specifics. The country subsidiaries dealing with issues like legal compliance in each country have limited power. Because the local marketing, operations, and R&D employees report to functional managers rather than the subsidiary managers, the employees' loyalty lies with their functional groups.

Advantages of the Global Functional Model Are:

Efficiencies—Because functional sets, such as marketing, are coordinated globally, each functional group is efficient. A good marketing idea that develops in a Japanese subsidiary will quickly move to the global marketing manager who can spread it to all the other marketing subsidiaries. Costs are kept low because there is little need to duplicate skill sets within the company.

Economies of Scale—The global functional model permits much larger economies of scale. Research and development and marketing can be developed in one place and quickly spread to all the subsidiaries. That allows for a more centralized control system and far greater economies of scale.

Rapid Transfer of Skills—The global functional model also permits faster transfer of skills between workers. Because everyone who does marketing for the corporation works together in the marketing department, it is easier for employees to see what others are doing and learn from it. The clear career ladder of a functional organization makes it obvious to employees what they need to learn if they want to move up.

Disadvantages of the Global Functional Model Are:

Inflexibility—A major disadvantage of the global functional model is its inflexibility. Because each management chain is headed by a functional manager and those functional managers are all competing to be the next CEO, there's some motivation for the functional managers to resist helping each other. That will often mean a good idea that develops in the Japanese marketing department will never find its way to the Japanese research and development department because the idea has to travel up to the marketing head, across to the research and development head and then back down to the Japanese research and development worker. Most ideas never survive the journey and so changes that are needed across departments never happen.

Local Dysfunctions—The lack of flexibility in department communications often leads to local dysfunctions. The Japanese marketing worker becomes frustrated that her ideas are never heard over in R&D. Research and development becomes frustrated that they never get help from marketing. Each of the functional areas becomes frustrated with the others, so local offices that combine the workers become quite dysfunctional. People not only won't work with each other, they often won't talk to each other and, at times, will sabotage one another.

Market Rejection—Another big problem is that the functional departments become very consistent. That consistency prevents products from being significantly modified for local markets. Local market preferences tend to get ignored and if those market preferences are important, the product ends up being rejected in the local market.

Bureaucracy—Although it is worse in the matrix models to be described later, bureaucracy can be quite bad in global functional models as well. Many of the functional workers work at subsidiary locations far from their functional managers, even though their functional managers are their bosses. That leaves the functional workers with the challenge of how to respond to subsidiary managers who have little control over their careers. As the stresses from the subsidiary managers become great, many workers fall to the bureaucratic solution. When functional employees have their functional manager telling them to do one thing and a subsidiary manager telling them to do another, they will often try to protect themselves with a form.

The employees will get their functional manager to describe their specific duties and the will then create a checklist. They will get a subsidiary manager to agree that, as long as they are completing the checklist, they are doing their job well. From then on the employees will focus on completing their checklist. When an employee eventually moves on, the person who replaces them is told the job is to complete the checklist. When the functional and subsidiary managers eventually move on, new managers replace them and the employees are stuck with the same problem. They often create new checklists. Eventually, the corporation is hiring five people to fill out checklists that no one is reading any longer, but no one knows that because the functional units aren't communicating with each other.

Discourages Initiative—Because of the frustrations of local dysfunction and bureaucracy, many employees in a global functional model decide their ideas are not really wanted. That discourages anyone from taking the initiative in trying to help the corporation move in new directions. Employees are "in the box" and find themselves thinking "not my job" when they could be helping the corporation.

GEOGRAPHICAL MODEL

The geographical model, like all the other models, has a corporate headquarters on top. Also, like the global functional model, the geographical model is used in companies with one operating division and in companies that would prefer a fairly simple organizational structure. The big difference between the global functional model and the geographical model is who makes up the first level of managers beneath corporate headquarters. In the geographical model, the highest level of managers are regional specialists rather than functional specialists. Reporting to a regional specialist is a country manager who is a regional specialist for a single country.

Regional specialists are people who have learned to adapt well to differing cultures and are responsible for making their operating groups adapt to their given region. Titles for this level of manager are often something like Vice President for Europe, Asia, or North America.

The geographical model works especially well for companies in which customers have substantial demands for customization to their region. For example, companies that sell food products quickly discover that some regions of the world like their food very spicy, other parts more creamy, and still others very bland. A food company needs to understand those regional differences and adapt their products to them. These sorts of companies are much better off having top level managers who understand the challenges of adapting to local tastes.

Because the highest level of management under the CEO is made up of people who are culturally skilled, lower level employees who are also culturally skilled are mentored and trained and, therefore, do better in the company. Technically skilled people are still needed in the company but their opportunities for advancement are more limited. Because functional skill groups are small, one country units, there is far less opportunity for functionally skilled people to learn from those around them.

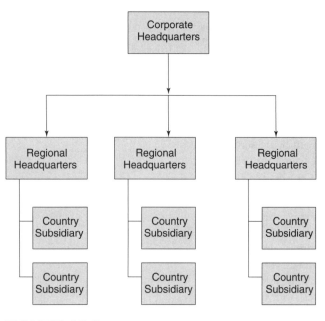

FIGURE 13.2 Geographical Model

Advantages of the Geographical Model Are:

Flexibility—Because the geographical model is built around country units it is extremely flexible. Each country manager has the freedom to adapt the company's products, promotions, human resources policies, or whatever else needs to change to make the company successful in that country.

Local Needs—The flexibility of the geographical model means country level managers can target local needs. If customers within the geographic location need smaller sizes, different flavors, or even just different supporting services, country level managers are expected to know about those needs and adapt to them. That means products are a much better match to local consumers' desires.

Quickly Adapts to Markets—The country level structure of the geographical model leaves people who work in a country able to make decisions about it. With marketing, product development, finance, and human resources all reporting to a country manager, the country manager has all the internal expertise needed to make changes. That means adaptations occur quickly within the geographical model.

Disadvantages of the Geographical Model Are:

Diseconomies of Scale—For all the advantages of the geographical model in adaptability, there are matching disadvantages in efficiency. The geographical model effectively duplicates its company in each country or region in which it operates. That is very expensive. It also lacks coordination between functional skill sets. That means that learning which might occur in the marketing department of the Asia unit may never get to the European unit. The efficiencies available in centralized global functions are not available to a company operating on the geographical model. That makes products coming out of the geographically-oriented company more expensive.

Duplication—The greatest diseconomy of scale is the massive duplication required to run the geographical model. Every single country or region in the geographical model has its own marketing staff, product development staff, research staff, HR staff, etc. Because of competition among country managers and regional managers, information is often not shared between country units. That means every invention made or process improvement discovered has to be remade or rediscovered in every country. That tends to make the geographical model very inefficient.

Poor at Serving Global Customers—Another major failing of the geographical model is its inability to serve global customers well. Global companies like IBM will often insist on global purchasing. IBM wants to go to one company in one place in order to buy a component for its operations all around the world. Because the geographically-oriented company has different product designs and prices in each country, it can't easily deliver one consistent product at a consistent price to a customer all around the world. That will lose it potential global customers.

SINGLE MATRIX MODEL

The efficiency of the global functional model makes it the one used most by single division companies whose employees need advanced technical skills. The adaptability of the geographical model makes it the one used most by companies whose customers have strong regional preferences. There are, however, some industries with both strong regional customer preferences and highly technical skills needed within the company. Companies in such industries tend to choose the single matrix model of organizational structure. A matrix is essentially a grid with boxes cut by vertical and horizontal lines. If you guessed that this creates complexity, you are right.

In the single matrix model, local managers each have two managers, one functional and one geographic (see Figure 13.3). The matrixed managers are equally responsible to each of their managers. In this model the functional managers and the subsidiary managers are equal powers, each with as much say over employees and equal chances of being promoted to CEO. As you may guess, it can be difficult for the matrixed managers to have

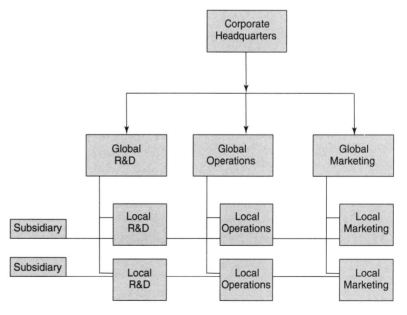

FIGURE 13.3 Single Matrix Model

two managers with equal say over what they're supposed to do when their two managers disagree. It is the matrixed manager who is left to figure out what to do and who pays the price when something goes wrong.

The political challenges inherent in the matrix model means those people with the greatest political skills tend to rise to the top. The best politicians, whether they are in the functional chain or regional chain, will be able to survive and thrive in a matrix.

Advantages of the Single Matrix Model Are:

Global Efficiencies—Because matrixed managers report to global functional managers, the matrixed model provides many of the global functional model's efficiencies. All the local marketing or operations managers are connected to each other through their functional managers so decisions and learning can occur globally.

Local Responsiveness—Because matrixed managers are also reporting to regional subsidiary managers, the matrixed managers are able, and required, to pay better attention to local needs. That allows greater customizations and adaptiveness on the local level.

Disadvantages of the Single Matrix Model Are:

Power Struggles—Providing both global efficiency and local responsiveness would appear to make the single matrix an ideal model. It has many problems, however, the biggest being the power struggles that occur within. The matrixed managers who have two managers themselves are constantly faced with opposing goals. Their functional bosses want efficiency; their regional bosses want local responsiveness. Occasionally, the two goals work together. Far more often, they work in opposition to one another. That leaves the matrixed managers to decide which of their bosses they are going to try to please. The power struggles that develop often leave matrixed managers spending 80% or even 90% of their time playing office politics. The people who report to the matrixed managers are often drawn into the conflicts and much of their time is wasted in office politics as well.

Role Ambiguity—One of the consequences of the constant power struggles is that matrixed managers and their employees are often left not really knowing what they're supposed to do. They might choose the safest route and do nothing. Those who do act won't feel confident in their actions and take them half heartedly. Little will get done well. Workers wait to try to figure out what they are supposed to do.

Dilution of Responsibility—There's also a severe dilution of responsibility in a matrixed organization. When something goes wrong the functional managers can say they gave good instructions, so it was the subsidiary manager's fault. The subsidiary manager can say the exact opposite. The matrixed managers can say they tried to do their best with conflicting instructions. Each ends up pointing fingers at each other saying it was someone else's fault and it is difficult to hold anyone responsible. That means the sources of problems are rarely detected or corrected.

Cost Inefficiencies—With so many resources sitting idle waiting for someone to decide what to do, a matrixed organization can become very inefficient. With so many people spending their time politicking, often little else is accomplished.

Cost of Compromise—The final major disadvantage is the cost of compromise. When people are stuck with competing goals they will often try to compromise between them. If the functional manager says to keep the cost of a product below $100 to meet the global market and the subsidiary manager says it needs to be at least $150 to include all the local modifications, the matrixed manager will often decide to make the product $125. The product, at $125, won't include enough local customizations to be successful and it won't be a low enough price for the global market. It will be a complete failure. That is what often happens with compromise. The solution in between solves neither problem and produces a market failure.

Each of the three main models for single product division companies have substantial advantages and disadvantages. The global functional model is efficient but doesn't adapt well to local differences. The geographic model adapts to local differences well but is inefficient. The matrix model is potentially efficient and adapts to local differences but comes with a very high political cost and a high risk of failure. Companies, therefore, choose among them based primarily on what types of products they sell and which model works best for their product type.

MULTI-BUSINESS GLOBAL PRODUCT DIVISION

The multi-business models use one of the three single division models and add the complexity of a multi-division company framework. The added size of a multi-division company can help make it more profitable and more powerful in its industry. But it comes at a high cost in management structure complexity.

The multi-business global product division model takes the global functional model and adds multiple product divisions. Technology-oriented companies with highly specialized skills required but few customer requirements for localization are likely to use this model. Being based on the global functional model, the multi product version has similar strengths and weaknesses. Weaknesses added by the multiple product divisions include even more bureaucracy and difficulty communicating ideas across functional groups. Added benefits include synergies across related product lines and the cross subsidization available from multiple products.

Advantages of the Multi-Business Global Product Division Model Are:

Flexibility—Having multiple product divisions can add flexibility to a corporation. By selling several related products, a company can learn more about customer needs. Separate product divisions can converge or share components to make the unique product for a specialized customer.

Local Needs—When done right, the added flexibility of the multi-business global product model can help a functionally-oriented company meet local needs. Various product divisions can combine their offerings in different ways to meet local standards. The functional approaches will still be less responsive than regionally-oriented models but multiple divisions usually do better than single division, functionally-oriented companies.

Global Coordination—Multi-division companies also have better resources available for global coordination. It can use a separate division to handle global coordination and global customers. That division will usually do a better job than a unit within a single division company.

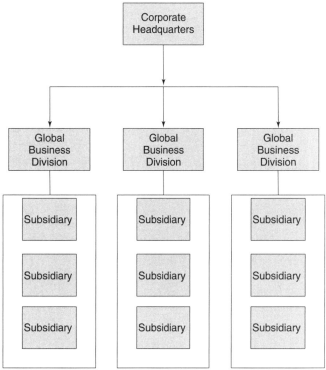

FIGURE 13.4 Multi-Business Global Product Division Model

Disadvantages of the Multi-Business Global Product Division Model Are:

Duplication of Effort—The multi-division approach means each functional group is repeated in each division. Having multiple marketing, finance, HR, and other groups creates the same duplication of effort found in geographically-oriented companies. Coordinating efforts across product divisions is often even more difficult than coordinating efforts across regions in a regionally-oriented company. That often means company divisions operate more or less as independent companies with most of the potential cost savings of an integrated company lost.

Lack of Local Responsiveness—As noted earlier multi-business global product division can better provide for local needs when the company's product divisions are integrated well. When they are not integrated well multiple product divisions make bureaucracy much worse and the company can become completely blind to local needs.

MULTI-BUSINESS GEOGRAPHICAL MODEL

The multi-business geographical model is the multi-division extension of the single product geographical model. Many of the issues and advantages for the single and multi-divisions geographical models are the same. Multiple divisions do add some unique twists, however.

Advantages of the Multi-Business Geographical Model Are:

Flexibility—The geographic approach in a multi-divisions company adds substantial flexibility to the company's operations. Each regional headquarters has multiple product divisions it can adjust to the local needs. Integration at the regional level allows country managers to choose which products will work best in their regions and to shift resources to them.

Adapts to Local Concerns—The added flexibility of multiple product divisions can make a regionally-oriented company even more responsive to local concerns. A single product line regional company manager has to find a way to make that one product line work in a country even if its political or cultural preferences do not favor it. With the multi-division company, regional managers can pick and choose which product lines will work best in their country and then adapt those product lines to local needs. The combination makes for highly customized goods.

Country Level Optimization—The added size and flexibility in product choice of a multi-division company allows a regionally-oriented company to optimize its performance within each country it operates. Companies that perform well in this model are often mistaken for local companies. For example, people in almost every country think Danone and Nestle are based in their country even though they are French and Swiss companies respectively.

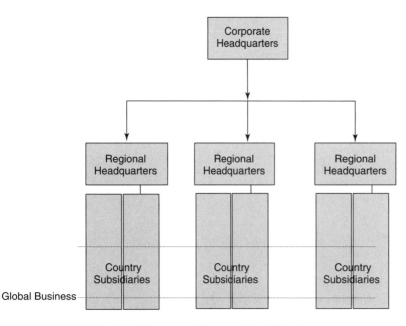

FIGURE 13.5 Multi-Business Geographical Model

Disadvantages of the Multi-Business Geographical Model Are:

Suboptimization of Global Businesses—Because the multi-business geographical model is optimized at the country level, by definition it is suboptimized at the global level. Adjusting to each country so well means global efficiencies are gone. The cost savings available from global scale can't be reached in a multi-business geographical model.

Delays in Product Introductions—Given the management complexity of trying to integrate ideas across multiple regions and multiple product divisions, most companies have great difficulty in introducing new products. Each regional manager wants to have input and must consult with numerous country and division managers. The delays inherent in the process tend to make geographically-oriented companies much slower to introduce new products than functionally-oriented companies.

Inefficient in Industries with Global Opportunities—Given the regional control, multi-division, geographically-oriented companies are even worse at handling global opportunities than their single division counterparts.

MULTI-BUSINESS MATRIX MODEL

Adding multi-division complexity to a matrixed company makes a model that is so complex that very few companies ever attempt it. In a multi-business matrix model, matrixed managers can have three managers instead of the two in a single division matrix. The third manager is a division manager. Think of a Rubik's Cube.

Matrixed managers, therefore, have to satisfy a division manager, a functional manager, and a regional manager. To say the political challenges are great is an incredible understatement. Three's a crowd. Few people are able to survive the pressures of the matrixed positions for very long. Companies that use this model, therefore, often have an up or out policy. Managers in matrixed positions are expected to get promoted fairly quickly (usually within a couple of years) or they're given opportunity's to seek employment elsewhere. It is survival of the politically astute individuals with a high tolerance for chaos and outside stressors (not unlike outside jobs combined with a personal life and college!).

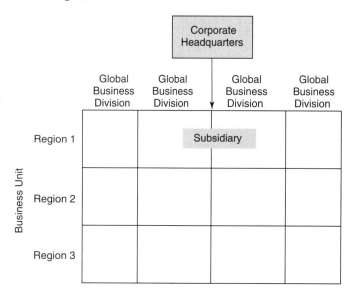

FIGURE 13.6 Multi-Business Matrix Model

Advantages of the Multi-Business Matrix Model Are:

The advantages of the multi-business matrix model are almost the same as for the single product matrix. That is—both global efficiencies and local responsiveness. The multi-product nature of the companies can emphasize both benefits because the company can combine efficiencies and local knowledge across product divisions.

Disadvantages of the Multi-Business Matrix Model Are:

Similarly, the disadvantages of a multi-business matrix model are almost the same as for a single matrix. The only real difference is that the power struggles, role ambiguity, dilution of responsibility, cost inefficiencies, and cost of compromise can be far worse. The size adds complexity, bureaucracy, and far more politics. Workers are really "in a box" surrounded by political forces.

HYBRID MODELS

The six models describe the general characteristics of the organizational structures of most international companies. Many companies, particularly multi product division companies, find the six choices too limited, however. These companies typically mix and match components of the six models to try to find something that will better fit their needs.

Companies choose components trying to maximize advantages while minimizing disadvantages for one particular business model. Particularly conglomerates with many unrelated product lines find some of their products require the local expertise available in a regional model and other product lines require the emphasis on specialized skills of a functional model, but they are unwilling to pay the high political cost of a matrix model in all their divisions. They, therefore, have different divisions operating under different organizational structures.

Most hybrid structures are so complex no one really has clear oversight of combined operations. It isn't uncommon to find people in the upper levels of a hybrid model who don't even know who their bosses are or who reports to them. No one in the company, including the CEO, could draw an organization chart. Such an organization may sound impossible, but many of them exist, and, although they can be frustrating to the people within them, sometimes they are the best solution for a complex mix of products.

The formal written organizational charts are the chain of command within an organization. They represent the formalized power of who reports to whom. To accomplish tasks, use political power, and become noticed, a worker or manager must also be aware of the informal influence systems and how to use them effectively. That involves more of the psychology, whispers, and cover-your-backside politics of organizational life. Nonetheless, where a position lands on the formal organizational chart of the company determines the formal report system with its inherent frustrations and challenges.

 **NOTES**

Concept	Definition	Example
Factors That Influence Structure		
Number of Lines of Business		
Product Diversity		
Customer Differences in Tastes		
Geographic Breadth		
Specialized Skills Involved in Production of Products		
International Organizational Structures		
Global Functional Model		
Geographical Model		
Single Matrix Model		
Multi-business Global Product Division Model		
Multi-business Geographical Model		
Multi-business Matrix Model		
Hybrid Models		
Global Functional Model		

Advantages
  Efficiencies
  Economies of Scale
  Rapid transfer of Skills		

Disadvantages
  Inflexibility
  Local Dysfunctions
  Market Rejection
  Bureaucracy
  Discourages Initiative		

Geographical Model		

Advantages
  Flexibility
  Local Needs
  Quickly Adapts to Markets		

Concept	Definition	Example

Disadvantages
  Diseconomies of Scale
  Duplication
  Poor at Serving Global
    Customers		

Single Matrix Model		

Advantages
  Global Efficiencies
  Local Responsiveness		

Disadvantages
  Power Struggles
  Role Ambiguity
  Dilution of Responsibility
  Cost in Efficiencies
  Cost of Compromise		

Multi-Business Global Product Division		

Advantages
  Flexibility
  Local Needs
  Global Coordination		

Disadvantages
  Duplication of Efforts
  Lack of Local Responsiveness		

Multi-Business Geographical Model		

Advantages
  Flexibility
  Adapts to Local Concerns
  Country Level Optimization		

Disadvantages
  Suboptimization of Global
    Businesses
  Delays in Product
    Introductions
  Inefficient in Industries
    with Global Opportunities		

Multi-Business Matrix Model		

Advantages
  Global Efficiencies
  Local Responsiveness		

Concept	Definition	Example
Disadvantages 　Power Struggles 　Role Ambiguity 　Dilution of Responsibility 　Cost Inefficiencies 　Cost of Compromise		
Hybrid Models		
Mix and match components of any of the above		
Try to maximize advantages while minimizing disadvantages for your particular business situation		
Most are so complex no one really has clear oversight of combined operations		

Global Operations Management

Although much of the world economy has shifted to a focus on service industries, the production and trade of physical goods remains a critical component of international business. Some services are traded across national borders in service industries dominated by large international companies but it is the trade of physical goods across national borders that still dominates international business. That makes production and operations management important to international business. Operations management will be the emphasis in this chapter.

The major difference between domestic production and production through international business is the size of the supply chain. With a truly domestic business all components would be purchased locally. In international business, components are purchased from the lowest cost and highest quality producers wherever they are in the world. Therefore, international producers must consider their supply chain to be global. A global supply chain adds challenges to production but has even greater advantages.

A global supply chain links the suppliers' suppliers with the customers' customers, accounting for every step of the process between the raw material and the final consumer of the good or service. The vertical, global supply chain seeks the best quality components for the best price all around the world. That adds challenges to the process. A company that is making cars, for example, might buy tires from Austria, steel from South Korea, glass from Mexico, and any of the hundreds of other components needed to build a car from as many as 100 different countries. The parts that go into the car are themselves built out of several subcomponents purchased from other parts of the world. Often those subcomponents themselves are made of several subcomponents and so on. A complex finished product like a car or computer could have pieces from all over the world. This makes the protectionist calls to "Buy American" difficult to understand or implement. Almost nothing is totally made in America today. Cars and computers are certainly an example of that. A factory might mean that a car is assembled here, but components are made worldwide.

(Earlier it was discussed why free and fair trade is better for overall world economies than is a protectionist attitude.)

If a company wants to maintain quality control over its finished product, paying attention to the quality of goods coming from its suppliers isn't enough. It has to pay attention to the quality of the supplies feeding into their suppliers and sometimes even the supplies feeding into the suppliers' suppliers. Failure to monitor components all the way back to their source can lead to failure of the overall product. A customer whose new car breaks down on the side of a highway doesn't really care that the breakdown was caused by a bolt sold to a valve maker who sold their valve to a carburetor maker who sold their carburetor to the car company. Traceability is important. Witness the recent lead paint (that is cheaper than allowed paint) that was used in China on children's toys sold in the United States. It was difficult to follow that back to its source. The same is true of agricultural products produced around the world. Genetically, modified corn produced in the United States is not supposed to find its way into the food supply, but it has. Europe will not take our chickens because of the hormones we feed them. A company that wants to protect its reputation with customers has to track and protect its supplies all the way back to their source.

Similarly, a company that wants to protect its quality image must watch its entire forward distribution network as well. In many countries, products pass through several levels of wholesalers before reaching final customers. If any one of those wholesalers is careless with the product, the customer ends up buying a broken or misrepresented good. Customers don't know which wholesalers the product went through; all they know is that the product has your brand name and it doesn't work. The entire supply chain, from raw materials to finished goods to transportation and distribution to the end user, must be monitored and managed.

ADVANTAGES OF A GLOBAL SUPPLY CHAIN

Establishing a vertical, global supply chain offers advantages to a company that include:

> **Lower Cost/Better Quality Supplies**—The biggest advantage of a global supply chain is the choice to purchase its components anywhere in the world. That means the company can purchase its components in whichever country offers the best quality for the cost value. Some countries have substantial advantages in producing certain goods. A global supply chain allows a company to buy its components wherever it can find deals it likes. Purely domestic companies are stuck buying locally produced components regardless of their cost or quality. That tends to make products coming from a global supply chain both better and less expensive.
>
> **Political Advantages**—A global supply chain also offers a company political advantages. When a company chooses to make subcomponents in a country, it brings jobs and wealth to that country. That allows the company to seek support from the country in exchange. Many countries offer to train workers, build roads, or sometimes even build a free factory for a company bringing in substantial jobs. The local political body might offer services like free schooling and day care, free health care on site, or even free lunches. Even if a company is buying components from an existing company in a country, it can use those purchases for political advantage. It can show the government the value of their component purchases and argue for support in selling the final product in the country.
>
> **Tax Advantages**—One of the biggest political advantages a company will seek in its global supply chain is tax advantages. Most countries will provide reduced taxes or, at times, even subsidies for companies bringing in new jobs. Similarly,

components purchased for export are often taxed at lower rates or taxes may be eliminated, or there may even be subsidies.

Customer Access Advantages—A global supply chain can also provide a company with better access to customers. As countries integrate into regions it can, at times, be advantageous to produce a good in a country within the region. The elimination of tariffs and freer flow of goods can give a company a substantial price advantage. A global supply chain makes it easier to produce in several different countries because components are already being moved around the world and only final assembly need occur inside each region.

RISKS OF A GLOBAL SUPPLY CHAIN

Building a global supply chain is not without risk, however. Some of the major risks are described here.

Language Problems—Who hasn't opened a product built in another country, turned to the product instructions, and found them unreadable? Even though all the words may have been English, together they made no sense. The instructions probably made great sense in their original language. Word for word translation, however, rarely works and the instructions, once translated, can be impossible to understand. As much as that problem is for instructions, it is far worse for production processes. Instructions are translated once and pretty much left alone. Production processes require constant interaction. When those interacting have a different first language, the translation process adds miscommunication to interactions. Accumulated miscommunications can cause serious production problems.

Differing Measurement Problems—A global supply chain can also be challenged when countries that build subcomponents are working in different measurement systems. Most Americans are familiar with the challenges of using the British system of measurements (feet, inches, ounces, gallons, tablespoons, etc.) when most of the rest of the world has shifted to the metric system (meters, centimeters, grams, liters, milliliters). There are many other sources of cross-cultural measurement error, however. For example, in the United States a period (.) is used as a decimal point and a comma (,) is used to separate each group of three zeros in a number. European numbering systems do the exact opposite. Therefore, the number 100.001 in the United States is 100 and one one-thousandth. In Europe it is 100 thousand and one. Serious errors can ensue when companies aren't very careful making sure they have precisely communicated not just the measurements they are using but also the standards on which those measurements are built.

Software Compatibility Problems—Another risk of a global supply chain comes with software compatibility problems. Most software is written in one country and then needs to be translated to other languages to be used in other countries. That often means there is a substantial lag between when software is first available in English (the language in which most software is written) and when it is available in other languages. The differing versions of software used within a global supply chain can create data compatibility problems that hide production problems. For example, a company using two different versions of a purchasing system would have to translate data between the two systems. If a company encountered a problem due to different measuring systems, the problem could be hidden because an older version of software might miss it.

Transportation Blockages—One final risk of a global supply chain is the risk that comes from transportation blockages. Most of the goods that travel the planet move between a small number of very large ports and railway stations. Those ports and railway stations become chokepoints. If something like a labor strike or major storm happens and shuts down the port, components can no longer get to factories that need them. With just-in-time systems, now the standard production process around the world, most factories carry a short inventory supply of subcomponents for factory production. The transportation blockage can quickly shut down all the factories dependent on the port or railway station.

THE MAKE OR BUY DECISION

As a company builds its global supply chain it must decide whether to make or buy each subcomponent in its final product. A company can choose to make every subcomponent itself and keep complete control over the entire product. Doing so has many disadvantages, however. There are instances where a company would be better off letting other companies build at least some of the parts of the final product. The major advantages of making or buying subcomponents are described here.

Make

When a company needs extremely tight control over a subcomponent in its product it is usually better off making the subcomponent itself. There are three major reasons why a company might need such tight control. They are:

Lower Costs—When a company is trying to win a market through a low-cost strategy, fractions of pennies count in each subcomponent. If a company bought a subcomponent from another company they would have to pay that companies profit margins as well as add their own profit margin. Companies competing for the very lowest cost will often find they can produce a subcomponent for less than they can purchase it because by making it they don't have to pay that additional profit to someone else. This only works when a company is really willing to focus on the costs in the subcomponent. If the subcomponent's cost can be easily passed on to the customer, a company may be better off purchasing it from someone else.

Proprietary Product Technology Protection—The much more important reason a company would choose to make its own subcomponent is because there's important proprietary technology embedded in the subcomponent or its production. Most advanced companies survive primarily on the technologies they have perfected that their competitors have not. It is where they gain their competitive advantage. If a company has important technology embedded in a subcomponent they would have to give that technology to another producer to be able to buy the subcomponent rather than make it themselves. That would make the technology available to competitors. Thus, where companies have important proprietary technology they are better off making their own subcomponents. Drug companies are an example of companies with proprietary product secrets. The company using proprietary product technology protection is said to be more vertically integrated, that is, it makes, and thus controls, most of its factors of production from raw material to finished good.

Improved Scheduling—With most companies running very tight just-in-time production systems scheduling the arrival of subcomponents can be a critical part of successful production. Where an industry has traditionally had unreliable suppliers, some companies have chosen to make their own subcomponents to smooth the flow of those subcomponents to their primary production process. Delays can be too costly to tolerate.

Buy

Where the three factors above do not play an important part, most companies decide they're better off buying subcomponents rather than making them. This logic is the logic behind the huge outsourcing movement that has swept through business in the last 20 years. The reasons for buying subcomponents rather than making them yourself are compelling. They're listed here.

Strategic Flexibility—By far the most compelling reason for buying subcomponents rather than making them is strategic flexibility. Strategic flexibility means that purchasing subcomponents from other companies gives a company far more flexibility in how they will handle the subcomponent. When a company makes a subcomponent itself it must build a factory, hire and train workers, provide research and development into techniques for improving the subcomponent, and spend money on all the basic business requirements and machinery needed for building the subcomponent.

When a company buys the subcomponent, however, the factories, research and development costs, and employees are not theirs. If the company decides to stop using a subcomponent it doesn't have to close a factory and lay off workers. The company will usually have multiple suppliers for the subcomponents so if one of them has labor or transportation problems the company can simply buy more of the good from a different vendor. The company can push the subcomponent makers to improve their quality and lower their costs by giving the majority of their orders to the supplier that does a better job or is willing to respond to competition and lower the price. The flexibility gained by using outside suppliers typically far outweighs any extra costs over making the subcomponent yourself. Wal-Mart uses strategic flexibility as one of its strategic advantages. Automobile manufacturers buy most of their production components from suppliers who often supply to multiple automobile competitors. This supply chain has been a factor in the U.S. Government's original decision to help Detroit. Not only were G.M. and Chrysler deemed "too big to fail," but the impact of the failure of suppliers was considered as well. Too many jobs were at risk for an already fragile economy.

Lower Costs—Sometimes you can even purchase a subcomponent for substantially less than you can make it yourself. If you only use a few thousand of the subcomponent in your product but large numbers of the subcomponent are used in other kinds of products, then the scale of factory needed to be most efficient is probably well beyond your needs. If there are others who need the subcomponent they will also share in covering research and development costs and other expenses you would bear yourself if you made the component. Think of Intel chips here. It is highly unlikely that you would try to make your own chip for your product. The precision and technology for clean room manufacture would make it cost prohibitive for almost all companies.

Potentially Higher Quality—Another important reason many companies buy rather than make subcomponents is that they can buy better quality. Unless a subcomponent is absolutely critical to the functionality of the overall good, it is unlikely a company would spend nearly as much on research and development and quality control improvements as a company solely dedicated to making the subcomponent. That means a company dedicated to the subcomponent will typically have a higher quality part than the company could make itself.

Offsets—One final advantage to buying subcomponents from other companies is buying subcomponents can provide offsets. Many small or less developed countries face severe balance of payments problems. Some try to improve their balance of payments by requiring companies that import into the country to export a similar amount. That export requirement is called an offset. A company trying to import its finished good can buy subcomponents in the country to generate offsets.

WHERE SHOULD YOU MANUFACTURE?

When a company decides it is going to manufacture its subcomponents or overall goods, there are many issues to consider when deciding where to build a factory. The issues are categorized into three different types: country factors, technological factors, and product factors. Each is described here.

Country Factors

Most of the country specific factors relevant to where a company should build its factories, natural resources, culture, law, and politics, have been covered extensively throughout this book. Issues such as the availability of natural resources, the culture of a country and its affect on the quality and availability of human resources, the laws and politics, and even the stability of a country all play an important role in deciding whether a country is the best location for a particular manufacturing process. A company must develop expertise in understanding and weighing all the factors relevant to making a site choice. Costs and benefits must be weighed.

Technological Factors

A number of factors specific to technologies being used in the production process affect the choice of factory location. Those factors include:

> **Infrastructure Requirements**—The availability, amount, and consistency of electricity and water, sewer, and disposal are important considerations when deciding the location of a production facility. A factory with a large amount of waste or a high need for power, such as a tire factory, needs to have reliable power.
>
> **Fixed Costs**—The amount of fixed costs required for a particular production technology can significantly affect the location for a factory. Some factories have very low fixed costs. For example, a typical clothing manufacturer needs nothing more than an empty building and several cutting and sewing machines. With such low fixed costs, a clothing manufacturer can focus on finding the lowest cost labor for production. If labor costs rise in an area, the factory can easily be moved. A car manufacturer, on the other hand, requires billion dollar factories. Once built, a factory is likely to remain in the same place for 20 or more years. With such high fixed costs, stability in the workforce and government around the factory is critical. It would be too expensive to move the factory if labor costs changed drastically or the government turned against the company.
>
> **Minimum Efficient Scale**—The minimal efficient scale of factory is the smallest size factory that can be set up and used efficiently in an industry. Some industries, such as dry cleaning, can use extremely small factories. An efficient dry cleaning factory can be set up to handle the needs of a limited number of customers. With such a small factory possible, factories can be set up anywhere and the efficiencies of being close to customers are the most prevalent concern. Other industries, such as microchip manufacturing, have a minimum efficient scale larger than the entire world's demand for the product. That being the case only one factory is needed to serve the entire world's demand for most types of chips. If only one factory is needed in the world, transportation costs and specialized labor needs become critical elements for determining factory location. In that case, reliability of the necessary quality of product and consistency of meeting demand is critical to its success.

Flexibility of Manufacturing Technology—The final technological issue in choosing where to place a factory is consideration of how flexible the manufacturing technology needs to be. Some technologies, such as robotics, can be used to produce a wide variety of products for the same line. Other technologies, such as metal stamping, can typically only be used to produce one good. The more flexible the technology used in manufacturing, the less a company needs to be concerned with local demand conditions for the particular product. The less flexible a manufacturing technology is, the more a company must be sure there's local demand for the good or inexpensive transportation to take it to other markets.

Product Factors

Product factors are traits of the product being produced which have an effect on where it should be produced. There are two primary product factors that most companies consider.

Manufacturing Skills Required—The most important product factor used in determining manufacturing locations is the manufacturing skills required to produce a good. Some goods can be produced with extremely limited skill sets. For example, McDonald's typically spends less than a day training its workers how to make a hamburger. When a product has such limited skill requirements, a company can seek the lowest cost labor available without particular concern for the skill level of the work force. Other production processes require extremely well-trained workers. An LCD factory, for example, requires several PhDs with very specialized skills. When a product requires such specialized skills, manufacturing needs to be placed where people with those skills can be found or are willing to move.

Value to Weight Ratio—The second important product factor used to determine manufacturing location is a product's value to weight ratio. A value to weight ratio divides a product's price by its weight. This ratio is critical to determine how important transportation costs are in a good. Some products, like cement, are very heavy and inexpensive. Such products need to be produced as close to where they will be used as possible. Otherwise transportation costs will overwhelm production costs in the good. Other goods are very expensive and light. Such goods can be produced virtually anywhere without regard to transportation costs. For example, no one worries about the transportation costs in the diamond market. Diamonds are cut wherever the skilled labor needed is most available.

Global operations management is a growing field of expertise. Engineers and specialists are needed to set up efficient and effective factories and to procure raw materials or parts from around the globe. The success of a company or its products depends heavily upon getting operations management down to the science it is and getting it right. Competition demands it in a global environment.

NOTES

Concept	Definition	Example
Global Supply Chain–links the suppliers' suppliers with the customers' customers, accounting for every step of the process between the raw material and the final consumer of the good or service		
Advantages		
Lower Cost/Better Quality Supplies		
Political Advantages		
Tax Advantages		
Customer Access Advantages		
Risks		
Language Problems		
Differing Measurement Problems		
Software Compatibility Problems		
Transportation Blockages		
The Make or Buy Decision		

Make
   Lower Costs
   Proprietary Product
     TechnologyPprotection
   Improved Scheduling		

Buy
   Strategic Flexibility
   Lower Costs
   Potentially Higher Quality
   Offsets		

Concept	Definition	Example
Where Should You Manufacture		

Country Factors
   Culture
   Laws and Politics
   Resource Availability
   Trade Barriers		

Technological Factors
   Fixed Costs
   Minimum Efficient Scale
   Flexibility of Manufacturing
     Technology		

Product Factors
   Manufacturing Skills
     Required
   Value to Weight Ratio		

International Marketing

As a company moves to overseas markets, it must reconsider what it thinks it knows about marketing. Because marketing is the primary interface to customers, it is crucial to get it right in terms of the multi-cultural interfaces it hopes to make. It must consider how different cultures, economic systems, and political and legal systems will affect its approach to marketing. It must also be aware of the perceived need for its products and whether or not the products must be pushed or pulled through the system. All of this analysis must include a consideration of the costs and benefits to the company.

RE-EVALUATE MARKETING MIX

The decisions made by a company's marketing arm entail four primary functions. Those four functions are often called the four P's of marketing even though realistically it is three P's and a D. The four P's of marketing describe the marketing mix— the adjustment of each of its primary marketing functions to create an attractive mix for customers. When a company moves into a new country, it must totally re-evaluate it marketing mix. Most mix elements are completely dependent on a country's culture, and its economic and political landscape. A company needs to consider how each element of the mix may be affected. The four P's are product, price, place (distribution), and promotion. In true marketing fashion, after the four P's were introduced, someone added "people." You can probably add other "P's" . . . penetration?

Product

There are obvious changes that a company must make to its product as it moves into a new country. All packaging, instructions, and any included software must be translated to the major languages of the country. Even if the country uses the same general language as the home-base country there are often minor differences in language usage to be adapted. For example, English speakers are aware when packaging developed for the UK is sent to the United States or vice versa because common spellings of words vary. For example, labor and labour. Similarly, most of the French speaking countries in Africa and Spanish speaking countries of South America have small differences in the way they use the language. Not adjusting to those small differences makes it appear as though the manufacturer does not know or care about the local market.

Beyond language, other product modifications are sometimes necessary. Electricity and plugs used around the globe vary considerably. Of course, the correct voltage and plugs must be installed. Countries routinely use larger or smaller sized goods. Some countries read up and down or right to left instead of left to right as in the European languages. Reading up and down or right to left teaches people very different scanning patterns. Those scanning patterns are critical to understanding where to put information you want customers to see first. That has serious implications for the design of safety features, warnings, and instructions.

Many products sell based on tastes. The obvious tastes are foods and fashions. Tastes are largely dictated by culture. Even colors have implications. For example, sports teams in the United States have team colors that can be captured for marketing purposes. Any food or fashion-oriented-product is likely to require adjustments for each new culture it encounters.

All these things considered, changing a company's product is expensive. Companies will necessarily try to make the fewest changes possible. An important part of being good at international business is to understand how to design products that fit many different tastes and that can be adjusted to different cultures with minimal effort.

Price

As a company reconsiders pricing while entering a new country, there are many factors that must be analyzed. The biggest discovery is the existing competition already in the market. If entering a poor country, there will often be local competitors selling a low quality good for a very low price to the multitude of "have nots." An international firm entering the market will usually be able to offer much better quality but probably won't be able to beat the local price. That will mean finding ways to make the international good comparatively reasonably priced even if not price competitive. That often means making a consumer good smaller or a stripped down version of a mechanical good. Of course the alternative is to price a quality good for the wealthier people, the smaller number of "haves" in the country.

When entering a wealthier nation, a company will have more pricing flexibility. Often, the international aura of a product will itself provide a quality mystique. That often leads companies to sell their products overseas at premium prices. The challenge is to always know what a market will bear and charge that price which maximizes long term return.

Place (Distribution)

Distribution in overseas markets is often a particular challenge for American firms. The United States has an extremely well developed retail and wholesale distribution system. Most U.S. manufacturing firms are able to pass their goods into the distribution system with little effort. Distribution systems in most other countries are far less developed. Manufacturers must take far greater care to make sure their product reaches the consumer in the condition expected. The best packaging can do little to protect and display a product that has been exposed to rain and cold in the back of an open truck. Similarly, surly clerks in a poorly lit, dingy store can damage the quality image of a good far faster than poor quality manufacturing. A company that wishes to maintain prestige imaging will need to work hard in most overseas markets to earn it. Where it is placed and how it is distributed matter.

Promotion

The promotion mix a company uses often needs to be adapted as the company moves from country to country. What promotion techniques work is dependent on a country's culture and state of economic development. In some countries, generating endorsements from local leaders is the only way to garner support. In others, printed ads work best. In still others, advanced electronic advertising such as location-specific cell phone advertising that is more sophisticated than what one typically finds in the United States is required. Understanding what works in a particular market in adapting a company's message is key to success.

People

The success of any marketing and the ability to get the product from manufacturing into the hands of the ultimate consumer depend on the right mix of people. That is intuitive, but critical to success. The people who work for or represent the company must be strong assets in the chain of product delivery and even afterwards for product service.

MARKET SEGMENTATION

In market segmentation, a company tries to divide its potential customers into meaningful groups with special needs or interests associated with its product. The key to good segmentation is figuring out how customers think of (or can be led to think of) your product. There are different approaches to segmentation. For example, some companies will segment purely by geographic region. While regional differences are often important to understanding customers' reactions to a product, there are other important differences between people that must be considered. International segmentation is typically done using the same or similar categories as segmentation done in a single country. You need to be careful, however, because while the same segments often exist in various countries they can have different meanings. The three main segmentation categories follow.

Traditional—Geographic, Demographic, etc.

With traditional segmentation, companies use factors like geographic differences or demographic differences to separate their customers. Customer groups are broken into areas such as Northern and Southern Italy which have substantially different cultures. Demographic groups, such as age, race, or gender, are also frequently used in international markets. Even though the same categories may exist, a company must be careful not to expect that categories will have the same meaning from country to country. For example, most advertising in the United States targets young Americans because youth in America defines cool. If you can sell your product to young Americans, older Americans eventually may purchase the product as well. Age works in other countries but often in the exact opposite direction. In many Asian countries, it is maturity that is honored rather than youth. In that case, products need to be sold to older people first, then the young will follow.

Psychographic—Lifestyle, Personality, etc.

In psychographic segmentation people are divided into groups based on psychological characteristics. Companies look for people who have chosen a particular lifestyle or developed certain personality traits that support a particular use of their product. Psychographic groups could be segments such as "soccer moms," sports enthusiasts, or technophiles. Again, similar groupings may exist across countries but not always with the same meanings, so a company must be careful to reconsider its segmentation for each country it enters.

A good example of what can go wrong without reviewing segmentation in the international market occurred with Mountain Dew. Mountain Dew is an old brand that for most of its life had a sleepy existence. When Pepsi acquired the brand they went looking for a way to significantly increase sales. In analyzing the soda they saw it had a much sweeter taste and higher caffeine than most other drinks of the time. They went looking for a segment for which these traits would be desirable. They settled on what was, at the time, the very small segment of extreme sports enthusiasts.

Pepsi advertised heavily in the United States to the extreme sports crowd and captured them. At the same time, they made extreme sports themselves much more popular and captured a very large chunk of the U.S. general population. In fact, they started the entire push towards high caffeine energy drinks.

Pepsi then tried to duplicate that success in other countries. They discovered another country with a significant extreme sports crowd was Germany. They tried transporting their marketing approach. However, the extreme sports crowd in Germany is very different. It is made up mostly of what the United States would call the biker crowd, that is, mostly male, mostly 50 or older, and mostly middle class. They were not the kind of people Germans considered cool and wanted to emulate. Mountain Dew caught on with the extreme sports crowd in Germany but the success never transferred to the general population. Mountain Dew remained a small niche market in Germany until Pepsi took an entirely different tact to advertising it.

Behavioral—Benefits Sought, Brand Loyalty, etc.

The final divisions frequently used around the world are behavioral segments. In behavioral segments, companies look to what customers hope to gain from a product. These segments are based on how the customers use the product and why they choose one product over another. For many fashion products, the prestige gained from a company's brand may itself be the benefit many customers pursue.

When considering the benefits sought, a company often discovers that customers use their product in different ways. For example, Arm and Hammer baking soda actually used to be used for baking. As working women stopped baking, Arm and Hammer had to suggest other uses. In the United States it suggested using baking soda as a refrigerator or freezer deodorant. The use kept the company alive but not healthy. In Europe, Arm and Hammer discovered segments who used baking soda as toothpaste, deodorant, and many other cleaning uses as well as personal hygiene uses. Arm and Hammer created or licensed a large number of baking soda products and sold them across Europe with such success they eventually moved many of the products into U.S. markets as well.

PRODUCT—PROMOTION MIX STRATEGY

As a company considers new approaches to market segmentation, it often finds it needs to modify its product and promotion mix to better target a particular segment. There are four options for modifying a company's product promotion mix as it enters a new country. Those four options are explained here.

Product-Promotion Extension

In a product-promotion extension, a company takes its existing product and its existing promotion mix and tries to use the same products and promotion mix in overseas markets. For example, Coca-Cola is basically the exact same product all around the world. The packaging may be slightly different from country to country but Coke works very hard to make sure all the packages looks similar and the product inside the package is nearly identical. At the same time, Coke develops many of its commercials so they can be translated to use all around the world.

Coke designs their advertisements so they have little or no text. They associate their product with ideas they hope will have universal appeal. For example, anyone can quickly recognize Coca-Cola Christmas ads. They're carefully designed to associate Coke with the positive feelings most people have about Christmas. Coke promotes the ads so strongly that they have developed Christmas traditions in many countries (such as Japan) with little Christian history.

Product Extension-Promotion Adaptation

If a company cannot use a product-promotion extension because a market will not accept it, the next least expensive, and therefore most common, approach is product extension-promotion adaptation. In this model, a company keeps its product untouched but modifies its advertising to fit local markets. This approach allows a company to address local market differences in perception. It allows a company to explain the advantage of its product designs. Most importantly, it creates a local market perception for a good that may not perfectly fit local needs.

Product Adaptation-Promotion Extension

Product adaptation-promotion extension is a fairly rare approach to the product promotion mix. Here the product is modified, but the promotion of it is more general to the brand image. There are a few companies who have determined that their brand is more important to sales than the products on which the brand is placed. For these companies product adaptation-promotion extension can work.

Take, for example, the Nike corporation. They face different sporting markets in many different countries. The cleats required for playing cricket are very different then those used for baseball. Nike must design and sell unique shoes for each market. Nevertheless, Nike considers their primary advantage to be their brand. Therefore, Nike creates ads that are used globally. Michael Jordan is used to sell shoes in countries that don't play basketball. In many worldwide polls he is the most recognized face on the planet, above those of the U.S. president, the pope, or any other celebrity.

Product-Promotion Adaptation

Some companies are unfortunate enough to be in industries where both product and promotion adaptation are required to succeed. The prospect of developing new products and promotions for each new market can make products that fall into this category expensive compared to locally made products. Thus, products in this category must show significant advantages over locally made products to survive. Premium foods and other consumer products sometimes fall into this category. International companies tend to compete in premium priced markets, leaving low-cost positions to local companies.

PROMOTION STRATEGY

As a company works on the details of its country specific promotion strategies, it selects advertising, personal selling, promotion, or publicity based on a number of factors. The primary concerns that affect the promotion mix are described here.

Laws

The first concern of a company designing its promotion strategy is laws of the country regarding promotion. Most countries have fairly extensive laws dictating what, when, where, and how products can be promoted. Some products, such as alcohol and cigarettes, can't be promoted at all or have limited promotional possibilities. Products may have restrictions on how they can be promoted. For example, many countries do not allow comparisons with competitor's products in advertising. Some don't allow door to door sales.

Media Availability

Next, a company must carefully consider what sorts of media are available and commonly used in a country. Many American companies are used to relying on television to promote their brand. In other countries, large portions of the population do not have regular access to TV so other sources like radio, print, or billboard ads may be needed to reach large segments of the population. In populations with high illiteracy rates or multiple common languages, writing of any sort may not work. In countries with less commonly used languages, a wide variety of print media may not be available for targeted advertising.

Cultural Preference

Cultural preferences will dictate what promotions' techniques will work within a culture. In some cultures, such as Russia, direct sales from friends are preferred, so door-to-door techniques like those used by Amway can be very successful. Other cultures prefer much less personal interaction, so techniques like TV or Internet advertising may be more successful. Still others prefer highly personalized interactions but not with other human beings. Person- and location-specific cell phone ads have worked very well in such countries. It is up to the promotion team to figure out what works in a culture and how best to convey their message within those cultural preferences.

Communication Practices

A company must also understand the normal communication practices of each country they enter. Some countries tend to believe sources of authority like teachers and politicians. In such countries product endorsements can push a brand ahead. Other countries have far less faith in authority and only trust communications from people they know. For example, in the Soviet Union the official government newspaper was called Pravda, which means "The Truth." People quickly learned they couldn't trust anything they were told by anyone but their closest friends. That makes communicating brand information in such cultures far more difficult.

Acceptable Level of Persuasion

A company must also carefully consider the level of persuasion acceptable in a population when choosing promotion techniques. Some cultures are comfortable with extremely aggressive sales techniques. In Egypt, it is not uncommon for a salesperson to stand inches away from a customer aggressively trying to convince that person that he sells the best product for the lowest price. In other cultures, it would be considered extremely rude to even mention competitors and doing so would instantly lose the sale. In many of these cultures, even mentioning a price would be disastrous.

Price

The level to which a company focuses on price in its promotions is also usually a country by country decision. Some countries are very price sensitive and appeals that don't mention price are likely to be ignored. Other countries are far more focused on other issues and appeals to price are likely to have little impact on sales.

Product Features

Finally, the product features upon which promotions should focus frequently need to be adjusted country by country. For example, cell phones have become the primary means of communications all around the world, even in the world's poorest countries. When advertising a cell phone in a very poor country, promotions usually need to focus on the phone's range because cell towers are often farther apart in poor countries. The phone's durability given the rough environment and high relative expense of replacing the phone must be considered. In rich countries, features such as the ease with which text messages can be entered or other fashionable traits are more likely to be emphasized.

DISTRIBUTION STRATEGY

In distribution strategy, a company must decide how it will get its product to end consumers. Distribution strategy includes plans for transporting a good through wholesale and/or retail outlets all the way to the end consumer. Distribution strategy is particularly challenging in international business for several reasons.

First, distribution is often across national borders so customs issues and government relations can become a challenge for international businesses. Second, most countries do not have nearly as developed a retail system as the United States, so American companies often have far greater difficulty finding acceptable outlets for their products. Finally, and perhaps most importantly, distribution is far more important to other economies than it is in the United States.

The United States is so large and diverse that manufacturers and service companies tend to dominate our economy. In smaller countries, there are rarely so many profit producing opportunities so the distribution system is a far more important part of the economy. With more of the wealth in the distribution system, so there is more of the political power. That means political systems heavily protect their national distribution systems and usually make them far less efficient than they could otherwise be. That often means international companies will have to spend far more time and resources on distribution in foreign markets than they do in their home market. It has been pointed out previously that bribes are commonly expected or demanded in the distribution systems of quite a few countries around the globe. Paying those bribes is illegal for U.S. companies. A fine line must be traversed in order to do business and still comply with laws.

As a company tries to plan its distribution strategy, there are four key issues they tend to focus on.

National Retail and Wholesale Structures Available

A company begins its distribution strategy by studying the existing retail and wholesale structures within the country. The company needs to discover what wholesale structures are required, both by law and tradition in the country. They need to understand the effects on their product's price and the quality of that wholesale structure. They also need to look at whether existing retail outlets present the image and level of service that is desirable for their product. If either the existing wholesale or retail structures is inadequate, the company will need to look for alternatives or decide against entering the country.

Competition with Others in Channel

As a company studies the wholesale and retail structures within a country, they must pay careful attention to what competition already exists in the channel. Smaller countries may only have one distribution system for a given product type. For example, many cities may have only one bottling plant. If Coke already has a contract with a city's bottling plant, Pepsi would not want to use the same sales channel. If they did, they would have no way to get favorable treatment for their product. They would probably have to set up their own bottling plant or have their product shipped in from another city at great expense.

Does Firm Normally Sell Direct

A question that arises far more commonly for international businesses is whether or not they normally sell their product directly to consumers. Most manufacturers are far more comfortable handing off their product to a wholesale or retail company and letting professionals in those industries deal with consumers. With inadequate wholesale or retail options in so many countries, more companies decide they need to sell directly to consumers in those countries. For a few companies, developing that retail expertise has been very profitable. For most, it has not. If a company does not have retail experience, it may be better off accepting either the limitations of a retail channel or the lower sales likely from a purely online approach.

Desirable Level of Channel Control

Ultimately a company's international distribution strategy will come down to a question of how much control is needed over a product throughout the distribution process. If a company sells a commodity, goods distribution will not be difficult. If, as is more common for an American company, the company sells prestige goods for a premium price, more control over the distribution channel will be needed. That means a company needs to be prepared for the political and competitive challenges of controlling a good through a challenging distribution environment.

NOTES

Concept	Definition	Example
Re-evaluate Marketing Mix		
Product		
Pricing		
Distribution		
Promotions		
New International Market Assessment		
Potential Need Screening		
Potential Satisfaction Screening		
Legal and Political Analysis		
Social Cultural Screening		
Ranking and Clustering of Markets		
Field Trips, Market Research, and Testing		
Market Segmentation		
Traditional—Geographic, Demographic, etc.		
Psychographic—Lifestyle, Personality, etc.		
Behavioral—Benefits Sought, Brand Loyalty, etc.		
Evaluating Market Segmentation		
Measurability		
Accessibility		
Reasonability of Size		

Concept	Definition	Example
Product-Promotion Mix Strategy		
Product-Promotion Extensions		
Product Extension-Promotion Adaptation		
Product Adaptation-Promotion Extension		
Product-Promotion Adaptation		
Promotion Strategy		
Select Advertising, Personal Selling, Promotion, or Publicity Based on:		
Laws		
Media Availability		
Cultural Preference		
Communication Practices		
Acceptable Level of Persuasion		
Price		
Product Features		
Distribution Strategy		
Select Channels Based on:		
National Retail and Wholesale Structures Available		
Competition with Others in Channel		
Does Firm Normally Sell Direct		
Desirable Level of Channel Control		

International Human Resources

One prevalent theme throughout this book has been the major effect of culture on international business. When we talk about culture, we're really talking about people and how they interact. Humans are more alike than different because we're a biological species. What makes us different is our specific genetics and the ideas and prejudices we've learned from our surroundings, experiences, and influences. Because the way people think and interact changes significantly from country to country, human resources is a great challenge for international business. Given the world of possibilities, a company must decide who it wants for employees and how to treat them. Handling international human resources is international business' great challenge and opportunity.

WHOM DO YOU WANT AS OVERSEAS EMPLOYEES?

The first human resources question is who to hire. Most companies want people from their home country in their overseas operations; and these people are expected to carry the home company values and culture and add it to the culture of the host country. There is an important balance to strike between home country employees vs. local employees.

How Many Should Be Home, Host, or Global Employees?

As a company tries to determine how many employees should be from their home country, from the host country, or global employees from third countries, there are factors to consider. Usually, host country employees are the least expensive. Even if a country has high labor costs, it is usually less expensive to use local employees because, as you'll see when we cover compensation later in this chapter, sending employees overseas is very expensive. Host country employees also have the advantage that they already know the local culture intimately and are closely tied to the community, so they will recognize the need for changes more quickly.

Most companies do want home country employees in any overseas operation. If a company feels they have something they can uniquely add by having an overseas operation, at least a small part of what they are adding is tied to corporate home culture. It is assumed home or global employees will be able to carry that corporate culture into a host country. For most companies, the question of how many home country employees to send usually comes down to the importance of home country culture vs. labor costs.

Usually Fewer than 10% Home Country—When companies do their analysis of home vs. host employees, most decide to send 10% or fewer employees from a home country. That 10%/90% mix provides enough interaction for host country employees with home country employees to transfer home country values where that is desirable. That ratio usually provides a large enough group of home country nationals to interact with each other and maintain the home country values the company is trying to support.

The high cost of home country employees usually prevents companies from going above 10%, but cost isn't the only reason companies try not to send more home country nationals. Companies find that if they go above 10% home country nationals, local workers feel less a part of the company and less willing to participate fully. There are few, if any, industries that can survive with no adaptation to local conditions. Sabotage can be a real problem from disgruntled workers.

Frequently Fewer than 1% Home Country—Although companies that really want to instil a home based culture into an overseas market may go as high as 10% home country nationals, most companies try for less.

For many companies, the fewest home country employees they try is two. Companies generally appoint as country manager a home country or global manager. They do so to ensure that the top person in the country will be loyal to company needs rather than local needs. Most American companies also want a U.S. financial officer in overseas operations. American companies use highly sophisticated financial systems which depend tremendously on being able to trust the data being entered to meet American expectations and standards.

Depending on the size and scope of the operation, some companies will include home country marketing managers, production managers, or other key positions depending on needs. Overall, however, many companies end up with less than 1% of their employees in overseas operation being home country nationals. That, obviously, can make it a challenge for those home country nationals not only to instil the needed home country culture in the host country employees, but also it can become a challenge for the home country employees to maintain the important aspects of their home country culture in themselves.

What Language Should the Company Use?

An important question an international business must consider when deciding whom it wants for employees is what language the company will use for its operations. Most international companies perform the majority of their lower level business in the dominant local language. Not doing so would require lower level workers who can function in multiple languages. That reduces the number of potential employees and, therefore, increases labor costs. The question for most companies is what language they use for higher level management.

Global Language Is English—The good news for most Americans is English has been widely adopted as the global language for business. Most multinational companies have adopted English for upper level management discussions. That has led to a wide adoption of English around the world. English is now, by far, the most widely spoken second language in the world, but, as a second language, facility and nuances with it is limited. That puts limits on the ability of those who speak only English to communicate.

Most Companies Require Managers to Speak Two or More Languages—The bad news for most Americans is that, although international business is largely conducted in English, most companies require international managers to speak at least two languages.

As you learn a second language, you quickly discover translation is far from perfect. Many ideas do not have direct translations in other languages. Word for word translations often do not convey the same message as the original language. People working in their second language often have a limited vocabulary in it that makes it hard for them to convey complex ideas. All these problems can be overcome as long as both people understand what it is like to be working in a language where you have limited skills. Patience with language problems comes from speaking more than one language. Thus, companies require of top managers that they speak more than one language because it is critical to be able to understand the challenges of translation and of working in a second language.

HOW DO YOU SELECT OVERSEAS EMPLOYEES?

When international companies select employees for overseas work, they consider a number of factors. The most important are described here.

Competence Factors

For overseas workers, companies first look at two types of competence—cultural and technical. These are not diametrically opposed but do tend to work against each other so it is unlikely to find someone who is good at both. Therefore, most companies look to each type of competence for particular positions and try to instill at least marginal competence in the opposing factor in those who are best at one of the factors.

Cultural Competence—Cultural competence is a measure of how quickly a person can adapt to new cultural environments. People with high cultural competence have a multidomestic perspective on life. They don't feel life has many fixed rules. They believe rules derive from culture. With that perspective, they are constantly searching for what the rules are in their current environment and adapting quickly to them. Cultural competence is a critical skill needed for country managers who are expected to understand and blend home culture and host culture.

Technical Competence—Technical competence is a measure of a person's technical proficiency in a given field. People who are technically competent understand and believe in the rules of their discipline and know how to apply them. Your best accountants, finance experts, and production managers are high in technical competence. International businesses need a great deal of it in their overseas operations to maintain quality control and consistency.

The challenge is that technical competence is based on believing in the rules but cultural competence is largely based on not believing in rules. Sophisticated international employees eventually develop the experience to tell which rules they should believe in and which rules they can ignore, but companies usually have to develop such sophistication over decades. That means companies need to sort their most culturally and technically competent people from average performers and steer the most culturally and technically competent people into the right positions. That can be a difficult challenge.

One approach taken to sort people is to put them into game situations they have not experienced. With each new game, you'll discover that the most culturally competent win the first few attempts at the game. They do so because they are constantly scanning the environment for the new rules and have the experience to adapt quickly to the new game's environment. Four or five rounds into the game, however, you'll find the most technically competent people constantly winning. They do so because, although it is more difficult for them to learn new rule sets, once they learn them they perfect their knowledge. The culturally competent waste too much time searching for new rules when they haven't changed and can't beat the efficiency of the technically competent. The vast majority of people who never gain a dominant position are typically those with limited ability for cultural and technical competence.

Adaptability Factors

Once a company has found its needed cultural and technical competency, it then tries to determine an individual's likely ability to succeed in an international environment. The most important factor it looks for is adaptability. Two types of adaptability are described here.

> **Able to Participate in New Culture**—Whenever an employee is sent to another country, there must be a willingness to adapt to a new culture. The first step in adaptation is a participation in experiences you don't understand. Those high on cultural competence will usually jump in and adapt quickly.
>
> The challenge comes with those you're considering for overseas assignments due to their technical competence. You need to be sure your technically competent people are willing to participate in the local culture. The technically competent usually won't agree that what the locals are doing is "the best way." They have to be willing to try it anyway. If not, there won't be enough interaction between host company employees and the home country technical employee so the host country employees won't learn and the technical employee won't adapt. Thus, if a highly technically competent person is unable/unwilling to participate in what, to them, is strange cultural events, you're probably better off leaving them in operations in the home country.
>
> **Family Adaptability**—A second important adaptability factor is family adaptability. Assuming you're sending an employee overseas for an extended period, rarely will they be willing to go without their family. That means if they have a spouse and children, the spouse and children need to be able to adapt to the new environment as well. Moving overseas is usually more difficult on families than it is on employees. Spouses who have been employed will usually find they can't get a work visa in the new country and are left in a strange environment with a great deal of time on their hands, making it even more likely that they'll miss family and friends. Most find it very difficult to adapt. Children are also sent into an environment they don't understand. They are forced to leave behind all their friends and comforting familiarity. If a spouse or child is unable to adapt to a new country, there will be tremendous pressure on the employee to give up and go home early. That means a company considering an employee for their first overseas assignment has to have very frank discussions with the employee about family.

Personal Characteristics

Another factor a company looks for in potential international employees is personal characteristics. When considering these factors a company must be careful. U.S. law makes it illegal to discriminate based on many of the factors in this category. Yet discriminating on some of the factors is a requirement in many countries. Fortunately, U.S. law does provide a safety valve for companies. Companies must show they do not discriminate in their overall operations, but not in each country where they operate. That allows a company to balance its operations across its entire global system. If discrimination is required on a factor like gender in a Middle Eastern country, for example, then a company can compensate for it by sending more females into

European operations. Factors a company may consider based on the country being considered include:

Age—One personal characteristic a company considers is an employee's age. Many cultures show a strong age bias that is opposite of that in the United States. Because in many countries if you do not have at least a few grey hairs you're not worth listening to, many American companies run into problems. Often, some of the best technical managers are young; but older employees in cultures with a strong age bias won't listen to them. That makes the young technical managers a poor choice for such countries.

Gender—There are many countries in the world that still have a strong bias against equality of women, and even more so against working women. Sending a female manager into such environments will make it likely the local employees won't listen to her and that she will become so frustrated with the experience she will insist on leaving or quit. Rarely is a company in a powerful enough position that it can force the local culture to adapt. Most of the time it simply must accept the country's system or the success of the company is at risk. Surprisingly, for most female managers this works to their benefit. Most of the countries that won't accept women managers are very traditional and slow growing. That means female employees have to be over represented in the more progressive countries that tend to have better opportunities.

Health—Another factor a company considers in overseas assignments is an employee's health. While American companies are still held to ADA requirements for American employees overseas, companies need to be realistic. Many poor countries have extremely bad medical systems. An employee with a chronic condition that requires constant care or which is likely to create an emergency need for immediate care can't safely be sent to a country with poor medical support. And, although American companies are held to ADA requirements, other countries are not. Some countries are simply impassable for those in a wheelchair, for instance. A company needs to know its employees' special needs and consider them in overseas assignments.

Race/Religion/Sexual Orientation—Other factors that more rarely play a role but must be considered in a few countries include race, religion, and sexuality. Race is rarely a concern in overseas assignments. Most overseas employees are categorized by their nationality rather than race. For example, an African American in almost any other country is just seen as American. If the country likes Americans, the employee is liked. If the country hates Americans, the employee is hated. Race is rarely a consideration. Surprisingly, the one group that can have problems in many parts of the world are those with blond hair and blue eyes. In many countries, blond hair and blue eyes really stick out and scream wealthy foreigner. In some countries kidnapping is an industry. Blond hair and blue eyes makes one an easy target for crime.

Religion is not often a factor either, with one caveat. Most countries are willing to accept an American regardless of religion so long as the American doesn't feel a need to proselytize. In many countries, trying to convince others to convert to your religion is considered very rude. In some countries it is illegal. A company doesn't have to worry much about religions as long as employees keep them to themselves. If they cannot, a company must consider how their evangelism will reflect on the company.

Finally, a company must also be careful with an employee who is openly gay. There are many countries where being openly gay is accepted and a few where it is even celebrated. There are many more countries where it is still illegal and/or dangerous. A company needs to know the employee and country well to know if the mix will work.

CULTURE SHOCK—PHASES OF ADAPTATION

Once a company has selected its employees for overseas assignment, it needs to prepare them. Although there are specific skills to acquire before being sent overseas, in the early phases employees may not even know they're being groomed for international assignment. At some point, when a company feels it has an employee ready for international work, it will suggest an initial assignment. That is when culture shock begins. Culture shock is an experience virtually all go through in the first overseas assignment. It is often repeated as they are moved from country to country but usually with diminishing effects. The culture shock experience generally hits people in a number of phases.

Initial Euphoria

The employee expects too much before leaving. When employees are told of their first international assignment they tend to get very excited for a number of reasons. First, companies usually only send overseas people they think have potential to become an executive. Large multinationals need executives who understand their international operations. The only way to get them is to send people who are being groomed for executive positions overseas. People who have the potential for executive positions usually know that an overseas assignment means upper level management is grooming them. Most people who get an overseas assignment have also worked very hard to earn it. The assignment itself becomes a reward. Finally, most people who get an overseas assignment have expressed interest over a period of time and are excited finally to be given the chance.

With all the excitement, employees usually jump headlong into their first assignment before they ever leave for it. They buy every tourist book available on the country along with every book they can find on its business practices. They usually create extensive plans for what they will do in the country and elaborate mental images of how they will adapt. When they finally reach the country their experience is what they anticipated. The unusual foods are all delicacies, the different architecture is all exciting, the cultural differences are an interesting challenge. Most people stay in this euphoric stage for somewhere around 3 to 6 months. Eventually, virtually everyone passes to the next phase—irritation and hostility.

Irritation and Hostility

Small aspects start bothering the employee. After a few months in a country, almost all international employees pass into the irritation and hostility phase where everything that seemed so wonderful in the euphoria phase now seems horrible. The foods that were so interesting now just taste bad. Instead of marvelling at the unique architecture they just wonder why a bathroom can't be built "right." The huge number of cultural differences overwhelms them and they feel like they'll never be able to fit in. This is the phase where many employees give up and go home, costing the company not only the large amount of money spent sending the employee overseas but also costing the company an employee they had spent a great deal of time and money training because they saw executive potential.

The irritation and hostility phase has a more variable time frame than euphoria. For the most culturally competent employees it may last only a month or two. Many people take 3 to 6 months before they get over it. Many others are still in it a year later when they give up and go home. Given the high cost of losing an overseas employee, companies need to plan ahead and try to prevent the irritation and hostility phase from chasing employees away.

Poor Family Adjustment

Even when employees have made it through the hostility phase it doesn't mean they are safe. As stated before it is usually much harder for the families to adjust than for the employees themselves. The employee at least has somewhat familiar surroundings and a support network at work. The family often has no such assistance. When one member of a family has a particularly bad experience, then the screaming, crying, or just quiet hostility makes everyone else in the family's irritation and hostility phase worse. A large number of spouses decide to return home for either their own sake or their children's sake. Employees are then left with the option of long distance relationships, divorce, or returning home themselves. None of the options work out well for the company because the employee is either distracted by a long distance relationship or divorce or is lost emotionally.

Re-entry—Return to Home Culture

Those employees who survive culture shock and are able to succeed in an international environment become a company's core international resource. They are often moved every couple of years to larger and more important countries in the company's business. If employees excel over a decade or so of international operations, then they have developed the skills needed in corporate executives. At some point, the company will bring them home for executive management positions. That is when re-entry shock occurs.

The phases of re-entry shock are identical to those of culture shock but the employees' experience in re-entry shock is usually much worse than their initial culture shock. Re-entry shock is worse for a number of reasons. First, employees moving overseas expect to encounter a culture they do not know. When they move home, however, they feel they know what to expect. But the country they knew existed ten or more years ago. Things will have changed and, when in the hostility phase, those changes won't be seen for the better.

Re-entry shock is also usually worse because even though the employee is usually brought back for an executive position, that executive position usually wields less power than they had as a country manager who operated with very little oversight.

Finally re-entry culture shock is usually worse because the types of people who succeeded overseas are the ones who enjoy the adventure of the position. They often see that adventure as dying when they return "home."

PREVENTING CULTURE SHOCK

Because of the high cost of culture shock, both in terms of money and the loss of promising employees, most international companies have elaborate systems for minimizing the impacts of culture shock. The more common system components are described here.

Train Employee

International companies will identify potential international employees either in the hiring process or very early in their careers with the company even though they will often not tell the employee about the designation. The company will then move the employees through several career steps that will help prepare them for an international assignment. When employees appear ready, companies often take a final preparatory step of moving them to an international division where they work with international accounts from the local office. If employees show the flexibility to adapt to the international environment in the home office, the company will move to final preparation for overseas assignment by designating a country and position and beginning to train an employee for it specifically. The employee will usually be sent to culture and language classes as well as cross-cultural classes that will help prepare for the culture shock about to be faced.

Train Employee's Family

As the employee enters the final preparatory phases of training for an overseas assignment, the employee's family will usually also be brought into the training process.

They will be offered language and culture classes to try to help prepare them. Companies who are the best at preparing employees for overseas assignments will often focus more on the families than on the employees themselves. They know the cross-cultural experience is usually harder on the family than on the employee and they usually lose the employee just as readily when the family fails to adjust.

Set Up Exchanges between Returning Employees and Those Leaving

Often, when a company has an employee they will be sending overseas, they have a more experienced employee they will be bringing home. When that is the case, most companies will bring home the overseas employee a month or two early to mentor the employee heading overseas. This has many benefits. It allows the employee heading overseas to ask questions that are specific to the country and personnel at the site. The insights gained are usually well beyond anything that can be gained from general theory. It also allows the employee, and often the family, to interact with the mentor's family and discover both the good and the bad of the country where they will be living from someone who has been there. Finally, it also provides to the returning employee close access to someone who understands headquarters as it is now rather than as it was when the employee left a decade or more ago.

Help Prevent Isolation in New Country

Because most international companies understand the process of culture shock, they will watch new overseas employees to determine when they reach the isolation and hostility phase. People's natural tendency in the isolation and hostility phase is to cut themselves off from social interaction. A wise company tries to prevent that from occurring. Companies will set up a regular series of events all new overseas employees must attend. They will include social gatherings, work events, and often cultral events that occur at least twice a week. The company uses these events as a way to get employees and their family out interacting with the culture. Most employees in the irritation and hostility phase find the schedule annoying but it breaks them out of their introverted cycle and shows them some of the benefits of the new culture.

Provide Security in Foreign Country for Employee and Family

It must also be recognized that violence is a part of many cultures. Overseas executives and their families are often among the wealthiest people in a community. That makes them a target for criminals. If employees and their families do not feel reasonably safe in their new environment, they will never overcome culture shock. That means the company must do what it takes to make employees and their families feel safe. Often companies must overdo the show of security to make the employee comfortable. Homes in secure compounds, armed guards, and other expensive measures may be needed and budgeted.

REPATRIATION

As mentioned earlier, the culture shock of returning home after a long tour abroad is often worse than the culture shock heading overseas. When a company brings employees home, it is usually because it wants them to assume executive positions. At this point, employees are among the company's most valuable and the company has spent literally millions of dollars preparing them for executive positions. Losing them now would be a disaster. The company must do what it takes to help them through the adjustment back to their home country.

Compensate for Lost Standard of Living

The first step a company must take in re-adapting employees to their home environment is to understand the employees. When they are being brought home, most employees have spent a decade or more overseas. By the end of the tour, they were probably country managers or higher who worked with very little oversight from the home offices and were probably among the richest people in their communities. If a company brings them home and asks them to become another average American, they will quit and seek another assignment overseas. That means the company must pay the employees enough that they can feel independent and among the wealthiest in their home community. Yes, that is often very expensive, but the company has decided it wants these people as executives. It needs to show that with compensation.

Compensate for Loss of "Adventure"

Next, the company has to understand that life overseas is exciting. The overseas employees usually work with limited oversight and take successful risks. Their friends and family back home talk of the brave explorer they know. When employees return home, they usually feel the excitement has been taken out of their lives. To prevent them from seeking that excitement with a competitor, companies need to provide it for them. For most companies, that means assigning them leadership of an important, high risk project at home. The high risk project both motivates the employee to re-adapt to the home environment quickly and serves as a test as to whether the employee really is ready for the company's executive ranks.

Assist Employees in Fitting into New Positions

Finally, a company needs to recognize that what makes executives successful is their understanding of the network of people within the company and the processes they use to get the company's work done. Being overseas for a decade or more means the employees probably do not know the headquarters network of people very well or their current processes. If the employees belong in the executive ranks they will be able to learn quickly, but the company will need to help introduce them to the existing people and processes. The approach most companies take to this is to make sure the high risk project they assign the executive cuts across many of the company's operating functions. Cutting across several operations itself makes the project high risk, but also forces the returning executive to learn the existing people and processes fast.

HOW TO PAY EXPATRIATES

An important human resources consideration a company faces when sending employees overseas is how to compensate them. Most companies know they can't expect employees to be willing to uproot their lives and move to another country for the same pay they would get at home, but there's always a question of how far beyond that to go. The pay considerations outlined below provide a model in determining overseas pay.

Salary

Salary considerations are cash or cash equivalents paid to employees annually for however long they are overseas. These are recurring expenses to the company.

> **Base Salary**—The first consideration in determining salary overseas is an employee's current base salary. Most employees who are being considered for overseas assignments have been with the company for a number of years. They have been high achievers who the company believes have the potential to become executives. They, therefore, usually have base salaries approaching $100,000 a year or so depending on the industry. Although there are many advantages for the employees going overseas there are also many risks and extra expenses. If the employees are American it is likely that wherever they will be first posted will have a lower cost of living. The company could, therefore, argue the employee's base salary should be less than their current salary. But if they did, who would go? Generally, the base remains the same or better.

Cost-of-Living Allowance—Even though the overall cost of living in most countries is less than in America, many specific costs are higher. Americans heading overseas rarely want to accept a lower standard of living. They, therefore, will argue for and usually receive a cost-of-living allowance that will allow them to maintain their American standards of living. For most countries, the cost-of-living allowance is simply added to base salary at a rate of somewhere between 20 and 50%. For the few locations like Hong Kong that are significantly more expensive than the United States, the cost of living increase can climb to 100% or more.

Foreign Service Premium—Most employees also recognize they are taking a substantial career and family risk by moving overseas. They will argue for, and usually receive, a foreign service premium to compensate for the risks they are taking. Depending on where they're being sent, the foreign service premium can be anywhere from 10% for going to a country like the UK, to 50% or more for going to an unstable developing country.

Hardship Allowances—Medical, Schools, etc.—Even though the cost-of-living adjustment provided extra cash for higher expenses, most countries have specific challenges that an employee can get a hardship allowance to cover. Most common of these allowances come for countries with poor medical systems forcing the employee and family to go elsewhere for medical care. Hardship allowances are also common for employees with school age children. Because the children will probably not be able to attend public schools due to language differences, they will attend expensive English language schools. The company would cover the additional costs.

Housing Allowance—Quality housing is usually more expensive in other countries. Companies want their overseas executives to be respected and safe. That usually requires even better housing than they would get in the United States. Some companies add to the salary to pay for high quality housing. Some companies buy housing and provide it for the employee. Either way, the company takes on substantial housing costs.

Mobility Allowance—Transportation Home Occasionally—Just because employees work overseas does not mean they will want to sever ties with family and friends back home. Most companies provide flights for employees and their families to return home once or twice a year. Because the employees are usually young executives, the company frequently will pay for business class tickets. Given the high cost of flights to anywhere but the world's most popular cities, flight costs can be substantial.

Tax-Equalization—With all the other costs above added to employees' salaries the tax burden can grow substantially. In some countries employees even face taxes from both their host country and home country. Employees obviously will not wish to take such a loss. Companies will often make tax equalization payments to reduce the taxes to what they would have been if they'd stayed in their home country.

All together the salary adjustments needed to keep employees overseas usually add up to 2-1/2 to 3 times their home salary. That means an employee who makes $100,000 a year at home will be compensated in the range of $250,000—$300,000 a year. As you can see, it is very expensive for a company to have employees overseas. That is why most companies try to keep the number of expatriate managers to a minimum.

Non-Salary Items

Along with all of the salary expenses a company must pay to keep an employee overseas, there are some non-salary expenses the company must pay just to get the employee overseas. These are one time expenses that the company incurs regardless of how long the employee stays. That means if the employee can't handle the culture shock and quits after four months, the company must pay these costs again to put someone else in place.

> **Relocation Allowance—Moving Expenses**—It is expensive to move overseas. Moving household goods and furnishings that an employee wants is expensive when the goods cross national borders. Both the cost of the physical move and customs duties are usually paid by the company. There are other expenses such as international cell phone plans, utilities connect and disconnect, and similar expenses that most companies will absorb. These expenses can range somewhere between $50,000 and $100,000 per employee.

> **Home Sale Allowances**—Because most employees being sent overseas have already been successful in the company, they usually already own a house in the home country. The company usually ends up paying a substantial fee of $20,000–$100,000 to a third company that specializes in buying employees' houses and reselling them.

ESTABLISHING PAY BALANCES

As noted throughout this text, multinational companies have many advantages over local companies. They also have several unique challenges. One of the biggest is establishing pay balances between home country and host country workers. Establishing that balance requires considering three unique perspectives. Whichever perspective a company takes, it always finds the other perspectives cause problems.

Home Nationals Expectations

One perspective is that of the home employee. The pay outlined above is substantial, but the people you're trying to attract into your overseas operations are your best and brightest. They know the risks they are taking when they go overseas. They wouldn't go if you didn't compensate them as described.

Host Employees Reactions

Next, you are faced with the perspective of your host country employees. If you're paying your host country employees something close to market rates in their country, it is likely they will be making 10 or even 100 or more times less than your home national employees. That is bound to create substantial tensions and resentment. A company can rarely afford to pay host employees too much above market rates without their costs going so high they can no longer compete with local companies, however. Most companies are stuck trying to bridge huge pay imbalances and all the political challenges they create.

Global Companies Standards

A few companies have attempted to create a global pay standard for particular skill sets. They attempt to pay all employees with the same skills the same wage regardless of where they are from or where they work. Although the solution appears "fairer" on its surface, it rarely works.

For instance, median pay around the world for a beginning accountant is about $10,000 a year. Therefore, a global standards company would attempt to pay all entry level accountants $10,000 per year. But $10,000 per year is nowhere near enough pay to attract a decent accountant in a wealthy country. Therefore, the company either needs to break its global pay scale or not have any employees in or from wealthy countries. In poorer countries the same wage would be more than is needed to attract the best and brightest. That will leave the company overpriced in poor countries and unable to compete with local businesses. That means the company would only be able to attract employees and remain price competitive in countries with wages near the world's median. That, in effect, says the company is just paying market rates but has severely restricted the markets it will enter.

UNIONS AND INTERNATIONAL BUSINESS

One final human resource issue for international companies is the effect of unions on business. Some countries have strong labor movements and strong political and legal protections for them. Other countries have much weaker labor coalitions. It is imperative that a company understands a country's labor strength before deciding to enter.

Labor Dominated Countries

As stated, some labor dominated countries have strong labor movements and laws to protect them. A company choosing to enter a labor dominated country needs to accept that it will be ceding a great deal of management control to the process of labor-management joint decision making. Labor will sometimes be overpriced in strong labor countries but much more critically, labor may have rigid work-rules and layoff policies. In some instances, working in such countries may be necessary but a company needs to monitor operations to be sure the rewards are worth the costs incurred. If a company is to choose a labor dominated country there are some steps it can follow to ensure a good outcome.

Laws Dictate Strong Labor Role—First, a company must recognize that a country that is labor dominated is so because the local laws require it. Labor movements do not survive without legal protections. If there are unique competitive or market advantages that make the country compelling, some companies may decide to enter the country regardless. When they do so, they still need to minimize their exposure to the country's labor and its laws protecting them, usually by using the least labor intensive production techniques available to them.

Cooperation—When in a strong labor country, it is best to cooperate with the union. Building a better relationship and building mutual trust will make the union more willing to work together on hard choices.

Develop Long Term Attitudes in Employees—It is also important for the company to take long-term approaches to their employees. In some countries it can be nearly impossible to fire poor performers. The company should, therefore, provide as much motivation and training as possible to keep employees productive. The company must also understand that workers in strong labor countries know the rules favor them and some will take advantage. The company needs to be prepared to isolate those employees to keep them from demotivating others. Teamwork with the union can sometimes help with dysfunctional and lazy employees.

Try to Make Employees Feel Profits and Losses—As a company negotiates with unions, they want to try to get a union buy-in to the company's profits and losses as much as possible. The union will usually resist, but the more one is successful the more the union goals will be in line with company goals, so it is worth the effort. Offering profit sharing with the union on top of agreed wages is one way to attempt doing this.

If Costs Go Too High, May Have to Go to Another Country—Costs within a strong labor country are a struggle to keep in check to make consistent profits in the country. Unless there's some unique labor or natural resource that the company needs in a country, it may have to decide it is better off elsewhere. If the unique advantage is a natural resource, the company may be stuck but will want to make sure it runs an operation in the country with the absolute minimum number of workers. The costs of labor are often cited as the reason U.S. multinationals have moved production overseas.

Weak Labor Countries

In weak labor countries, the laws and political system are not nearly as protective of workers. In these countries, a company can operate more freely to meet the company's goals. Management will be much freer to make the decisions that maximize company performance. Even in a country with no labor laws, however, a company will want to follow two basic labor tenants. They are:

Avoid Creating a Need for Unions—When in a country with weak labor laws a company's major goal should be to avoid creating a need for unions. If an international company treats its employees better than local companies, it is unlikely to be challenged. The strategy is to treat employees better than local competition without driving costs so high that the company cannot compete with local competition. That usually means finding a balance that absorbs some of the margin international branded goods can often receive without so depleting margins it is not worth doing business in the country.

Adhere to Cultural Norms of Host—The one place multinational companies have to be particularly careful in weak labor overseas operations, is paying attention to cultural norms in the host. Some companies make the mistake of trying to treat employees "better" by treating them according to their home standards. Often, what is seen as very beneficial in the home country is detrimental in the host. For example, a few western companies extended domestic partner benefits to their employees all around the world. In some of the more conservative countries it was seen as an imperialistic attempt to influence their culture and created a political backlash that led several host countries to restrict freedom of action for companies. Many a labor movement has been started over such a cultural misunderstanding.

Ultimately, labor and management are both concerned about wages, hours, and working conditions. The laws of countries vary greatly in support of these ideas. To get the most teamwork and contain costs, company leaders and managers must work for the blend that shows a valuing of all employees, their inputs, and their cooperation. The need for unions is then reduced greatly.

 **NOTES**

Concept	Definition	Example
Whom Do You Want as Overseas Employees?		

How Many Should be Home, Host, or Global Employees?
    Usually Fewer than 10%
        Home Country
    Frequently Fewer than 1%
        Home Country		

What Language Should the Company Use?
    Global Language is English
    Most Require Managers
        to Speak at Least Two
        Languages		

How Do You Select Overseas Employees?		

Competence Factors
    Cultural Competence
    Technical Competence		

Adaptability Factors
    Able to Participate in New
        Culture
    Family Adaptability		

Personal Characteristics
    Age–Many Cultures Care
    Sex
    Health
    Race/Religion/Sexuality		

Culture Shock–Phases of Adaptation		
Initial Euphoria–Employee Expects Too Much before Leaving		
Irritation and Hostility–Small Aspects of Culture Bother Employee		
Poor Family Adjustment		
Re-entry–Return to Initial Culture Not Well Planned		

Concept	Definition	Example
Preventing Culture Shock		
Train Employee		
Train Employee's Family		
Set Up Exchanges between Returning Employees and Those Leaving		
Help Prevent Isolation in New Country		
Provide Security in Foreign Country for Employee and Family		
Repatriation		
Compensate for Lost Standard of Living		
Compensate for Loss of "Adventure"		
Assist Employee in Fitting into New Position		
How to Pay Expatriates		

Salary
   Base Salary
   Cost of Living Allowance
   Foreign Service Premium
   Hardship Allowances—
     Medical, Schools, etc.
   Housing Allowance
   Tax-equalization		

Non-Salary Items
   Relocation Allowance—
     Moving Expenses
   Mobility Allowance—
     Transportation Home
     Occasionally
   Home Sale Allowances		

Options on Payment Process
   Pay all in host currency–
     good if low tax and strong
     currency
   Pay part in host, part home–
     better if high tax host
   Pay all expenses in host, all
     salary in home–high tax
     or risky currency host		

Concept	Definition	Example
Establishing Pay Balances		
Home Nationals Expectations		
Host Employees Reactions		
Global Companies Standards		
Unions and International Business		
Labor Dominated Countries 　Laws Dictate Strong Labor 　　Role 　Cooperation Best 　Develop Long Term Attitudes 　　in Employees 　Try to Make Employees Feel 　　Profits and Losses 　If Costs Go Too High, May 　　Have to Go to Another 　　Country		
Weak Labor Countries 　Avoid Creating a Need 　　for Unions 　Adhere to Cultural Norms 　　of Host		

International Accounting and Finance

INTERNATIONAL ACCOUNTING

This section on international accounting may be surprisingly short. It is not short because international accounting is incredibly simple or easy to understand. International accounting is so complex there is little meaningful that one can learn about it in a few pages. For those who will be managers in an international business, what you need to know most about international accounting is that you need to find someone who is skilled at it that you can trust.

For those who will be going into international accounting as a profession, you need to understand how complex an endeavor you're undertaking. Consider all the education in accounting you have had thus far and still need to enter the accounting profession. Some portion of that was learning accounting theory. The rest of it, however, was learning the rules of the American accounting system. Every other country has its own set of accounting rules. That means to be an international accountant you have to gain complete understanding of two or more country's accounting systems' rules and figure out how to translate between them. The bad news is that it is very difficult to do. The good news is few people have mastered it so those few people tend to have very lucrative careers.

ACCOUNTING SYSTEMS IN A MULTINATIONAL COMPANY

As you try to understand international accounting, it is important to remember that most companies run several parallel accounting systems. Each revenue stream and expense is booked in different ways in each system. Most international companies run all of the following parallel systems.

Tax Accounting System–Unique to Each Country

Each country has its own tax system that allows some expenses to be deducted immediately, some depreciated over time, and some disallowed or allowed only as a percent of the actual expense. Similarly, rules dictate what revenues can be booked and when. All those tax accounting rules are country specific so a company must code each expense and revenue appropriately for the country's tax system. If a company is in many countries it will need a separate set of tax rules built into its system for each country. If taxable expenses cross borders, the company will need ways to translate accounting entries from one country's tax coding to another.

Public Accounting System–Unique Elements in Each Country

Each company also maintains separate accounting for its public reporting system. Because what is publicly reported is usually driven by national laws and those laws are usually separate from tax laws, a company must generate separate income statements, balance sheets, and cash flow statements for each country that requires public reporting. That means a company that operates in only one country needs two accounting systems, one for tax reporting and one for public reporting. A company in two countries probably needs at least four accounting systems, one for each country's tax reporting system and one for each country's public reporting rules. As the number of countries a company operates in climbs to 100 or more, it can get very difficult to keep up with all the rules. To add complexity, a company may have subsidiaries domiciled in different countries. More tax codes enter the mix under that scenario.

Managerial Accounting System–Hopefully Consistent across Company

Most companies will also maintain a managerial accounting system. The managerial accounting system will try to keep managers well informed about the company's real cash flow. Most companies will have only one of these. It will try to talk to all the other country specific systems in the company to help managers make well informed decisions. Needless to say, creating an integrated system that can bring together the data and rules from a wide variety of countries is far from easy.

ACCOUNTING STANDARDS

As you look into international accounting, one thing you quickly discover is most countries use different accounting systems. Each country has its own basis for rules, therefore accounting numbers are not comparable across countries without a great deal of adjustment. Just because two countries' balance sheets both say accounts receivable, for example, doesn't mean they are reporting similar things. The rules for what goes into accounts receivable could be drastically different between the two countries.

Each country has its own accounting standards. For example, companies in the United States follow **Generally Accepted Accounting Principles (GAAP)** dictated by the **Financial Accounting Standards Board (FASB)**. GAAP lays out tens of thousands of pages of rules for how each accounting issue should be decided. Most of Europe follows **International Accounting Standards Board (IASB)** standards but IASB standards are much broader than GAAP so each country implements them slightly differently.

Even the U.S. FASB has agreed to move accounting rules towards IASB standards, but they are doing so slowly, and again, IASB standards are fairly broad so even when the United States implements them, there will still be significant differences between accounting standards in the world.

Most countries of the world use some variation of IASB standards or GAAP. Virtually every country has added its own twists, however. That means jobs translating between countries' accounting systems looks safe and necessary for a very long time.

WHY ACCOUNTING SYSTEMS VARY

As you look at the different accounting standards around the world, you'll discover many of the differences in the systems exist for a good reason. Understanding those reasons can help you better anticipate changes to accounting systems and help you group countries with similar accounting systems as you build a company's accounting infrastructure. The primary forces that affect an accounting system are described here.

Political and Economic Ties with Other Countries

The dominant factor in determining a country's accounting system is the other countries with which the country trades. When companies frequently trade with companies in another country they often need to share accounting information. For example, one company that wants to start importing from a company in another country will want to examine the books of that vendor to make sure it is strong enough to be a reliable source. The more such interactions occur, the more frustrated businesses become with drastically different accounting systems that make it hard to understand each other's financial position. The more frustrated companies become with the differences, the more they lobby to have rules changed so they are more similar. That process, over time, makes countries which trade frequently with one another seek convergence to similar accounting systems.

Relationships between Businesses and Providers of Capital

Another force pushing accounting systems to be similar is the relationship between businesses that borrow money and the providers of that capital. The providers of capital will want to regularly review the books of the borrowing companies. The greater the differences in accounting systems between the borrowing and lending countries, the more difficult the reviews. That leads most countries that are large providers of capital and the country where they lend to develop similar accounting standards.

Levels of Inflation

Another factor that substantially influences an accounting system is the long-term inflation rate of the country. A country with a low inflation rate can safely use conservative accounting. If an asset is put on the balance sheet at book value and left there that way, the book value may not perfectly reflect the market value of the good but it will be close enough. Leaving the item at book value is more efficient and reduces the opportunity for companies to game their books.

A country with a high inflation rate, however, has to look at accounting differently. If an asset is put on the books at book value and left that way after the country has faced 100% inflation, the asset is now 50% undervalued on the books. Countries with high inflation, therefore, must accept the inefficiency and risks of frequent marks to market in company books.

National Culture–Optimism vs. Conservatism

A country's culture also has a significant effect on its accounting standards. Some cultures, such as the United States, are naturally optimistic. They, therefore, use optimistic accounting standards. For example, the United States values companies as "going concerns." That is to say, we assume a company will exist out into the indefinite future, so we value assets at what they are worth to a surviving company. Many more conservative cultures do not take that leap. They value all assets as if the company will be liquidated tomorrow. Liquidation values are usually well below going concern values.

Level of Economic Development

The final factor that has a substantial effect on a country's accounting system is the level of economic development in the country. A wealthy country with a complex economy requires elaborate accounting rules to deal with the many different possibilities. A country whose primary business is small farmers does not require anywhere near as complex a system. Some countries' accounting standards are still less than 100 pages long instead of the tens of thousands of pages in the world's most developed economies.

INTERNATIONAL FINANCIAL MANAGEMENT

International financial management faces many of the same problems financial management faces in just one country. In international financial management there are many added problems and added opportunities a company must consider. Given the multiple currencies, tax systems, and economic systems available, international financial management needs to be far more sophisticated to succeed.

FUNDING SOURCES

One of the first financial questions a company faces is how to fund its new operations. Most of the funding sources a company has available in its home country are still available for international operations but there are unique resources available for international operations as well. The major potential funding sources are described here.

Equity Capital—Home Market, Host Market

Equity capital is funding operations through selling a piece of a company through mechanisms such as stocks or venture capital. When funding an overseas operation, most companies can sell stocks or other equity instruments in their home country. They can then use that money for their overseas operations. They also have the option of selling equity in the host country. For example, if they will be opening up operations in Germany, they can sell corporate stocks in Germany and use the money there.

Debt Capital—Home, Host, or Third Nations Market

A company can also fund itself through debt capital such as selling bonds or taking out bank loans. Debt capital does not surrender ownership control the way equity capital does but requires a fixed repayment schedule so in many ways is a higher risk for the selling company. When a company tries to fund overseas operations it can get loans or sometimes sell bonds in its home market and use the money overseas. It can sell bonds or get a loan in the host country where it will be setting up operations. It can even go to third countries it has no operations in and get loans. With so many options for debt capital, a company must carefully consider not just the interest rates and repayment terms of loan offers but also currency risks, accounting standards, and political risks of each source of funds. The challenge of finding the least expensive funds can be daunting but much cheaper funds are available for companies that do their homework.

Development Banks and Government Agencies in Host Country

As companies move into poorer countries, or sometimes even wealthy countries with poor neighborhoods, they can, at times, find funding from development banks or other government agencies within the host country. Development banks are set up by governments to try to bring employment to underperforming areas. Governments, through development banks or other agencies, will often provide funding at well below market rates or other incentives like infrastructure or tax breaks to try to attract large employers to impoverished areas. It would be foolish not to consider such funds if a company was considering setting up in those areas anyway. Sometimes funding is so inexpensive through a development bank or other government agency that it is worth a company setting up operations in an impoverished area it might not have otherwise considered. When making such decisions, however, a company must be careful to make sure it has considered all the security and employee training costs that are likely to be necessary to make the site work.

Export Credit Agencies, Banks, and Financiers

When searching for funding for overseas operations, most companies will also carefully look at export credit agencies, banks, and financiers. Many governments have set up funding sources to provide low-cost capital to companies who will export from their country. The government agencies may be neomercantilistic, but in this case it works to the company's benefit, so if a company is eligible for such funds it should probably take them.

International and Regional Development Agencies

Finally, there are some countries that are in such dire straits economically they have little hope of being able to turn things around themselves. Neighboring governments or other governments that have relations with the countries have, at times, created international or regional development agencies to provide low-cost funding for companies willing to do business in the countries in such dire straits. The international and regional development agencies are effectively charity organizations. The countries they work with often have severe tactical problems companies must work around, but if they're able to, they can usually get funded more or less for free and usually get very low cost labor in the country.

HOW MUCH PROFIT SHOULD YOU BRING HOME? — REMITTANCE STRATEGY

A company may choose to enter a country for many reasons but ultimately the bottom line is they enter the country because they believe they can be profitable there. Once a company makes profits in a country, at some point it will want to take the profits out and use them somewhere else. Figuring out how and when to take profits out of a country is called remittance strategy. Remittance strategy is a separate field because, at times, it can be very difficult. Almost every country is happy to have outside companies invest and create jobs for its people. Most are far less happy to allow the company to take out the profits they generated from the investment. That means a company must plan ahead before it even makes an investment for when and how it will bring its profits home. Listed here are some of the factors considered in deciding when profits should be brought home or redeployed.

Opportunities for Growth Outside Country Where Profits were Earned

The first factor a company looks at when trying to decide where to leave profits is where its best opportunities for growth are. New growth leads to new profits so a company will try to send its profits to where it has the best growth potential. If the best growth potential is in the country where the profits were generated, then the company will leave the profits there. If the best growth opportunities are elsewhere, then the company will need to figure out how to move the money to the market with better potential.

Firm's Objectives

The second factor considered in determining when to send money is the firm's objectives. If the company is trying to grow in a country or region it will probably leave profits there to be reinvested. If a company is moving out of a country or region it will want to move profits out to other places.

Availability of Capital from Local Sources

A company will also consider the availability of capital from local sources when designing its remittance plan. If profits were generated in a country with available low cost capital, the company might be better off moving profits to another country where capital is more expensive. If capital is expensive or difficult to get in a country, the company may be better off leaving profits in the country for future investment needs.

Stability of Currency Exchange

A company also needs to consider how stable the currency is in the country where the profits were earned. If the currency of the country is stable, the company can make its remittance strategies based on other factors. If the currency is unstable, the company probably wants to get its profit out as quickly as possible. That will allow the company to store its money in a more stable currency. When you listen to multinational companies report quarterly results, you will learn about adjustments made for currency exchange and/or hedges made profitably or not. Substantial adjustments to profit and loss are often needed.

Economic and Political Conditions at Home and Abroad

A company also needs to consider the economic and political conditions, both at home and abroad. If the company is based in a country with poor political relations with the country where profits were earned, country political struggles could affect the company's ability to take profits out. Similarly, changing economic conditions in either country can affect the company's ability to move money. Both economic and political considerations mean a company must pay careful attention to international relations and move money accordingly. We have previously discussed substantial bribes that can be expected, and although illegal in the United States, are a "shrinkage" cost to profit.

Cost and Ease of Currency Translations

Some currencies, such as the Yen and Euro, are easy to get into and out of, that is, they are highly liquid. If that is the case for a currency where profits are generated, then currency factors will have little to do with remittance strategy timing. Currencies with higher translation costs or greater difficulty in performing translations will have a greater effect. Companies will need to find ways to move money in and out of difficult currencies with the least cost and disruption of normal business processes.

Host Government Restrictions on Remittance

Host government restrictions can also play an important role in remittance strategy. Many governments will try to make it difficult to take profits out of their country. Particularly smaller and weaker countries will use their legal systems to make it difficult, if not impossible, to get profits out. Where that is the case, timing and methods of remittance need to be much more sophisticated.

Tax Systems in Host and Home Country

A company will also carefully consider the tax systems in their home and host country when devising their remittance strategy. As you will see, the remittance techniques described later will make it obvious that companies can use differences in countries' taxing systems to their advantage. The timing and techniques of remittance strategy are, therefore, highly dependent on the differing tax systems.

Impact on Image in Host Country

One final factor companies don't want to forget when devising their remittance strategy is the impact of that strategy on a company's image. Many companies are wealthier than the countries where they operate. When a wealthy company takes profits out of a poor country, it can be easy for politicians or other interested parties to make the company look bad. Even in the richest countries you'll often find politicians railing against the "evil corporations" who are doing nothing more than taking the profits from investments the country begged them to make. A company must, therefore, be careful as it devises its remittance strategy to consider its image. While there will always be a segment of any population who understands investment and profits, there will also be a large group who do not and are willing to make profits look like a company is stealing wealth from a country's people for its own political gain.

REMITTANCE TACTICS

Because of the political and image impact of taking profits from a country, many companies have devised methods to maneuver profits to more favorable perspectives. These techniques also allow corporations to avoid most taxes. The three techniques described below should be considered categories rather than specific prescriptions. They are general approaches companies take to minimize taxes and show profits where they are desirable. Because these techniques are highly dependent on the interaction of each country's laws, the specifics change frequently. Corporations acting on an international stage can usually change fairly quickly so they have largely been able to outmaneuver countries who can only affect their own laws and usually in a fairly slow process. That has kept these and many other techniques as viable alternatives even though the specifics change from year to year.

Transfer Pricing

Transfer pricing depends on a problem we saw in Chapter 9 when we considered customs valuation. Customs valuation is a problem because it is impossible to know the "right" price for a good as it enters a country. Because the good has not been sold to the final consumer yet, it is impossible to know its ultimate worth. Part of this shipment may be sold through discounters and part through high end retailers so ultimate price is not only unknowable but inconsistent. If the good has been sold from company subsidiary to company subsidiary within the same parent organization, whatever cost is being reported for the good is equally unreliable. Therefore, there is no true way to know the "right" price as a good reaches customs at a country's border. That fact allows transfer pricing schemes.

In transfer pricing, a company adjusts the cost-of-goods sold and price of a good as it moves from subsidiary to subsidiary and country to country. It does so in a way to minimize taxes and move profits from country to country in undetectable fashions. Consider the example of a German TV manufacturer who wants to sell its product in the United States.

In Germany, the TV manufacturer could build a television for $100 in components purchased from other companies and $50 in labor and other expenses. In the United States it can sell that television for $250 with $50 marketing and administration fees. In the most straightforward transaction, the German company would report to the German government it had produced a TV for $150 with $100 in cost-of-goods sold and pay value added tax on $50 to Germany. It would report to the United States it had sold a TV for $250 with $150 cost of goods sold and $50.00 in marketing and administrative costs for a total cost of $200. It would pay income taxes in the United States on the $50.00 profit.

Using transfer pricing, however, the company would set up a small subsidiary in the Bahamas. It would still build the TV in Germany but not complete a vital step. It would still require $100 in subcomponents, but because the TV isn't finished it would sell it to its Bahamas subsidiary for $100. That would leave no value added in Germany and so no German value added tax. It would ship a mostly done TV to the Bahamas, then add that one vital step that makes the product a finished TV. Because it is now a valuable TV, the Bahamas subsidiary would sell it to the United States for $200. The Bahamas subsidiary bought the TV for $100 and sold it for $200, so now the company would show $100 in profits in the Bahamas. But the Bahamas has no income tax, so the company would not have to pay tax on that $100. The $200 TV would arrive in the United States, the company would sell it for $250 but still claim $50.00 marketing and administrative costs. That means the company will have no profits in the United States and pay no income tax.

With transfer pricing the company was able to eliminate its tax bill and only show profits in a country with no remittance problems. As stated before, real life examples are usually more complex, but if you look at the real tax rates on most large international companies, you'll find them paying 2 or 3%. They rarely have problems outmaneuvering much slower moving national governments and even the United States government.

Swaps

Transfer pricing works well for product oriented companies but is more difficult for service oriented companies to use. Many of them will use swaps as a remittance technique. In a swap, a company uses a bank as an intermediary much as companies use third country subsidiaries in transfer pricing.

Consider a U.S. computer services company that wants operations in Venezuela. Venezuela has very high taxes and does its best to block remittance. Let's say the U.S. company believes a one million dollar investment in Venezuela would generate $100,000 per year in profits. If the U.S. company made a one million dollar investment they would pay high taxes on any income they generated and whatever they had left they would have a hard time getting out of Venezuela.

Instead, what the company would do was have its home office deposit $1 million dollars in a bank with offices in the U.S. and Venezuela. The Venezuelan branch of the bank would make a one million dollar loan to the company's Venezuelan subsidiary. The company would work out interest rates with the bank ahead of time to allow it to transfer money through bank rates. In our current example, the company might agree the subsidiary would pay 10% interest on the Venezuelan loan. That loan payment would erase the profits that would have otherwise been reported in Venezuela. The bank would then pay the U.S. parent company 9.5% interest on its deposits in the bank, much higher than regular market rates. That will have moved the $100,000 ($95,000 after the bank's $5,000 cut) from Venezuela to the United States. In practice, what the U.S. company would do is have its Bahamas subsidiary make the deposit so it doesn't have to pay U.S. taxes on that dividend payment either.

Unbundling

Transfer pricing and swaps work well for moving money the company planned on earning. Sometimes a company makes more profits than expected, however. For those instances, unbundling is a popular technique. In unbundling, a company charges its subsidiaries for services that might normally be provided by the parent corporation as standard operations.

For example, in normal operations a U.S. company with Italian operations would use transfer pricing to move profits between countries. But one year a competitor in Italy suffered, prices increased, and the Italian operation made a surprise one million dollar profit. In normal years the parent corporation provides all sorts of services to the Italian operation, corporate accounting, management reviews, and productivity reports being some of the standard services. But in years when there are surprise profits the parent corporation can unbundle those services and charge the Italian operation for them. Because they show up as expenses on the Italian balance sheet, the extra Italian profitability can be erased. They would show up as revenue on the parent corporation's books. Many companies would take the added step of having the services based out of the Bahamas or some other country with no corporate income taxes. That way the profits are all reported in a country where they are not taxed and no profits need to be shown in a country with remittance problems.

TYPES OF INTERNATIONAL CASH FLOWS—INTRACOMPANY

A large multinational company with many country subsidiaries will be faced with constant challenges in controlling the flow of money between subsidiaries. Strategies that maximize profitability of each subsidiary could substantially reduce the profitability of the overall corporation. An important job of any international financial manager is to control the cash flows between subsidiaries to maximize overall corporate returns. A few of the common techniques for doing so are described here.

Netting

Netting is canceling inflows and outputs to reduce transactions. In a company with many national subsidiaries, each subsidiary will develop revenue from and payments due to most of the other subsidiaries. A company wants to prevent subsidiaries from regularly paying each other in cash. Each cash transaction carries a currency risk and transaction cost the company does not need to face. For example, a company might have a U.S., a German, and a Japanese subsidiary. The U.S. subsidiary may owe the Japanese subsidiary one million dollars, the Japanese subsidiary may owe the German subsidiary $500,000, and the German subsidiary may owe the U.S. subsidiary $500,000. Instead of shipping around a total of two million dollars, the company can net it out and say the U.S. subsidiary owes the Japanese subsidiary $500,000 and all else is a wash.

Keeping Cash in a Subsidiary

Another international cash flow technique is storing cash in subsidiaries. Given the transaction cost of moving money from country to country some companies choose not to do so. For the most part, they leave cash where it is generated. This holds some obvious risks in countries with unstable currencies but for companies that only deal with a small number of stable countries it is an option.

Pooling

Pooling all funds in a subsidiary with the best tax laws or security is an option. Larger companies will usually choose to pool their money in the country that has the best tax laws, political system, and financial security. There are countries that have specialized in banking and other financial services and that charge little or no taxes on investment income. Large companies logically choose to pool profits from all their subsidiaries into those countries. Switzerland is a major player in this expertise.

Leading and Lagging

Accelerating or slowing payments to take advantage of currency movements is called leading or lagging. A slightly more complex approach to international cash flows has a company constantly monitoring currency movements and adjusting the speed of payments between subsidiaries based on them. For example, a U.S. company might have a subsidiary in Argentina. Argentina's currency is traditionally unstable. That means a company would want its money to be in Argentinian pesos for as short a time as possible. Therefore, when the U.S. subsidiary owes the Argentinian subsidiary money, it severely lags the payment. If the payment is recorded January 1 and is due February 1, the company won't pay until June 1. By then the Argentinian peso may have dropped 10% against the dollar and the dollar cost of the payment will be 10%

less. When Argentina is paying the United States, the exact opposite happens. The Argentinian subsidiary substantially leads the payment so it is made sometimes even before the goods or services are exchanged. All of this is done in an effort to keep money in the strongest currency the longest.

TYPES OF INTERNATIONAL CASH FLOWS— INTERCOMPANY

All of the above cash flow techniques work well for subsidiary to subsidiary payments. Frequently, however, a company must make payments to an unrelated company where it can't control both sides of the cash flow. In those instances, far fewer options are available. Two primary considerations in such cash flows are listed here.

Prevent Other Companies from Leading and Lagging

Leading and lagging as described in intracompany cash flows were even better in intercompany cash flows because in intercompany cash flows the company doing the leading and lagging is capturing profits from suppliers or customers. Everyone knows this. However, there's constant competition to out lead or out lag suppliers and customers. Ultimately, that means the companies with more power in their industry can take advantage of others. If you're a powerful company in your industry, you need to consider carefully which companies you'll lead and lag and when. If you're a weaker company in your industry you'll need to do everything you can to prevent stronger players from leading and lagging you into bankruptcy.

Minimize Currency Exchange Transaction Costs

Besides preventing leading and lagging, the other major focus of intercompany international cash flows falls into the general category of minimizing transaction costs. Sometimes that is done through currency hedging and at other times through other techniques. Cash flow managers are challenged to keep transaction costs low.

TYPES OF CURRENCY EXCHANGE RISK

Because currency exchange risk is one of the biggest challenges of international financial management, it has been carefully studied. Those studies have shown that there are actually three types of currency exchange risks a company faces and must manage.

Translation Exposure

Translation exposure is paper gains and losses on the balance sheet. This is the currency exchange risk many companies fear most. International company assets usually are produced and held in host country currencies. Its corporate balance sheets, income, and cash flow statements are all denominated in home country currency. That means every currency exchange rate change affects home country financial reporting even when it had no effect on company production or sales. For example, if an American company owns a factory in France worth one million Euros and at the time the Euro and dollar are at parity, if the Euro drops against the dollar by 10% the value of that factory will still be one million Euros but it will only be $900,000. That has to be reflected on the company's balance sheet. The balance sheet value has changed so it will also be reflected on the income statement. That could show the company losing $100,000 when in fact nothing but the currency exchange rate changed. With large multinational companies that translation exposure can be huge. It can make balance sheets and income statements for multinationals difficult to compare from year to year especially for multinationals based in countries with unstable currencies.

Transaction Exposure

These are actual gains and losses, actual cash flow losses a company takes due to currency movements. For example, a company based in dollars might agree to pay $1,000,000 to a Spanish company in six months. If the company does not hedge that price and the dollar drops 10% against the Euro during that time the company will actually have to pay 10% more in dollar terms. That is a real cash flow loss the company has to bear.

Economic Exposure

The economic exposure of a company is the total costs of exchange fluctuations to a company, including hedging costs. It includes translation and transaction exposure. It also includes hedging costs and other costs incurred in attempts to reduced translation and transaction exposure. Many large multinationals have very large financial operations whose sole purpose is reducing currency risk. Those financial operations are also part of economic exposure. Good financial management requires a company to understand its economic exposure and not spend so much on managing translation and transaction exposure that they pay more in managing costs than the risks warrant. Overall, getting international financial management right is hugely important to the success or failure of an international business.

 **NOTES**

Concept	Definition	Example
International Accounting		
Accounting Systems in a Multinational Company		
Most companies keep several sets of books including:		
Tax Accounting System— Unique to Each Country		
Public Accounting System— Unique Elements in Each Country		
Managerial Accounting System—Hopefully Consistent across Company		
So a company with offices in 5 countries will probably be keeping at least 11 sets of accounts. Each of which needs to be translated to most of the others.		
Accounting Standards		
Important Note—Most countries use different accounting systems. Therefore, accounting numbers are not comparable across countries without a great deal of correction.		
US—FASB and GAAP— "moving towards" IASB		
Many Others—Variations of IASB		
Most countries use unique variations of above or something completely idiosyncratic.		

Concept	Definition	Example
Accounting Systems Vary Because of:		
Political and Economic Ties with Other Countries		
Relationships between Businesses and Providers of Capital		
Levels of Inflation		
National Culture—Optimism vs. Conservatism		
Level of Economic Development		
International Financial Management		
Financial System Must Consider:		
Political Risks		
Variations in Sources of Funding		
Foreign Exchange Rate Fluctuations		
Restrictions on Capital, Exchange, and Profit Flows		
Differences in Tax Systems Faced		
Variations in Economic Systems and Economic Conditions		
Differences in Inflation		
Varying Interest and Discount Rates		
Funding Sources		
Equity Capital—Home Market, Host Market		
Debt Capital—Home, Host, or Third Nations Market		

Concept	Definition	Example
Development Banks and Government Agencies in Host Country		
Investment and Commercial Banks in Host Country		
Export Credit Agencies, Banks, and Financiers		
International and Regional Development Agencies		
How Much Profits Should You Bring Home?—Remittance Strategy		
Opportunities for Growth Outside Country where Profits were Earned		
Firm's Objectives		
Availability of Capital from Local Sources		
Stability of Currency Exchange		
Economic and Political Conditions at Home and Abroad		
Cost and Ease of Currency Translations		
Host Government Restrictions on Remittance		
Tax Systems in Host and Home Country		
Impact on Image in Host country		
Remittance Accomplished Through:		
Transfer Pricing		
Swaps		
Unbundling		

Concept	Definition	Example
Types of International Cash Flows—Intracompany		
Netting—Cancelling Inflows and Outputs to Reduce Transactions		
Keeping Cash in Subsidiary		
Pooling—Pooling All Funds in Subsidiary with Best Tax Laws or Security		
Leading and Lagging—Accelerating or Slowing Payments to Take Advantage of Different Inflation Rates		
Types of International Cash Flows—Intercompany		
Prevent Other Companies from Leading and Lagging		
Minimize Currency Exchange Transaction Costs		
Types of Currency Exchange Risk		
Translation Exposure—Paper Gains and Losses on Balance Sheet		
Transaction Exposure—Actual Gains and Losses		
Economic Exposure—Total Costs of Exchange Fluctuations Including Hedging Costs		

Foreign Direct Investment vs. Export/Import

In this last chapter of the book we wrap up by covering the basics of foreign direct investment and import/export businesses. Foreign direct investment and import/export businesses have been discussed throughout the book. There are a few key concepts and vocabulary that have not yet been addressed and are covered here. The first issue within the topic is why a company would choose import or export over foreign direct investment or vice versa. We start with exporting because that is how most companies initially get involved in dealing directly with overseas markets.

WHY EXPORT?

The first question a company faces when considering exports and making their first move into international business is "why bother?". Hopefully, by this point you are very aware of the many reasons to enter international business. There are a few that can be added now for why a company might choose to make the initial steps into exporting. They follow.

To Serve Markets Where You Have No Production

The most common reason companies begin exporting is to serve an overseas customer who has found them. It is fairly common for an overseas customer to find a unique product on the web or through some industry contact and to approach the company in an effort to bring the product to their market. The company being approached won't have production capacity in that country and will rarely want to build it given their limited international experience. The logical choice is to set up an export relationship. It allows the company to serve the market and provides a knowledgeable point of contact in the country.

To Remain Price Competitive at Home

Another important reason companies take up exporting is to improve their product price at home. Most industries have economies of scale that allow bigger companies to produce more efficiently. If a company is faced with larger domestic competitors it may find it difficult to remain price competitive. The company may choose to begin exporting its product simply to increase its scale and be able to lower its domestic price.

To Test Foreign Markets Inexpensively

Companies may also choose to start exporting simply because they have decided they want to try selling in foreign markets but they want to test their skills inexpensively. Exporting is much less expensive than setting up overseas operations, especially if the company can export to overseas partners who handle the product once it arrives.

To Offset Domestic Cyclical Sales

Other companies will get into exporting to try to offset a highly cyclical domestic sales market. Some goods, such as snowboards, can only be sold for a few months a year in any one country. Producing in the northern hemisphere but exporting to the southern hemisphere, however, allows a snowboard producer year round sales. Other industries have domestic cycles that are longer but can still be offset through exporting. For example, many lower upper class products like Coach Purse sales are highly dependent on economic cycles. When times are good in a country, the products sell well. When the economy in the country goes bad, sales tank. Many such companies take to exporting to smooth out sales across economic cycles of several countries.

To Respond to Foreign Competitors

Another reason companies will begin exporting is to respond to foreign competitors. Often a domestic company will suddenly find new competition in its market from overseas competitors. When that happens, many companies will find their best strategic response is to counterattack by exporting to the foreign competitors' home markets. Other times the company discovers it cannot defend its domestic market well but might have growth opportunities in other parts of the world that the foreign competitor has not addressed.

To Improve Efficiency of Manufacturing

Finally, as new technologies continue to increase the most efficient scale of manufacturing, many companies will jump into exports just to increase the efficiency of their manufacturing process by creating a larger market.

EXPORT ASSISTANCE

As companies first jump into exports they discover the process is nowhere near as simple as it should be. As small companies discover the challenges of exporting they usually decide they need help. A few sources for that help are described here.

Market Access and Compliance (MAC) Specialists

The most effective source of help in exporting is called Market Access and Compliance (MAC) specialists. MAC specialists are companies that do nothing but help other companies export their products. Most MAC specialists focus on a country or region of the world. They become experts on those markets and governmental systems. A company that hires a MAC specialist usually finds someone who can help it identify customers in the country, make appropriate introductions, and help the company work through all the international contracts and legal paperwork necessary to get the product overseas. The problem with MAC specialists is they can be very expensive and, as with any service, the level of quality can vary tremendously. If it can possibly afford it, a company first entering an export business should probably use a MAC specialist. As a company develops experience with exporting, it may discover MAC specialists are too expensive for its needs.

Trade Development Office

If a company cannot afford, or no longer needs, a MAC specialist, it can still get help from various government agencies. Governments at various levels, including many cities, counties, and states, offer help to companies wishing to export products. Most agencies are called something similar to trade development offices. Because most governments want the jobs and tax dollars that come from expanding business, they understand the importance of local company's exporting and try to promote it. The specific services and competence of those services vary even more than the quality of MAC specialists but the services are usually either low cost or free. A company wishing to get into exporting should at least check the trade development offices for each level of government to which they are subject.

U.S. Commercial Services (USCS)

American companies also have the option of help from the U.S. Department of Commerce—U.S. Commercial Services. The U.S. Commercial Services helps American companies start or expand exporting. Many companies find market research available from the USCS to be very useful. They also provide some assistance through the export process.

International Trade Office of the SBA

For small companies, the international trade office of the Small Business Administration can also be of use. The Small Business Administration provides advice to small businesses wishing to begin exports. More importantly, the Small Business Administration can, at times, help secure funding for new export endeavors.

EXPORT VOCABULARY

The actual process of exporting can, at times, seem like a mountain of paperwork. With multiple governments involved, the number of forms that need to be filled out, boxes that need to be checked, and approvals that need to be obtained can often seem unending. Unfortunately, the processes for countries vary and often each product is different. That means there isn't much a general text such as this can teach you to help. There are, however, a few vocabulary words you'll want to know as you begin your search. This vocabulary is used throughout international business and not knowing it could make people question your international exposure. The key phrases follow.

Shipping

Somewhat surprisingly, international negotiations frequently come to the price of a good fairly quickly. Most companies within an industry know the costs of producing a good and the price the market will bear. It isn't that difficult to agree on a price point. In export markets, however, there are the substantial additional costs associated with transporting the good. Often, the vast majority of negotiations comes down to who has to pay for transportation and face the risks associated with it. The four most frequently heard shipping terms over which companies will negotiate follow. These are not the only shipping options but are the most commonly used.

> **FAS—Free Along Ship, Port of Call**—Free Along Ship, Port of Call means the exporter will pay to get the product to the shipping dock and then it is the buyer's problem. That means the buyer has to pay to have the good loaded on the ship, pay for the ship transportation, pay for insurance on the good while it is

in transport, pay to have it unloaded, and pay customs duties or whatever other import costs are associated with the product. Obviously, FAS is very favorable to the sellers, so they will try to argue for it as shipping terms. In virtually any international business discussion, you will never hear the phrase Free Along Ship, Port of Call used. Everyone simply uses FAS as they use the acronym for all the shipping terms.

CIF—Cost, Insurance, Freight, Foreign Port—Cost, Insurance, Freight, Foreign Port means the product exporter is responsible for all the costs associated with getting a product to the foreign port. These terms are very favorable to the importers and what they will be arguing to achieve.

CFR—Cost and Freight, Foreign Port—Cost and Freight, Foreign Port is a popular in-between ground many importers and exporters settle on when neither is powerful enough to make the other agree to the terms most favorable to them. In Cost and Freight, Foreign Port the exporter is responsible for all the costs of getting a good to the foreign port except insurance. Given the high risk of goods at sea with the possibility of shipping containers falling overboard or more frequently disappearing at a poorly secured dock, insurance is often as expensive as all the other shipping costs. In effect, CFR splits shipping costs between the importer and exporter.

DAF—Delivered at Frontier—One other international shipping phrase commonly heard in the United States is Delivered at Frontier. DAF, in practice, is exactly like FAS except goods will cross the border by train or truck. With Mexico and Canada as the United States' biggest trading partners, many exported goods are never placed on a ship.

Payments

Besides shipping terms, people first moving into exporting must also get used to a new vocabulary in payment terms. Because banks are regulated by national governments, there is no such thing as a truly international bank. Many banks have subsidiaries in several countries and do their best to hide the differences they must have in their operations to meet the requirements of each national government. But because they're following different sets of laws, they can't standardize the way they can within one country. That means systems like checks within one country can't function between countries. Therefore, new processes as well as a new vocabulary are needed.

L/C—Letter of Credit—Companies sending goods overseas are taking more legal risk than if they stay within their own country. If the company where they send the goods never pays them, then their only hope for recovering their money is likely to be suing the company in their own country. In many countries that is a tremendous risk. That being the case, most companies won't send goods overseas until they have very high confidence the purchaser will pay for them. An important step in that process is the letter of credit. The letter of credit is issued by a bank saying the purchasing company has sufficient credit with the bank to pay for whatever goods they are ordering. The letter of credit doesn't guarantee the exporter will be paid, but it significantly increases the odds, so most exporters require it.

Export Draft—Almost an International Check—As stated above, there is no true international check. Once a check crosses national boundaries it crosses legal jurisdictions. That being the case, banks and companies have devised other techniques for international payments. Electronic payments are coming to dominate the field but there are still many operations where a paper transaction is preferable. For those transactions, the export draft is the closest thing to an international check that there is. An export draft looks much like a check but with far more information on it. It is a claim on a foreign bank account much as a check is a claim on a domestic one. Given legal differences, however, and the sophistication of some counterfeiting rings, a company should not believe itself to be paid just because it received an export draft.

Factoring—Selling Accounts Receivable—One other important exporting payment difference is factoring. When a company is owed money by another company or individual, that debt is an account receivable. Factoring is a selling of accounts receivable so someone else becomes responsible for collecting debts due. It puts a payment on the books but for less than the total of the actual receivable. Factoring is available in domestic business but is much more common in exporting markets. Export markets usually have longer time frames between shipping products and receiving payments. They also have greater default risk because of the difficulties of international collections. Therefore, many more exporters choose to factor their international accounts receivable even though it is a fairly costly discount to take.

IMPORT VOCABULARY

The flip side of every export transaction is an import transaction. As every good is shipped out of one country it is eventually shipped into another. Oil tankers can float at sea for months before that happens. Often, the paperwork for importing is far more onerous than for exporting. Most governments want to increase exports but want to decrease imports. They often make importing even more difficult. If you want to get into importing you're going to need to spend time figuring out the paperwork for your product for the two countries involved. Importers usually rely on the assistance available to exporters as their primary aid because it is more reliable and readily available. That said, there is a unique vocabulary to importing just as there is to exporting. A few key phrases you will need to know follow.

Bonded Warehouse

Place to Store Imported Goods before Customs are Paid—One important tool for importers is the bonded warehouse. When a company imports goods, it is required to pay import duties as the goods enter the country. Because the company is importing from an overseas manufacturer, it will often get substantial discounts for buying large quantities.

Large quantity purchases can substantially reduce the costs of paperwork, transportation, and insurance. Unfortunately, large quantity purchases can increase tariff related expenses. They increase tariff costs because, if a company imports a year's worth of a good, it must pay the tariff upfront. That means it must finance the cost of the tariff for the year. A bonded warehouse is a way to eliminate that cost. A bonded warehouse is a government controlled warehouse where the government acts as though the goods in the warehouse have not arrived in the country yet. A company, therefore, does not have to pay tariffs until they take goods out of the warehouse. For products with high tariffs a bonded warehouse can save a company a great deal of money. For products with low tariffs the cost of a bonded warehouse probably isn't worth the savings.

Automated Commercial System

Electronic Tracking of Imports Used by the United States—For American companies, another important phrase to know is the automated commercial system. Goods coming to the United States are not allowed to just show up at a dock as they can in many other countries. The U.S. government wants time to check out products before they get here. That means any product coming to the United States must be entered into the U.S. automated commercial system when they are put on a ship to the U.S.

The U.S. government uses the automated commercial system to track the good and predict potentially problematic shipments.

Harmonized Tariff Schedule of the US

Classifies Products to Determine Tariff Rates—When importing to the United States, a company also needs to know about the harmonized tariff schedule of the United States. The harmonized tariff schedule classifies all products coming into the Unites States and assigns them tariff rates. Anything that tries to classify every single product entering the United States is obviously going to have grey areas. For most goods, the grey areas don't matter because tariff rates are similar. For some goods with particularly high tariff rates, however, being classified differently can change tariff rates by 50% or more. Companies importing products in those grey areas need to pay careful attention to how their products are categorized.

FOREIGN DIRECT INVESTMENT AND COLLABORATIVE STRATEGIES

For companies directly participating in international business, the alternative to importing/exporting is setting up shop in foreign countries. Such foreign direct investment faces all of the cultural, political, legal, and economic challenges you have seen throughout this book. Given all those challenges, one might wonder why any company would bother. Why not just export? You have seen many reasons for entering into business in another country throughout this book. They are consolidated here along with a few you have not yet seen.

Supply Factors

One important group of reasons for foreign direct investment are supply factors. Many companies choose to expand into foreign countries because those foreign countries provide better access to needed supplies. Specific supply factors follow.

> **Production Costs**—One of the most common supply factors that lead companies into foreign direct investment is lower production costs. Most lower production costs are achieved in foreign markets through lower labor costs and even through lower real estate costs and lower legal costs due to a more favorable legal climate. Companies sometimes find they can capture lower costs better themselves by putting operations in a low-cost country than they can by importing from it.

> **Logistics**—Companies also move operations into foreign countries for logistical purposes. Suppliers to an industry tend to cluster in specific countries and even cities of those countries. A company working in an industry will find logistics much easier when it has plants in the same cities as its suppliers. That reduces transportation times and inventory costs but, more importantly, allows the company to interact more regularly with suppliers and suggest or learn new production techniques and product designs.

> **Availability of Natural Resources**—There are some natural resources that are very rare on this planet. Companies working in industries dependent on those natural resources frequently must go wherever the natural resource is. Companies often find governments of countries with rare natural resources require some higher level manufacturing based on the natural resource occurring within their country. The governments do this to capture more of the jobs and wealth that come from the natural resource. Companies often must make foreign direct investments to comply.

> **Access to Key Technology**—Just as suppliers to an industry tend to cluster around a small number of cities, so do the research and development labs of new

technologies for the industry. Companies that utilize technologically advanced products or production systems usually go to where new technology in their industry is being produced. Many industries depend on just two or three universities or government labs for the majority of their innovation. Companies must have operations near those universities or labs if they want to prevent falling behind competitors. That means they must put facilities in whichever country those universities or labs are located in.

Demand Factors

Another category of reasons for choosing foreign direct investment is demand factors. Sometimes having operations closer to customers is an advantage. Some reasons for those advantages follow.

Multidomestic Strategy—One important demand condition that will lead a company to foreign direct investment is customers' demand for products designed specifically for their country or culture. When a company sells a product that requires a multidomestic strategy, it is pretty much required to accept foreign direct investment as part of that strategy. Trying to export products in a multidomestic strategy would leave the company too far from customers to understand their developing needs.

Customer Access—Another important demand condition that can lead a company to foreign direct investment is customer access. Being close to customers can provide a company useful insights. Regularly receiving customer feedback and having employees who live among customers gives a company access to information that would be hard to get through exporting. That information can be used to adjust products, prices, services, or any other business processes to match customer needs.

Marketing Advantage—Sometimes having foreign operations can itself be a marketing advantage. Some customers prefer to buy local. Others just want a company they feel understands them. Having a local operation can make a customer feel a company understands them and their needs even when the company is selling a globally standardized product. For example, there are still many people who prefer to buy "American" cars even though many cars from "American" companies are now produced overseas and many cars sold by "Japanese" or "German" car makers are now built in America.

Exploitation of Competitive Advantage—Companies will also choose to move overseas because they believe they have some unique competitive advantage they want to duplicate. Most service companies couldn't use their competitive advantage in international business through exporting. The only way for a service company like FedEx to exploit its competitive advantage overseas is to set up operations there.

Customer Mobility—Sometimes a company will choose foreign direct investment simply because a large customer has done so. When a company is a supplier to another large company and that company chooses to set up operations overseas, the supplier company must follow or risk being replaced. Many companies are forced into foreign direct investment before they're ready by this very process. Any company that has a single customer who makes up a large proportion of its sales needs to be prepared to face the situation.

Political Factors

Sometimes companies choose foreign direct investment due to political factors. Companies are always adjusting to the governments around them and sometimes those governments will be the deciding factor in a foreign direct investment decision. The two most common political factors follow.

Avoidance of Trade Barriers—The most common political reason a company will choose foreign direct investment is to avoid trade barriers. Even though the most powerful trading countries and many international organizations are constantly fighting to reduce trade barriers, substantial tariff and nontariff barriers still exist in almost every country.

Such neomercantilistic approaches make both the countries using them and the world poorer but they serve some group within the country that has the power to get them implemented. That being the case, companies rarely have any choice but to deal with the environment they face and at times that means setting up operations in a country to avoid local trade barriers. Because the economics of such decisions are dependent on political conditions that can change rapidly, a company must be very careful. It will want to keep such investments as liquid as possible so when political conditions change, it can make rational economic decisions quickly.

Economic Development Incentives—Whereas trade barriers may lead a company to choose foreign direct investment over exporting to avoid costs, economic development incentives can lead to the same outcome but through incentives to foreign direct investment rather than through punishing tariffs. Countries sometimes offer substantial tax breaks and funding assistance for foreign direct investments.

Such incentives can swing the economics of a manufacturing decision toward foreign direct investment. If the company is better off accepting such incentives, it should do so but always with a wary eye. The political support for such incentives can disappear quickly and can drastically affect the economics of a decision. Companies are usually better off making economic decisions disregarding such political advantages. If incentives are offered on a project that otherwise makes economic sense, the company should grab them. If the project only makes sense due to the political incentives, the company needs to be very sure of the long term political situation in the country before accepting.

APPROACHES TO DIRECT INVESTMENT

Once a company has chosen to make a foreign direct investment it has several options in how to do so. Because each option has substantial advantages and disadvantages, a company needs to consider its choice carefully.

Outright Purchase

One option to entering a country through foreign direct investment is an outright purchase. In an outright purchase, a company finds another company within their industry in the country they're interested in that does things similar enough to themselves and buys them. This has several advantages. An outright purchase provides the purchasing company an already built facility, an established brand, a trained workforce and expertise in the country. Those advantages make an outright purchase very attractive.

The major disadvantage of an outright purchase is that you purchase the company's entire history as well. All labor/management problems that exist in the company are now yours. Any unmotivated or under-trained employees of the company are now yours as well as the government regulations of the country that may constrain you from dealing with the problems. Any skeletons in the company's closet are also yours. For example, Germany was a popular country for American companies looking to expand into Europe in the 1980s. Many U.S. companies bought well established German brands. In the 1990s it was discovered many old line German companies had used Jewish slave labor during World War II. Many American companies had to pay restitution for their German purchases that far exceeded the value of the companies bought. Another disadvantage can be in the blending of cultures that are unwilling to be merged. Think of Daimler-Chrysler.

Greenfield

In a Greenfield approach to foreign direct investment, a company starts from scratch. It finds a grass covered (green) field somewhere in the country of interest and builds its own factory, hires its own workers, and builds up its entire production process from scratch. A Greenfield operation eliminates all the historical problems of an outright purchase. It allows the company to train its workers to its standards and develop its own management team.

On the downside, however, a Greenfield operation gives the company none of the country expertise it gains with an outright purchase. It also requires the very slow growth of building the infrastructure and facilities, training all new workers, and more importantly, training a new management team. Therefore, Greenfield operations can be successful when a company has decades to develop within a country. It is much less successful when competitive pressures require a more rapid solution.

Collaboration

Given the risks and challenges of both an outright purchase and a Greenfield operation, many companies attempt to gain the country expertise of an outright purchase along with the advantages of starting over by collaborating with companies that exist within the target country. There are four primary approaches to collaboration used in international markets. The differences between them primarily hinge on how much authority each company has over operations.

Private Label—A simple way to avoid tariffs and get your product produced in another country is to have an existing manufacturer make your product under your private label. For example, Toyota could have asked GM to manufacture its Lexus brand for them here in the United States. You surely can think of reasons Toyota chose instead to build its own factories here. But sometimes the solution of having your product produced by an existing overseas factory as your private label to your standards is the least costly and most effective.

Licensing—In a licensing operation, a company sells a foreign company the right to distribute its product within that country. A licensee agreement can be set up quickly. It allows the licensee the most authority to adapt to their local market conditions. It allows the licensor the ability to generate profits in another country with the least amount of effort. The primary problem with licensing is the licensor loses most of the control over the product. If the licensee is not selling the product in a fashion consistent with the desired image, there is little the licensor can do about it. If the licensor grows rapidly and feels they could increase sales in the country with a different approach, the company is largely stuck. Thus, licensing agreements usually only work out when the company licensing the product is significantly more developed than a licensor.

Franchising—Many companies looking to expand through collaborations overseas will want greater control than provided through a license and will choose franchising instead. In franchising, the foreign company will still own the operation but the franchising agreement will give the franchisor far more control over operations. The franchisee agreement will give the franchisor rights to review operations and close franchises that do not meet a company's standards. Franchises are an improvement over licensing as far as control goes but still have many problems. Disputes over rights have to be enforced by foreign courts, which in many countries can be a challenge. A franchisee who doesn't meet standards can drag down the company's image for years while trying to get it closed. Franchising provides more control than licensing but still less than many Western companies feel is necessary to protect their brand image and the premiums they charge for them.

Joint Ventures—In a joint venture, two companies create a third company and split ownership rights in it. Joint ventures are the form often chosen when two large companies believe they can gain by collaborating. Joint ventures are most commonly formed between companies with product and research skill in one country and one with production and marketing skill in another.

The percent of control owned by each company varies based on the laws of the country where the joint venture is set up but they are often 50/50 ownership splits or something close to them. That gives both parties the presumed equal interest in making a joint venture work. Joint ventures often work in the short run. The company with the product and research skills, usually in a very advanced country, gains quick access to production capacity and marketing skill in a less developed country. The production and marketing company gains advanced products to manufacture and sell and training in advanced production techniques. Most joint ventures don't work in the long run however, in part because there is no way to resolve equal 50/50 votes when disputes arise They fail for many other reasons but mostly they fail because they are the most prone to the problems outlined in the following section on foreign direct investment problems.

FDI PROBLEMS

Most foreign direct investments, whether outright purchases, Greenfield, or collaborations, run into substantial problems. The problems are usually worse and manifest themselves more quickly in collaborations but they affect all types of foreign direct investment. A company wishing to profit from foreign direct investment will have to monitor these problems and deal with them as they arise.

Conflicting Cultures

The most prevalent problem of foreign direct investment, like all international business, is that of conflicting cultures. Different cultures emphasize different things. Foreign direct investment forces people from different cultures to try to come to agreement. Sometimes that works—sometimes it doesn't. It always takes a great deal of time and upsets many people along the way. All foreign direct investments end up changing the cultures of the countries receiving them. There's always some pain involved in the transitions.

Control Issues

Foreign direct investments will also almost always lead to struggles for control. Control issues are most prevalent in collaboration but they even arise in Greenfield operations. Struggles for control invariably grow from a conflict of cultures. Each culture tries to maximize its goals within the operation. The members of each culture, therefore, try to gain control of operations so they can do what so obviously needs to be done to maximize their cultural values. Even when a company starts out Greenfield and imports its entire management team, struggles for control arise from unions or less organized employee groups. When management is split between local and international managers, rallying around the local manager who most defends local culture is common. Making the local manager or managers more powerful by giving them their way where possible is a good tactic both to adapt your company to local culture and to win support for the areas where you can't give in.

Differing Goals

Ultimately, the challenge of foreign direct investment comes down to the fact that the two countries involved have different goals. The company making the investment is looking for new markets, increased sales, or reduced costs. They are primarily profit motivated. The country and company accepting the investment is usually trying to learn how to make profits in the industry. For a while the relationship works. The investing company grows in the country and generates profits from it. Eventually, however, the people of the country invested in learn the business. When they do, they don't really need the investing company any longer. They then have every motivation to make things so uncomfortable for the investing company that it chooses to leave. The only defense investing companies have is strong brand names that customers won't surrender or research and development that constantly improves products and processes so the adopting countries are always catching up and still need the investing company.

Unmotivated Partners

A corollary to the problem of differing goals is many companies using foreign direct investment feel their partners are unmotivated. The problem is rarely that the people are unmotivated, but it's that their culture has them motivated differently. American companies entering foreign markets are ultimately there for one reason, to increase profits. Countries accepting the investments are not motivated to increase the American company's profits. They may want the income from jobs, they may want the prestige of the American company, or they may have any of hundreds of different motivations for wanting the investment, but increasing profits going to America is not one of them.

That means an American company that wants to make money overseas is going to have to figure out what their overseas partners and workers are trying to get from the relationship. They then have to figure out how to give them that in a way in which the improvement of their cultural goals also increases the American company's profits. If they can, they will be incredibly successful. If they cannot, they will always feel their partners and/or employees are unmotivated and the foreign direct investment will underperform or fail.

 **NOTES**

Concept	Definition	Example
Why Export?		
To Serve Markets Where You Have No Production		
To Remain Price Competitive at Home		
To Test Foreign Markets Inexpensively		
To Offset Domestic Cyclical Sales		
To Respond to Foreign Competitors		
To Improve Efficiency of Manufacturing		
Export Assistance Exporting is hard. You will need help. Get it from:		
Market Access and Compliance (MAC) Specialists		
Trade Development Office		
U.S. Commercial Services (USCS)		
International Trade Office of the SBA		
Department of Commerce Export Assistance Program (EAP)		
Export Vocabulary		

Shipping
    FAS–Free Along Ship, Port
        of Call
    CIF–Cost, Insurance, Freight,
        Foreign Port
    CFR–Cost and Freight,
        Foreign Port
    DAF–Delivered at Frontier		

Concept	Definition	Example

Payments
    L/C–Letter of Credit
    Export Draft–Almost
      an International Check
    Factoring–Selling Accounts
      Receivable		

Other
    Free Trade Zone–Country
      designates area to be
      outside its customs
      territory
    Customs Drawback–Rebate
      on customs duties		

Why Import?		
Lower Cost of Goods		
Needed Natural Resources		
Unique Cultural Goods		
Overseas Efficiencies		
Import Vocabulary		
Bonded Warehouse–Place to store imported goods before customs are paid		
Automated Commercial System–Electronic tracking of imports used by the United States		
Harmonized Tariff Schedule of the United States–Classifies products to determine tariff rates		
Foreign Direct Investment and Collaborative Strategies		
Why Foreign Direct Investment?		

Supply Factors
    Production Costs
    Logistics
    Availability of Natural
      Resources
    Access to Key Technology		

Concept	Definition	Example

Demand Factors
  Customer Access
  Marketing Advantage
  Exploitation of Competitive
    Advantage
  Customer Mobility		

Political Factors
  Avoidance of Trade Barriers
  Economic Development
    Incentives		

Why Not Export Instead?		
Lower Transportation or Production Costs		
Multidomestic Strategy		
Access to Resources		
Host Country Policies		
Approaches to Direct Investment		
Greenfield		
Outright Purchase		

Collaboration
  Licensing
  Franchising
  Joint Ventures		

FDI Problems		
Conflicting Cultures		
Control Issues		
Differing Goals		
Unmotivated Partners		

Index